Miracle Girls 4

by Nami Akimoto

TOKYOPOP® Presents
Miracle Girls 4 by Nami Akimoto
TOKYOPOP is a registered trademark of Mixx Entertainment, Inc.
ISBN: 1-892213-82-6
First Printing February 2002

10 9 8 7 6 5 4 3 2 1

This volume contains the Miracle Girls installments from
Miracle Girls Comics No.13 through No.17 in their entirety.

Translator - Ray Yoshimoto. Retouch Artist - Jinky DeLeon.
Cover Retouch - Rod Sampson.
Graphics Assistants - Dao Sirivisal and Anna Kernbaum.
Graphic Designer - Akemi Imafuku.
Associate Editor - Robert Coyner.
Editor - Stephanie Donnelly.
Senior Editor - Jake Forbes.
Production Manager - Fred Lui.
Art Director - Matt Alford.
VP of Production - Ron Klamert.
Publisher - Stu Levy.

Email: editor@Press.TOKYOPOP.com
Come visit us at www.TOKYOPOP.com

TOKYOPOP®
Los Angeles - Tokyo

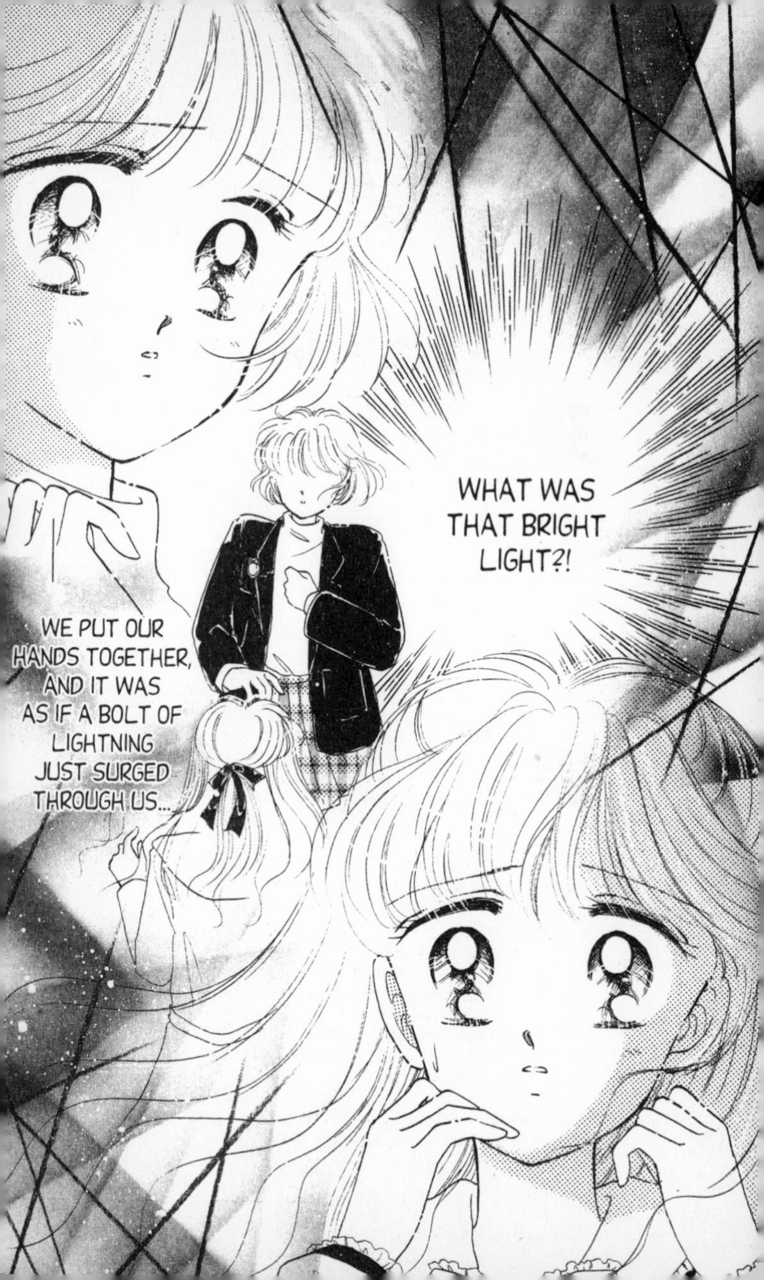
WHAT WAS THAT BRIGHT LIGHT?!
WE PUT OUR HANDS TOGETHER, AND IT WAS AS IF A BOLT OF LIGHTNING JUST SURGED THROUGH US...

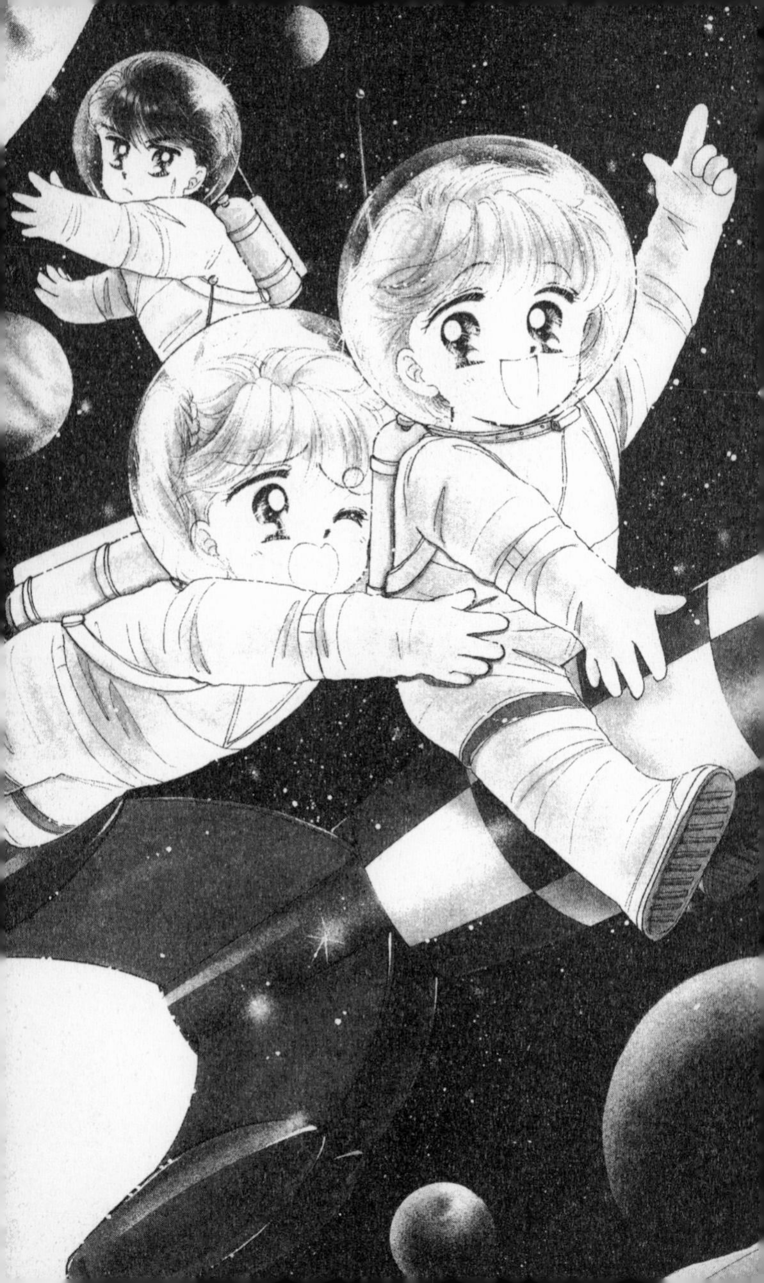

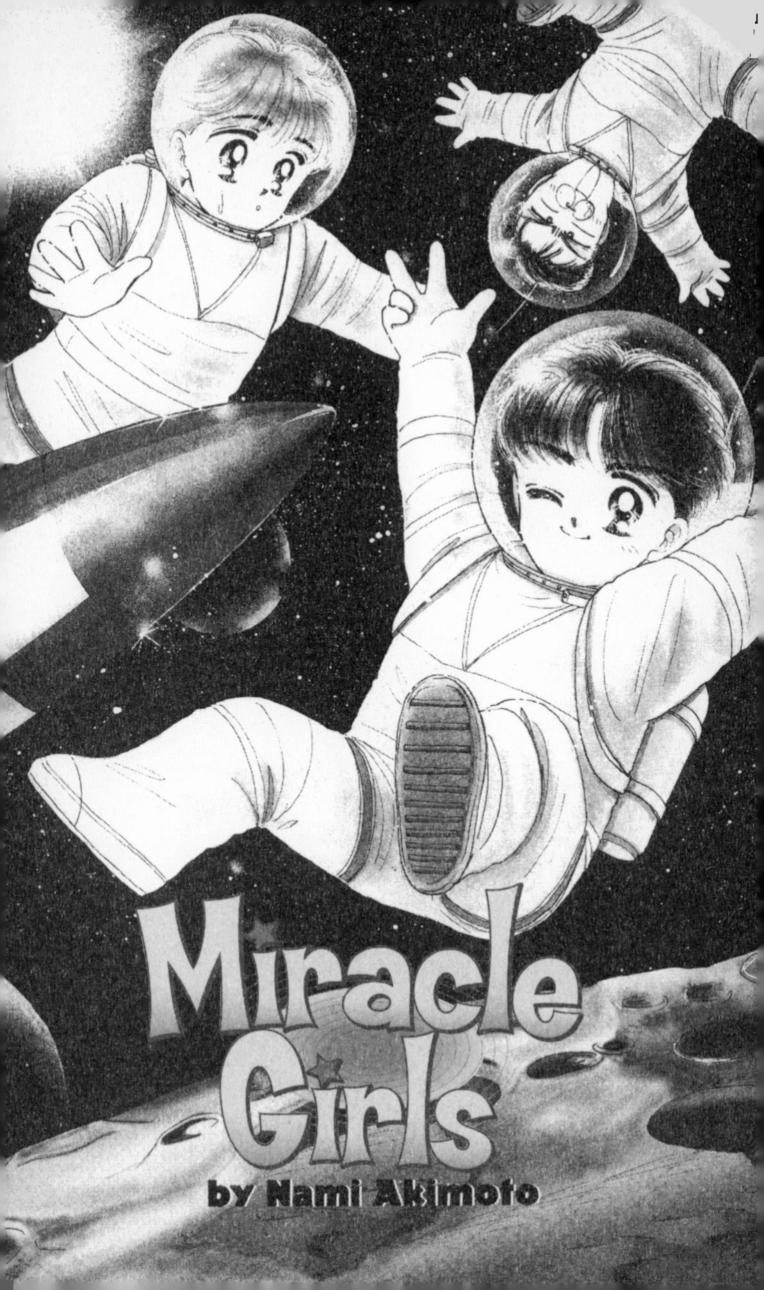
Miracle Girls
by Nami Akimoto

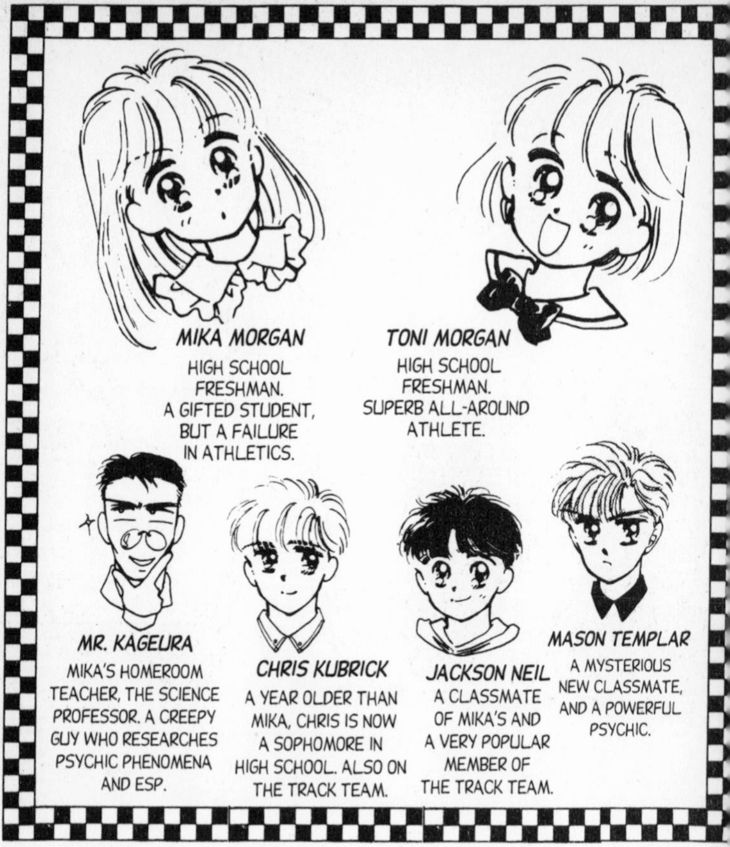
MIKA MORGAN
HIGH SCHOOL FRESHMAN. A GIFTED STUDENT, BUT A FAILURE IN ATHLETICS.
TONI MORGAN
HIGH SCHOOL FRESHMAN. SUPERB ALL-AROUND ATHLETE.
MR. KAGEURA
MIKA'S HOMEROOM TEACHER, THE SCIENCE PROFESSOR. A CREEPY GUY WHO RESEARCHES PSYCHIC PHENOMENA AND ESP.
CHRIS KUBRICK
A YEAR OLDER THAN MIKA, CHRIS IS NOW A SOPHOMORE IN HIGH SCHOOL. ALSO ON THE TRACK TEAM.
JACKSON NEIL
A CLASSMATE OF MIKA'S AND A VERY POPULAR MEMBER OF THE TRACK TEAM.
MASON TEMPLAR
A MYSTERIOUS NEW CLASSMATE, AND A POWERFUL PSYCHIC.

THE STORY SO FAR...

TONI AND MIKA ARE IDENTICAL TWINS WITH PSYCHIC POWERS. THEY ARE ABLE TO TELEPORT AND COMMUNICATE TELEPATHICALLY, BUT THEIR POWERS WORK ONLY WHEN THEY'RE TOGETHER. UNBEKNOWNST TO THE MORGAN SISTERS, MASON TEMPLAR, ANOTHER PSYCHIC WITH THE POWER TO LEVITATE OBJECTS, SCHEMES TO ROPE THE TWO INTO HIS PSYCHIC POWER ORGANIZATION. JACKSON UNCOVERS MASON'S PLOT, BUT HAS HIS MEMORY ERASED. ON THE FIRST DAY OF THE NEW SEMESTER, TONI AND MIKA, LATE AGAIN, RESORT TO TELEPORTATION. BUT AS THEY ARE ABOUT TO MAKE THE JUMP, A STRANGE LIGHT APPEARS...

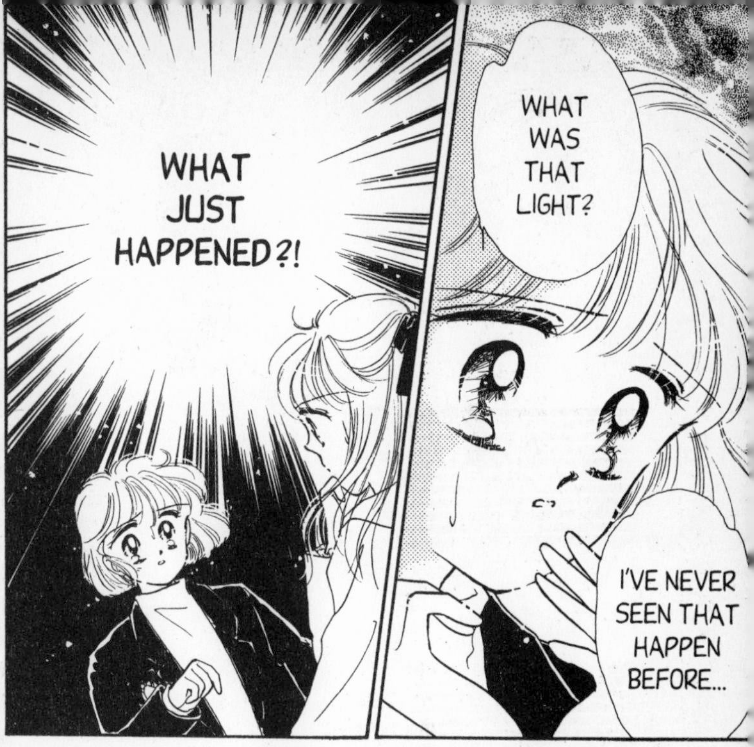
WHAT JUST HAPPENED?!
WHAT WAS THAT LIGHT?
I'VE NEVER SEEN THAT HAPPEN BEFORE...

BONUS

Hello everyone!
We're now into the home stretch of part 2, book 4.
On your next trip, on those long winter nights
(it doesn't have to be winter, but that's when it goes on sale!),
make sure you have a copy of Miracle Girls!
Heh heh - gotta advertise...

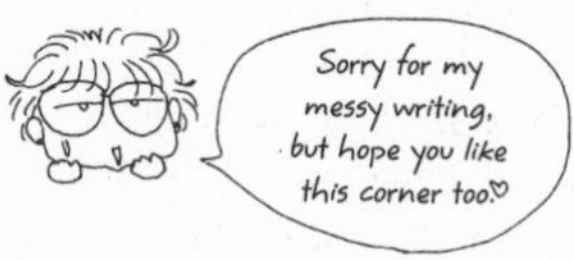
Sorry for my messy writing, but hope you like this corner too♡

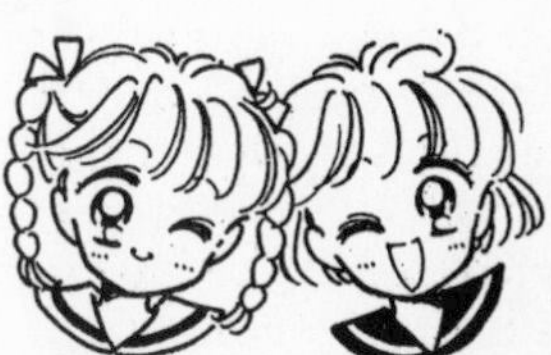

Toni & Mika

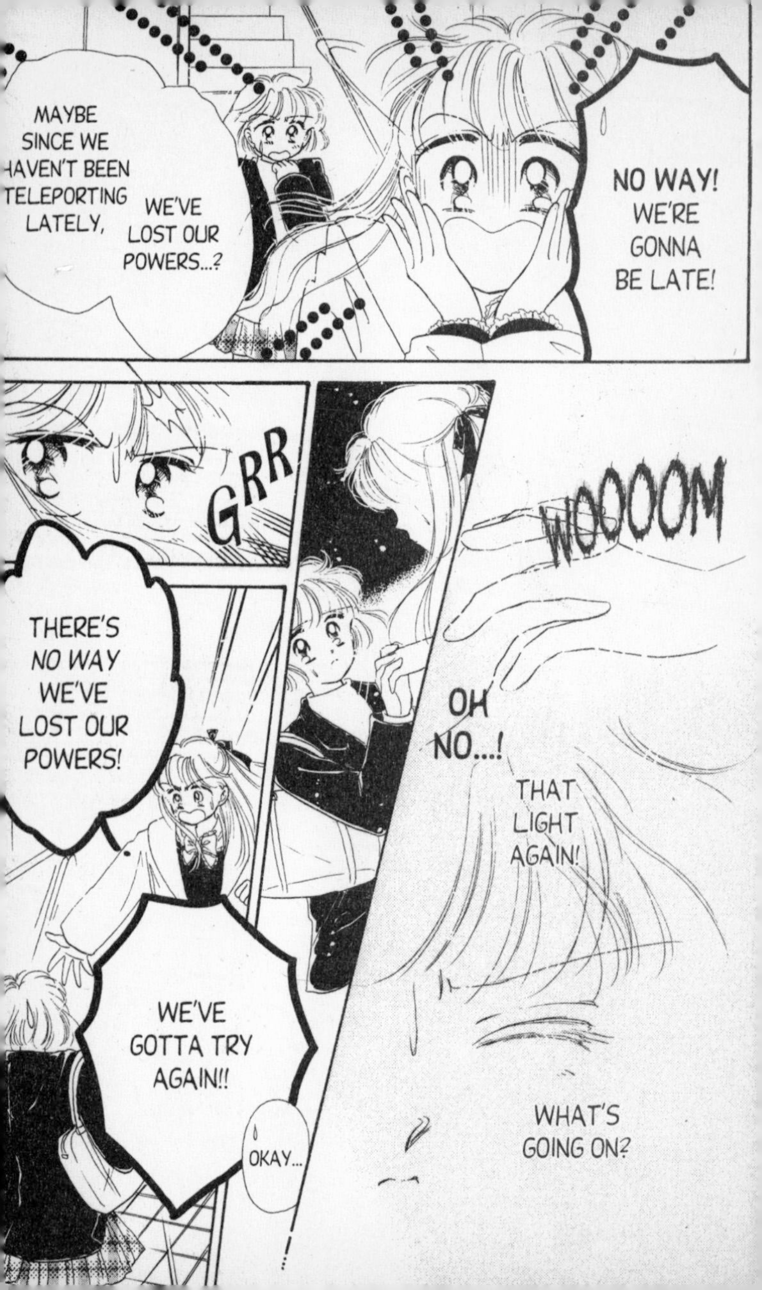
MAYBE SINCE WE HAVEN'T BEEN TELEPORTING LATELY,
WE'VE LOST OUR POWERS...?
NO WAY! WE'RE GONNA BE LATE!
GRR
THERE'S NO WAY WE'VE LOST OUR POWERS!
WE'VE GOTTA TRY AGAIN!!
OKAY...
WOOOOM
OH NO...!
THAT LIGHT AGAIN!
WHAT'S GOING ON?

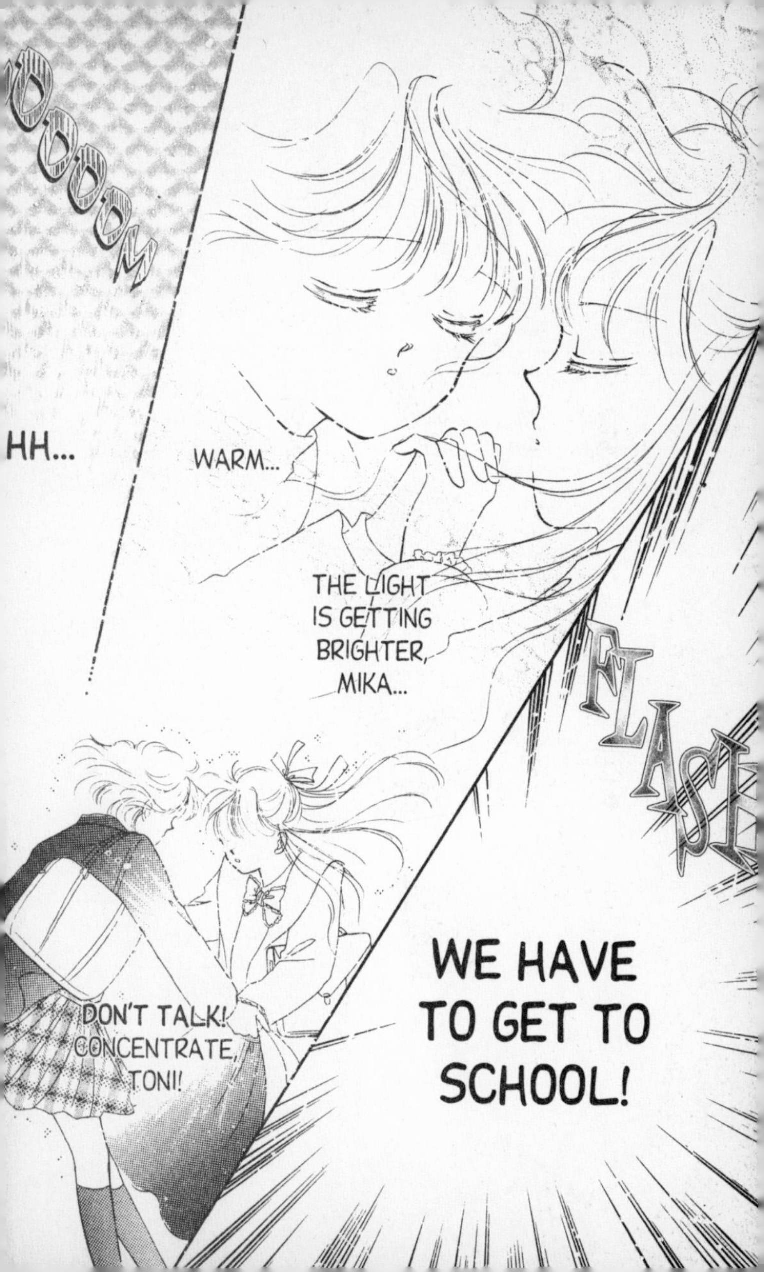

VOOOOM
HH...
WARM...
THE LIGHT IS GETTING BRIGHTER, MIKA...
FLASH
DON'T TALK! CONCENTRATE, TONI!
WE HAVE TO GET TO SCHOOL!

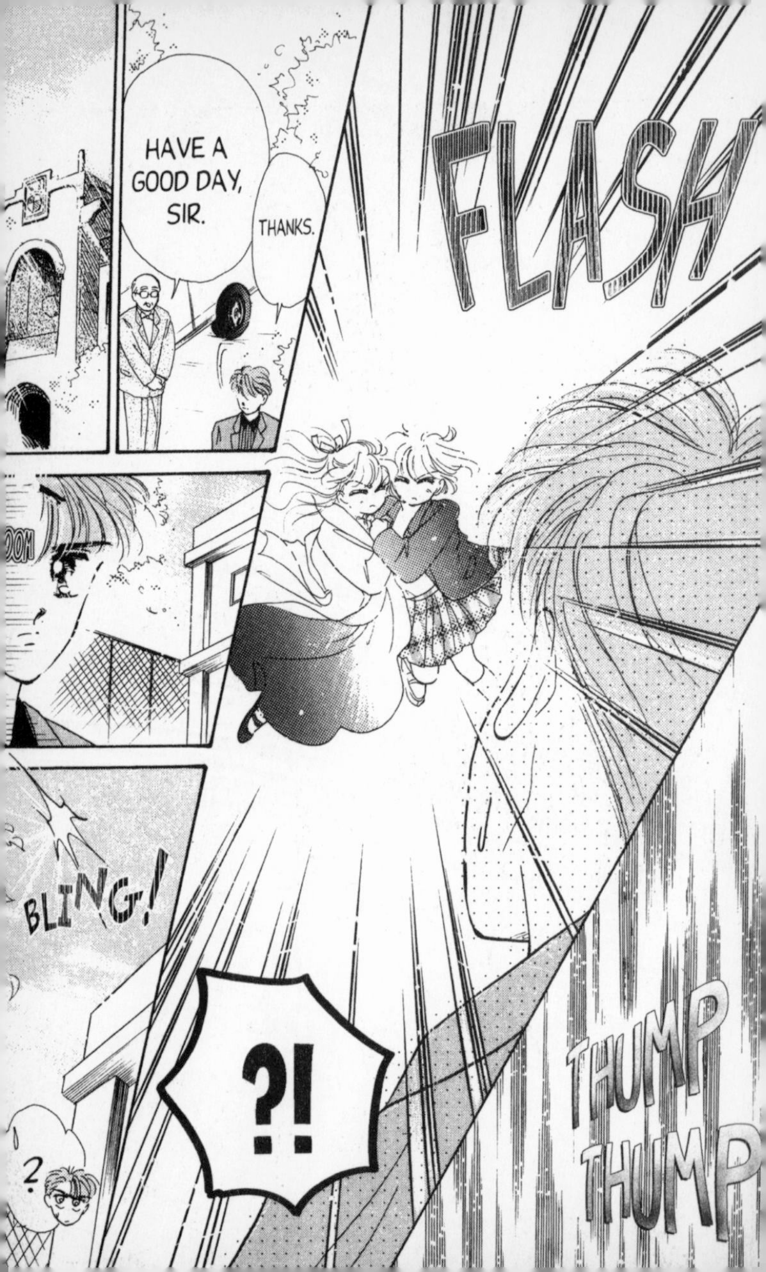
HAVE A GOOD DAY, SIR.
THANKS.
FLASH
BLING!
?!
?
THUMP THUMP

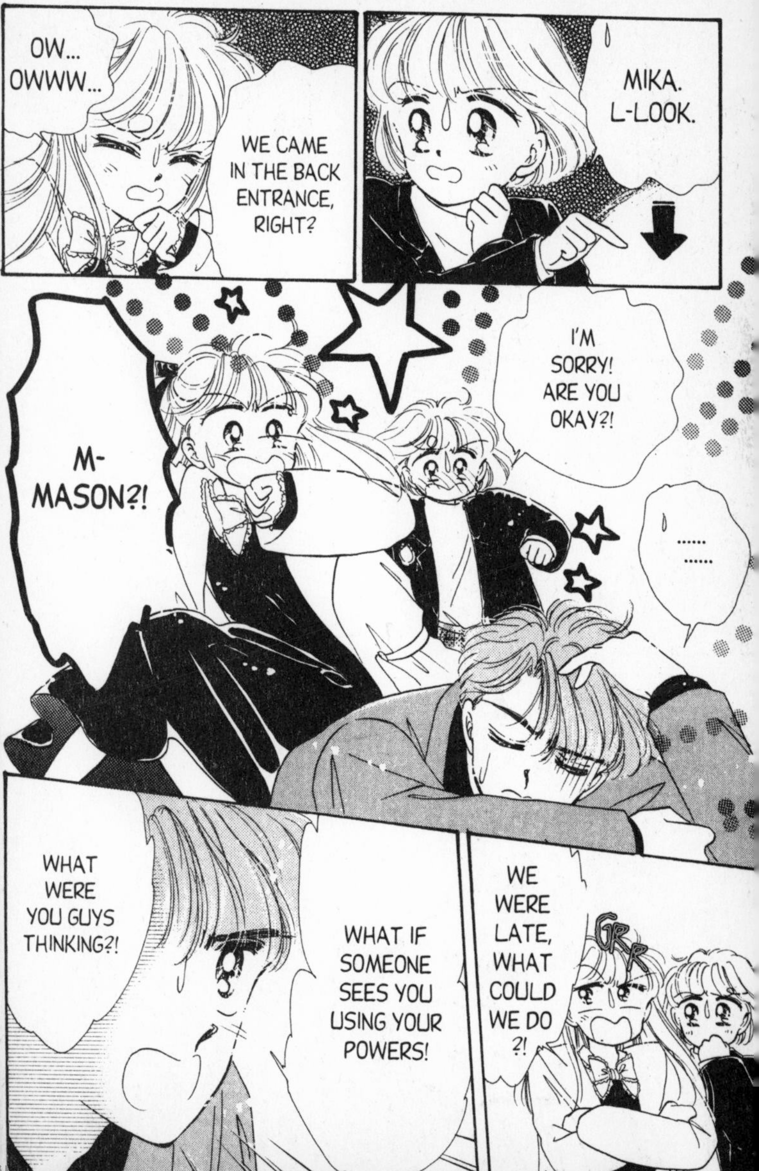
OW... OWWW...
WE CAME IN THE BACK ENTRANCE, RIGHT?
MIKA. L-LOOK.
M-MASON?!
I'M SORRY! ARE YOU OKAY?!
....
WHAT WERE YOU GUYS THINKING?!
WHAT IF SOMEONE SEES YOU USING YOUR POWERS!
WE WERE LATE, WHAT COULD WE DO?!
GRR

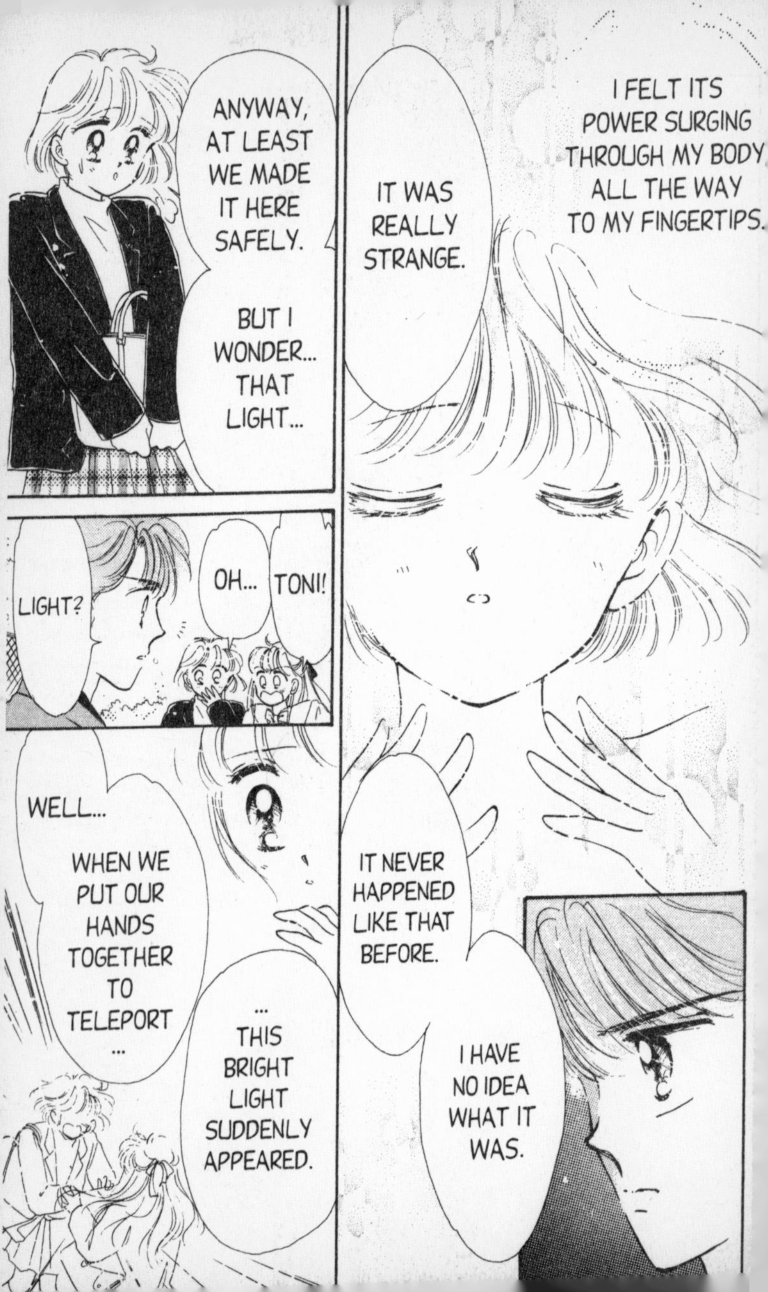
ANYWAY, AT LEAST WE MADE IT HERE SAFELY.
BUT I WONDER... THAT LIGHT...
LIGHT?
OH...
TONI!
WELL...
WHEN WE PUT OUR HANDS TOGETHER TO TELEPORT ...
... THIS BRIGHT LIGHT SUDDENLY APPEARED.
IT WAS REALLY STRANGE.
I FELT ITS POWER SURGING THROUGH MY BODY ALL THE WAY TO MY FINGERTIPS.
IT NEVER HAPPENED LIKE THAT BEFORE.
I HAVE NO IDEA WHAT IT WAS.

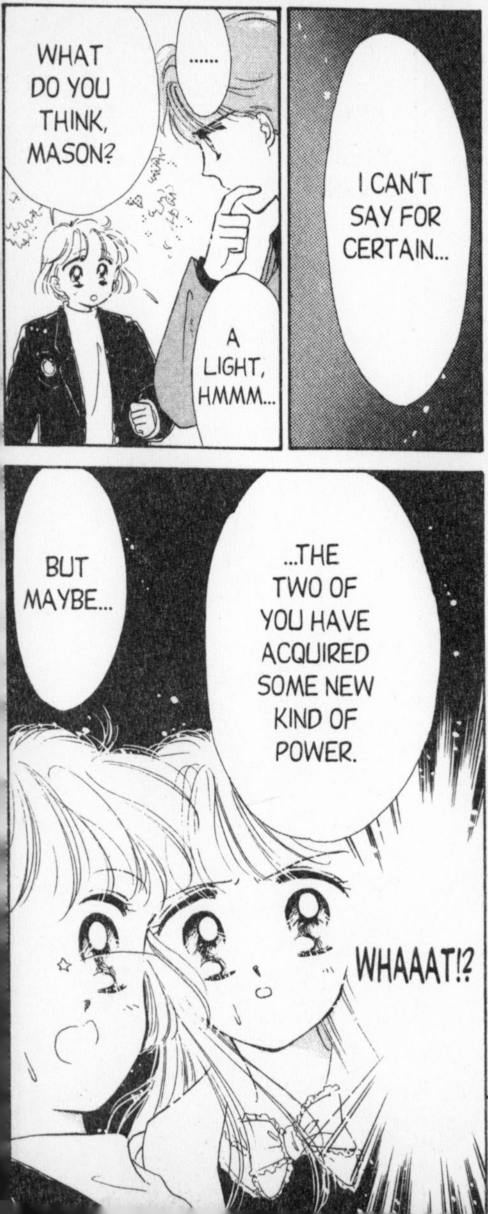
WHAT DO YOU THINK, MASON?
......
A LIGHT, HMMM...
I CAN'T SAY FOR CERTAIN...
BUT MAYBE...
...THE TWO OF YOU HAVE ACQUIRED SOME NEW KIND OF POWER.
WHAAAT!?

BONUS

Thanks to everyone who came out to my signing booth at the Nakayoshi Festival!! To everyone who couldn't make it, I'm sorry! I'm not really comfortable in front of crowds, but seeing everyone really made me glad to be there. I'm going to continue to work hard. But manga artists are just people too. I'm really a shy person!

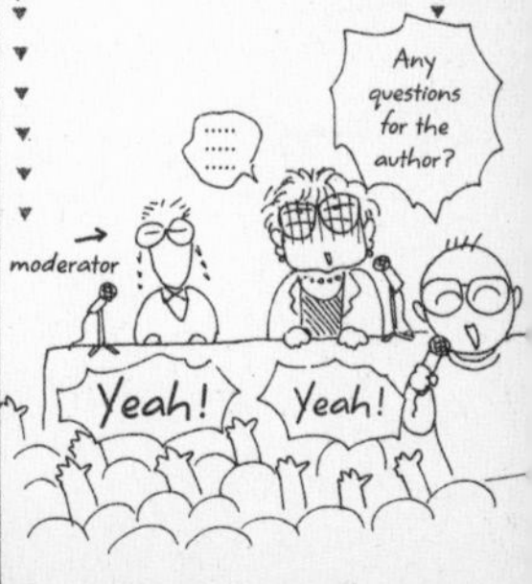
Any questions for the author?
......
moderator
Yeah!
Yeah!

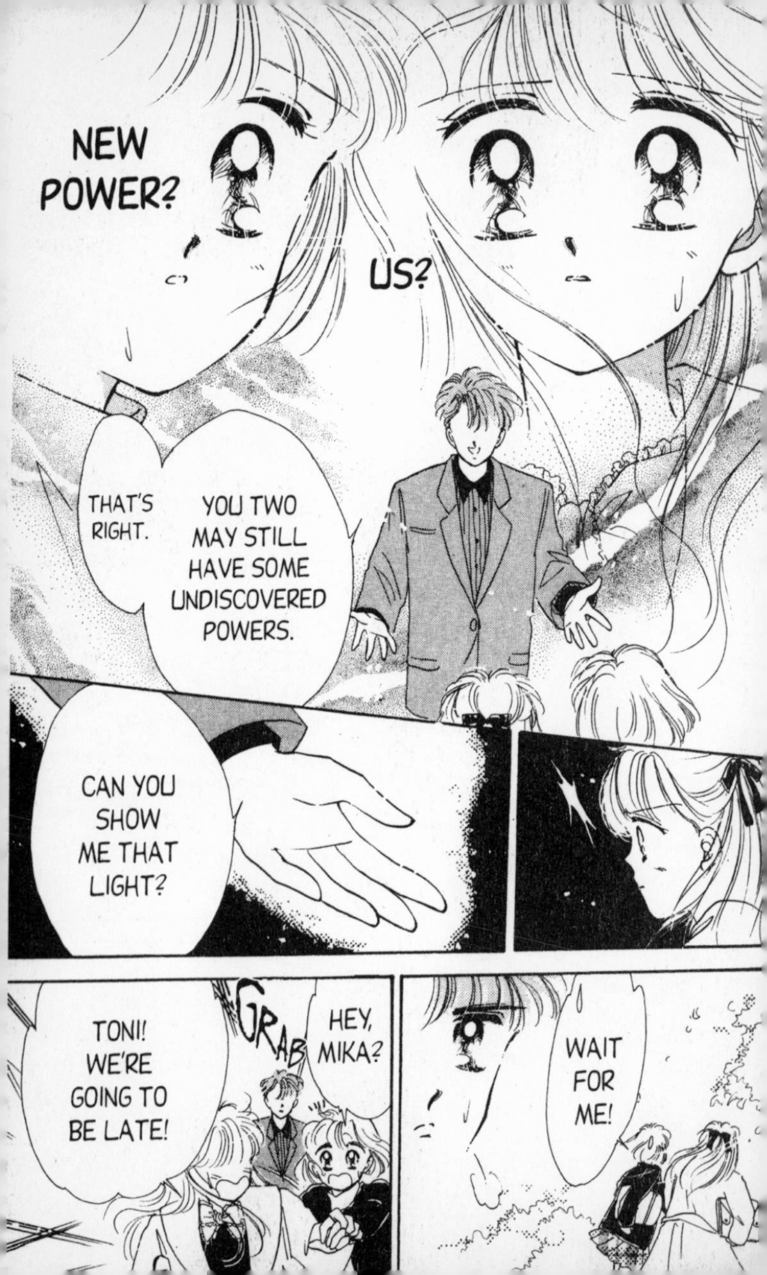
NEW POWER?
US?
THAT'S RIGHT.
YOU TWO MAY STILL HAVE SOME UNDISCOVERED POWERS.
CAN YOU SHOW ME THAT LIGHT?
TONI! WE'RE GOING TO BE LATE!
GRAB
HEY, MIKA?
WAIT FOR ME!

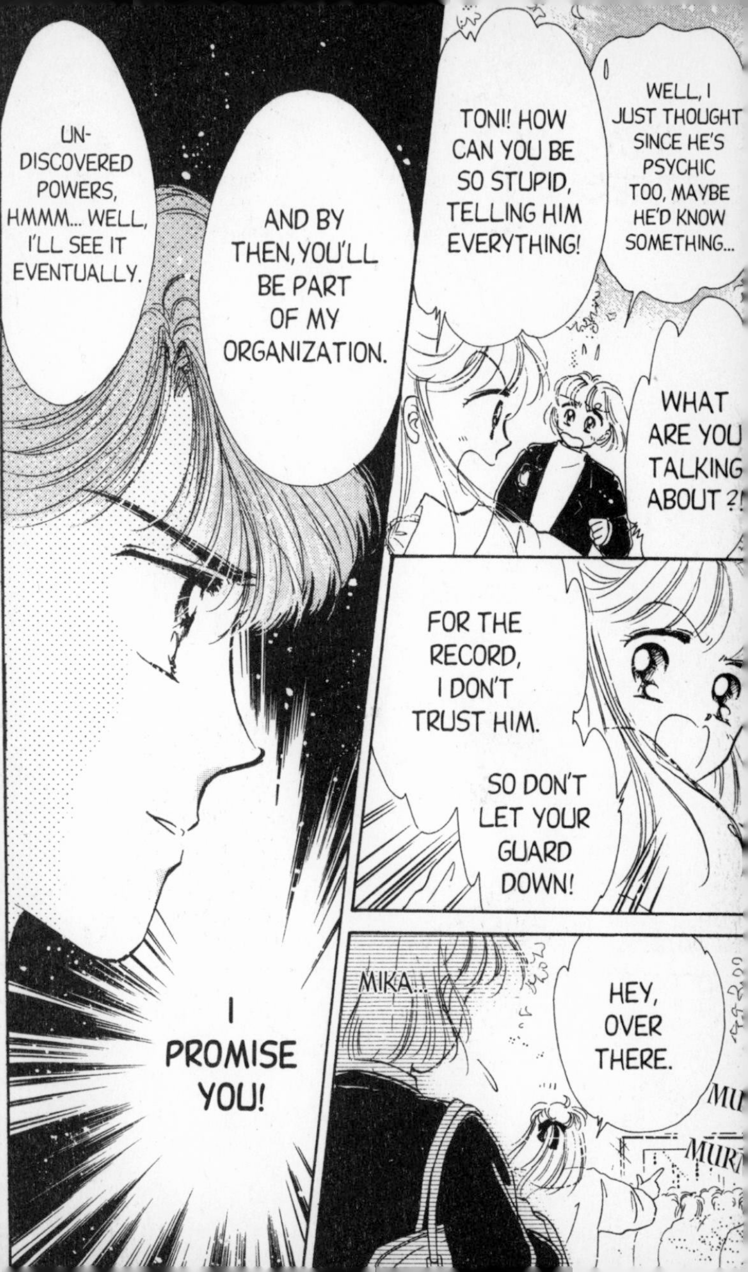
UN-DISCOVERED POWERS, HMMM... WELL, I'LL SEE IT EVENTUALLY.
AND BY THEN, YOU'LL BE PART OF MY ORGANIZATION.
I PROMISE YOU!
TONI! HOW CAN YOU BE SO STUPID, TELLING HIM EVERYTHING!
WELL, I JUST THOUGHT SINCE HE'S PSYCHIC TOO, MAYBE HE'D KNOW SOMETHING...
WHAT ARE YOU TALKING ABOUT?!
FOR THE RECORD, I DON'T TRUST HIM.
SO DON'T LET YOUR GUARD DOWN!
MIKA...
HEY, OVER THERE.

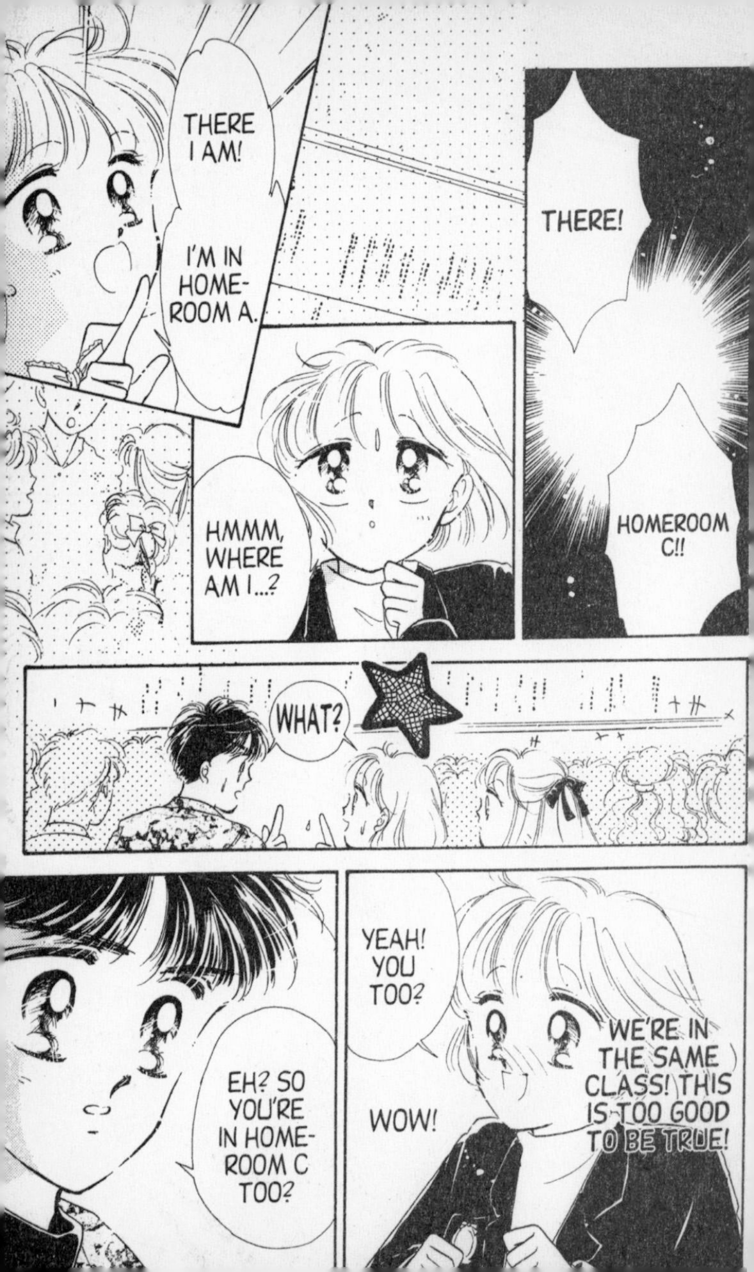
THERE I AM!
I'M IN HOME-ROOM A.
HMMM, WHERE AM I...?
THERE!
HOMEROOM C!!
WHAT?
EH? SO YOU'RE IN HOME-ROOM C TOO?
YEAH! YOU TOO?
WOW!
WE'RE IN THE SAME CLASS! THIS IS TOO GOOD TO BE TRUE!

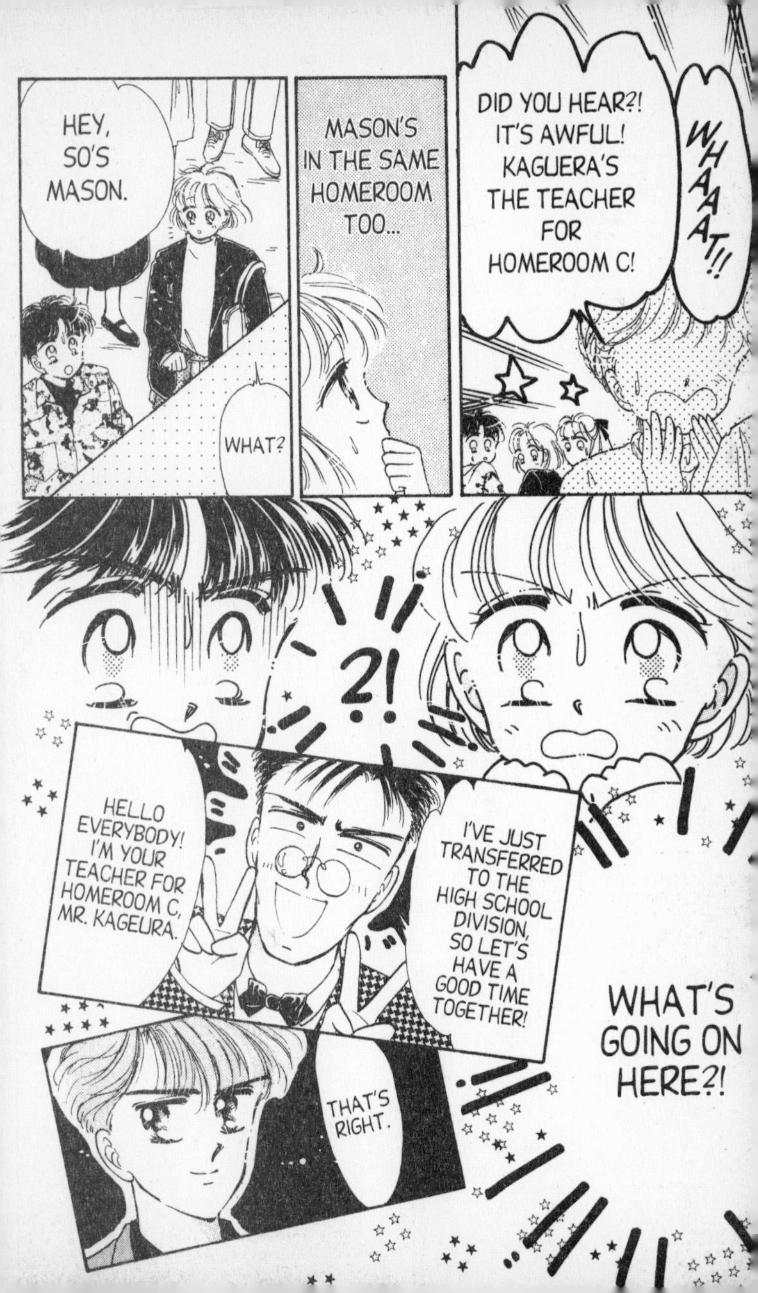
HEY, SO'S MASON.
WHAT?
MASON'S IN THE SAME HOMEROOM TOO...
DID YOU HEAR?! IT'S AWFUL! KAGUERA'S THE TEACHER FOR HOMEROOM C!
WHAAAT!!
?!
HELLO EVERYBODY! I'M YOUR TEACHER FOR HOMEROOM C, MR. KAGEURA.
I'VE JUST TRANSFERRED TO THE HIGH SCHOOL DIVISION, SO LET'S HAVE A GOOD TIME TOGETHER!
THAT'S RIGHT.
WHAT'S GOING ON HERE?!

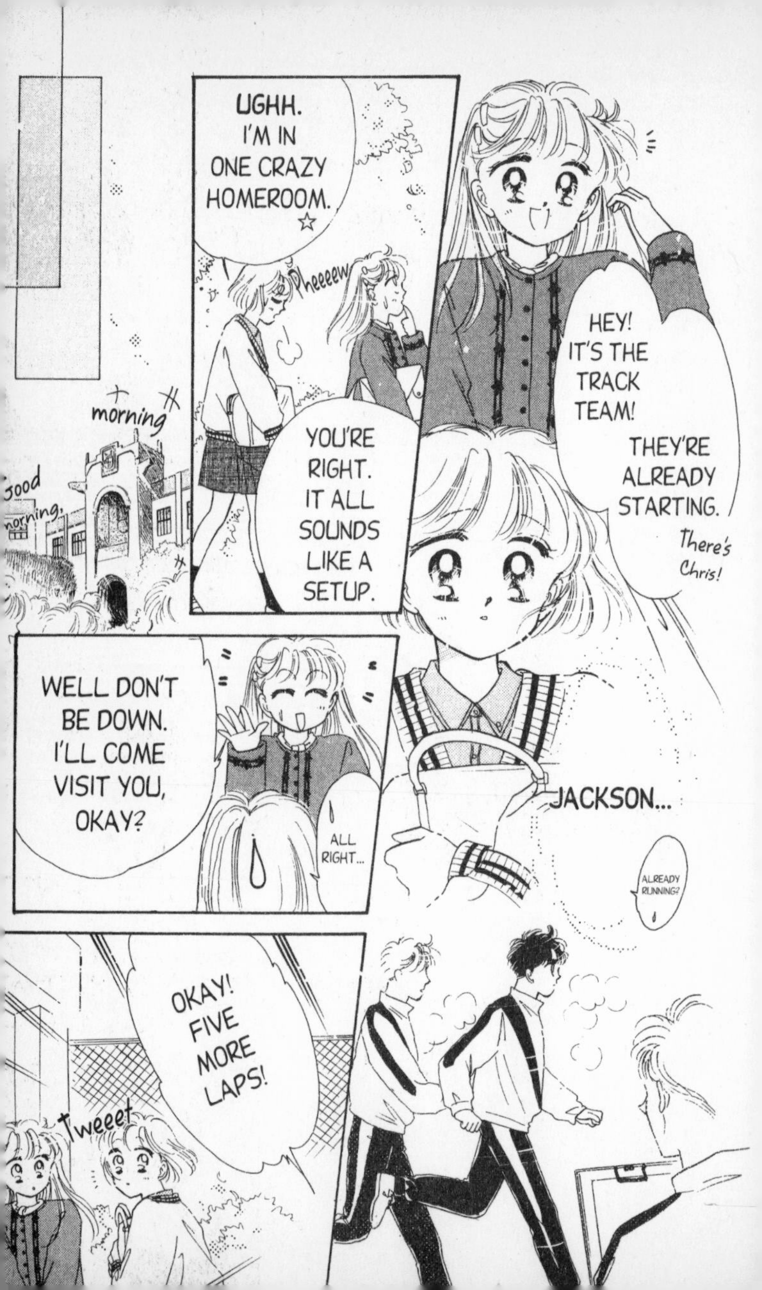
morning
Good morning,
UGHH. I'M IN ONE CRAZY HOMEROOM. ☆
Pheeeew
YOU'RE RIGHT. IT ALL SOUNDS LIKE A SETUP.
WELL DON'T BE DOWN. I'LL COME VISIT YOU, OKAY?
ALL RIGHT...
HEY! IT'S THE TRACK TEAM!
THEY'RE ALREADY STARTING.
There's Chris!
JACKSON...
ALREADY RUNNING?
OKAY! FIVE MORE LAPS!
Tweeet

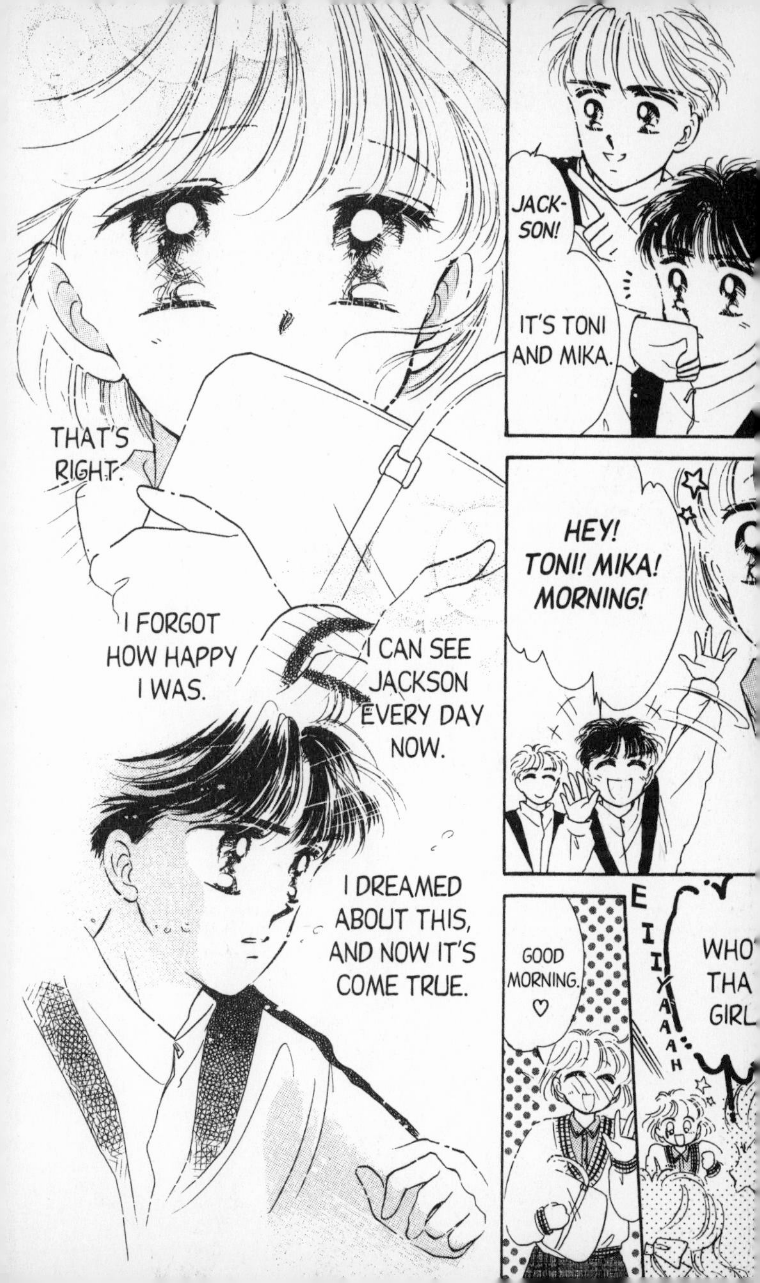
THAT'S RIGHT.
I FORGOT HOW HAPPY I WAS.
I CAN SEE JACKSON EVERY DAY NOW.
I DREAMED ABOUT THIS, AND NOW IT'S COME TRUE.
JACK-SON!
IT'S TONI AND MIKA.
HEY! TONI!! MIKA! MORNING!
GOOD MORNING. ♡
EIIYAAAH
WHO THA GIRL

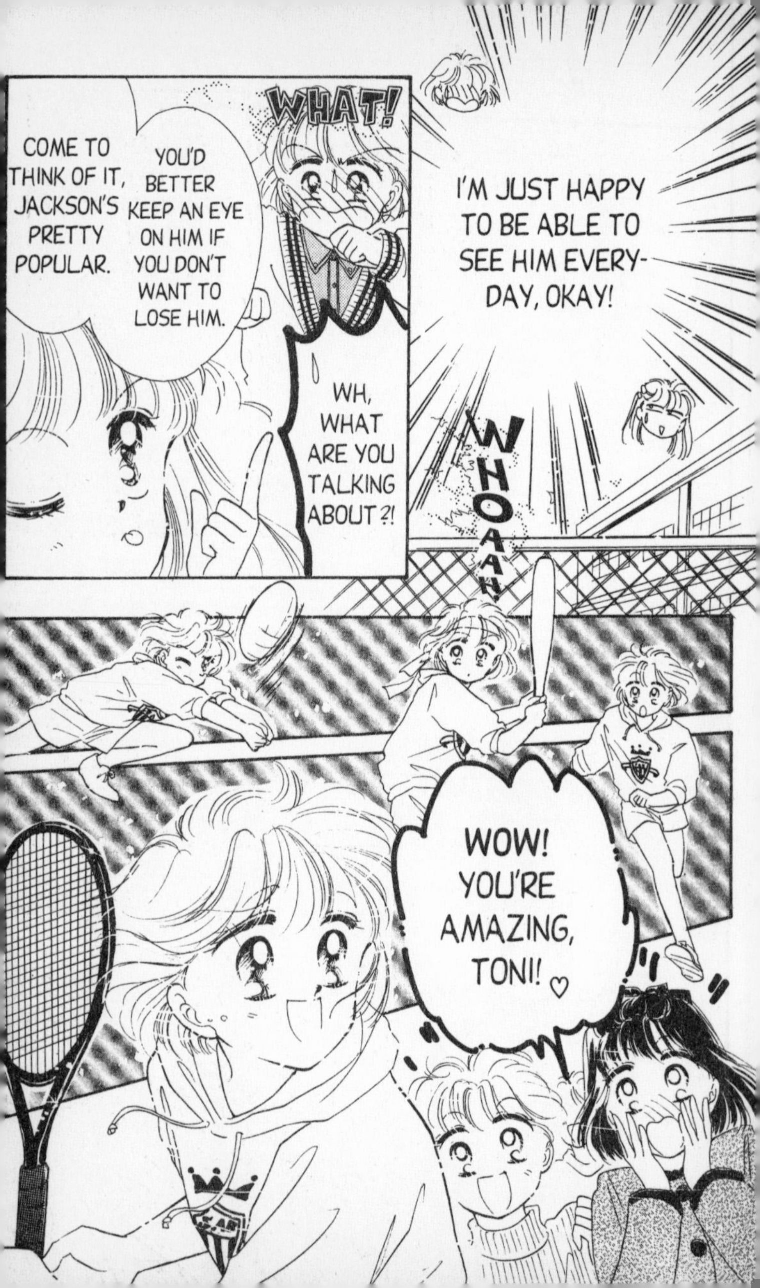
COME TO THINK OF IT, JACKSON'S PRETTY POPULAR.
YOU'D BETTER KEEP AN EYE ON HIM IF YOU DON'T WANT TO LOSE HIM.
WHAT!
WH, WHAT ARE YOU TALKING ABOUT?!
I'M JUST HAPPY TO BE ABLE TO SEE HIM EVERY-DAY, OKAY!
WHOAAH
WOW! YOU'RE AMAZING, TONI! ♡

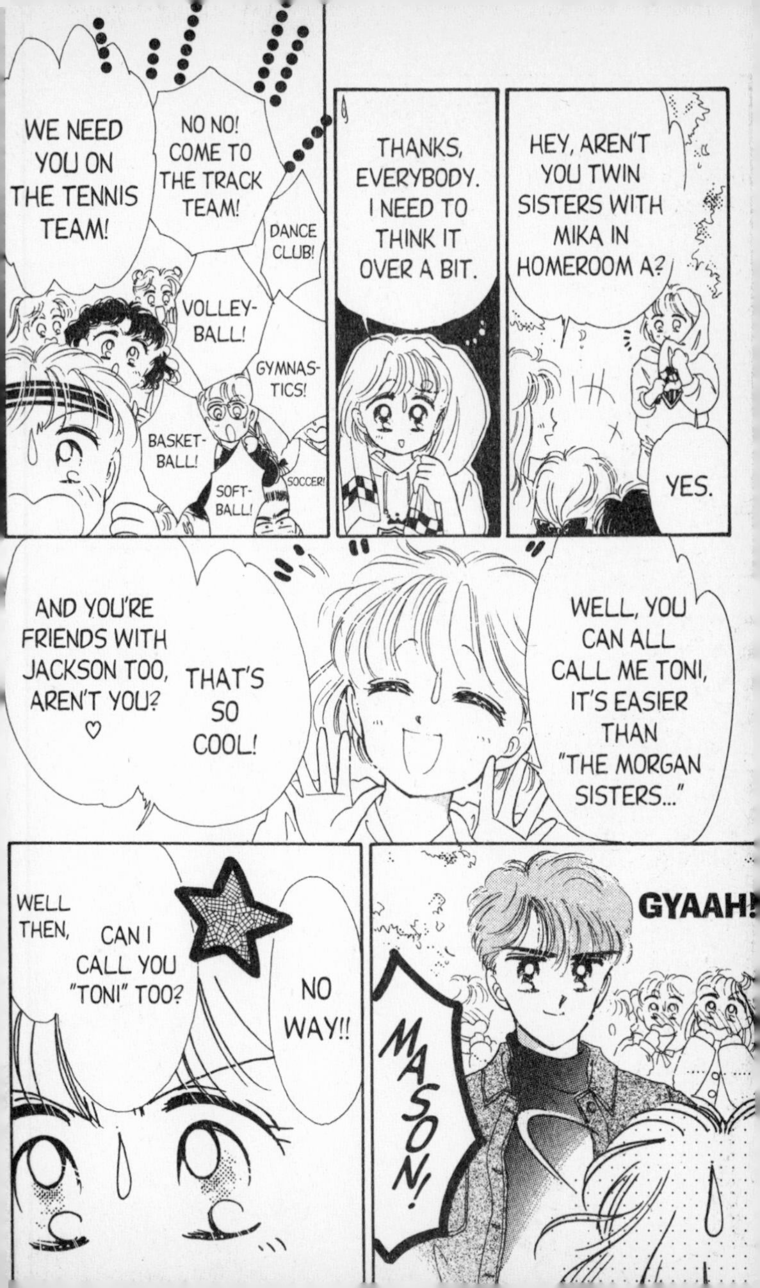
WE NEED YOU ON THE TENNIS TEAM!
NO NO! COME TO THE TRACK TEAM!
DANCE CLUB!
VOLLEY-BALL!
GYMNAS-TICS!
BASKET-BALL!
SOFT-BALL!
SOCCER!
THANKS, EVERYBODY. I NEED TO THINK IT OVER A BIT.
HEY, AREN'T YOU TWIN SISTERS WITH MIKA IN HOMEROOM A?
YES.
AND YOU'RE FRIENDS WITH JACKSON TOO, AREN'T YOU? ♡
THAT'S SO COOL!
WELL, YOU CAN ALL CALL ME TONI, IT'S EASIER THAN "THE MORGAN SISTERS..."
WELL THEN,
CAN I CALL YOU "TONI" TOO?
NO WAY!!
MASON!
GYAAH!

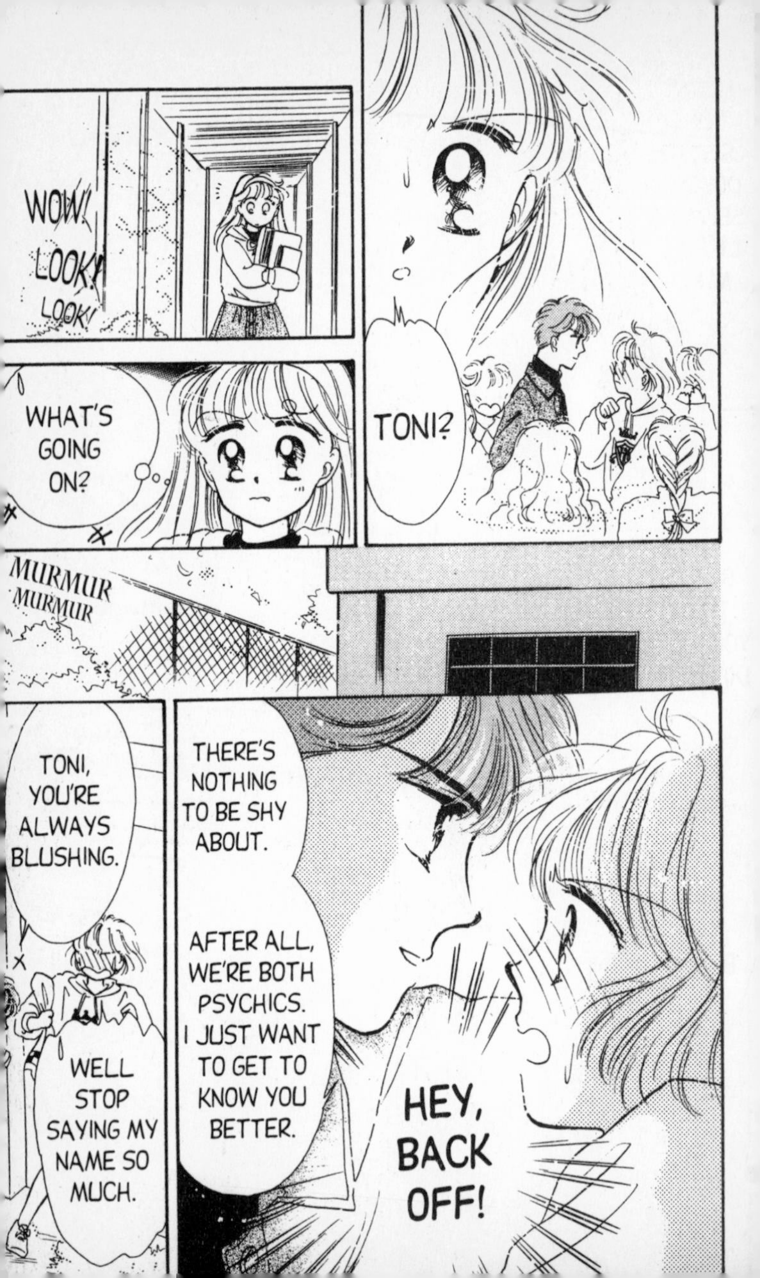
WOW! LOOK! LOOK!
WHAT'S GOING ON?
TONI?
MURMUR MURMUR
TONI, YOU'RE ALWAYS BLUSHING.
WELL STOP SAYING MY NAME SO MUCH.
THERE'S NOTHING TO BE SHY ABOUT.
AFTER ALL, WE'RE BOTH PSYCHICS. I JUST WANT TO GET TO KNOW YOU BETTER.
HEY, BACK OFF!

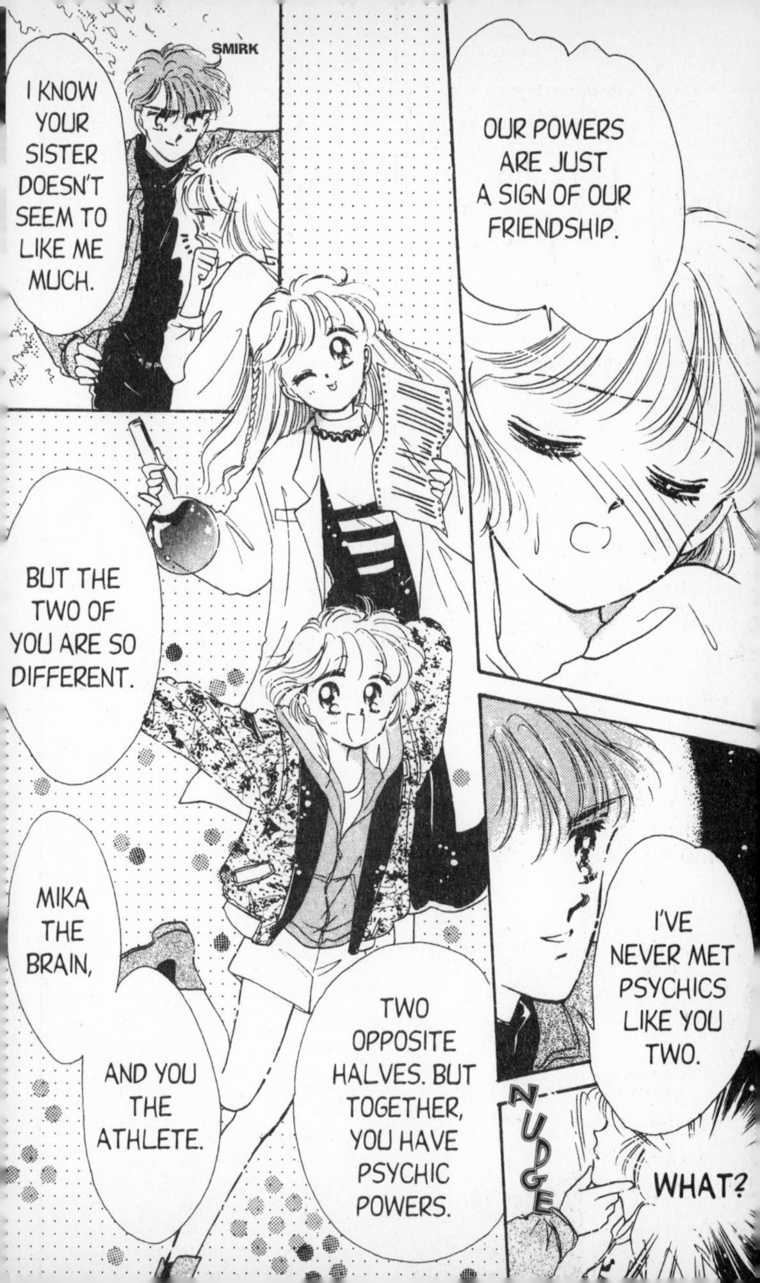
SMIRK
I KNOW YOUR SISTER DOESN'T SEEM TO LIKE ME MUCH.
BUT THE TWO OF YOU ARE SO DIFFERENT.
MIKA THE BRAIN,
AND YOU THE ATHLETE.
TWO OPPOSITE HALVES. BUT TOGETHER, YOU HAVE PSYCHIC POWERS.
OUR POWERS ARE JUST A SIGN OF OUR FRIENDSHIP.
I'VE NEVER MET PSYCHICS LIKE YOU TWO.
NUDGE
WHAT?

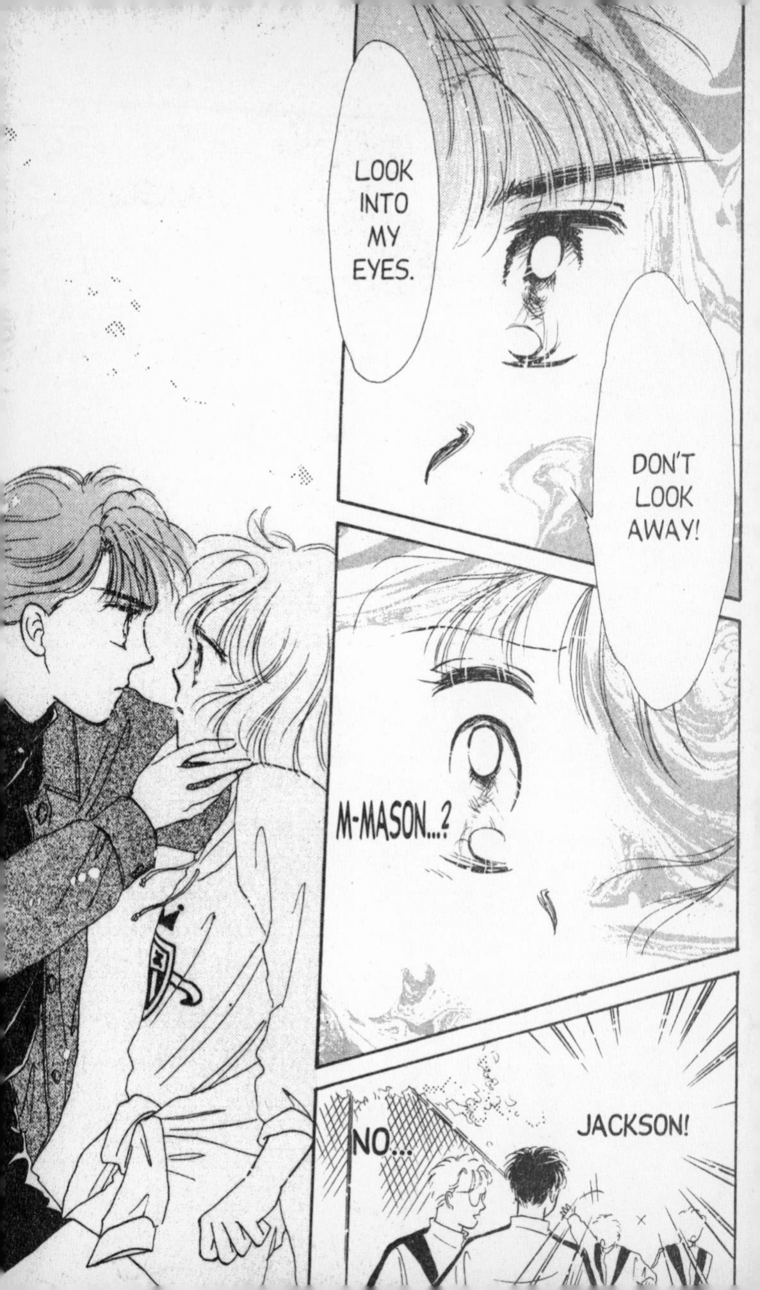
LOOK INTO MY EYES.
DON'T LOOK AWAY!
M-MASON...?
NO...
JACKSON!

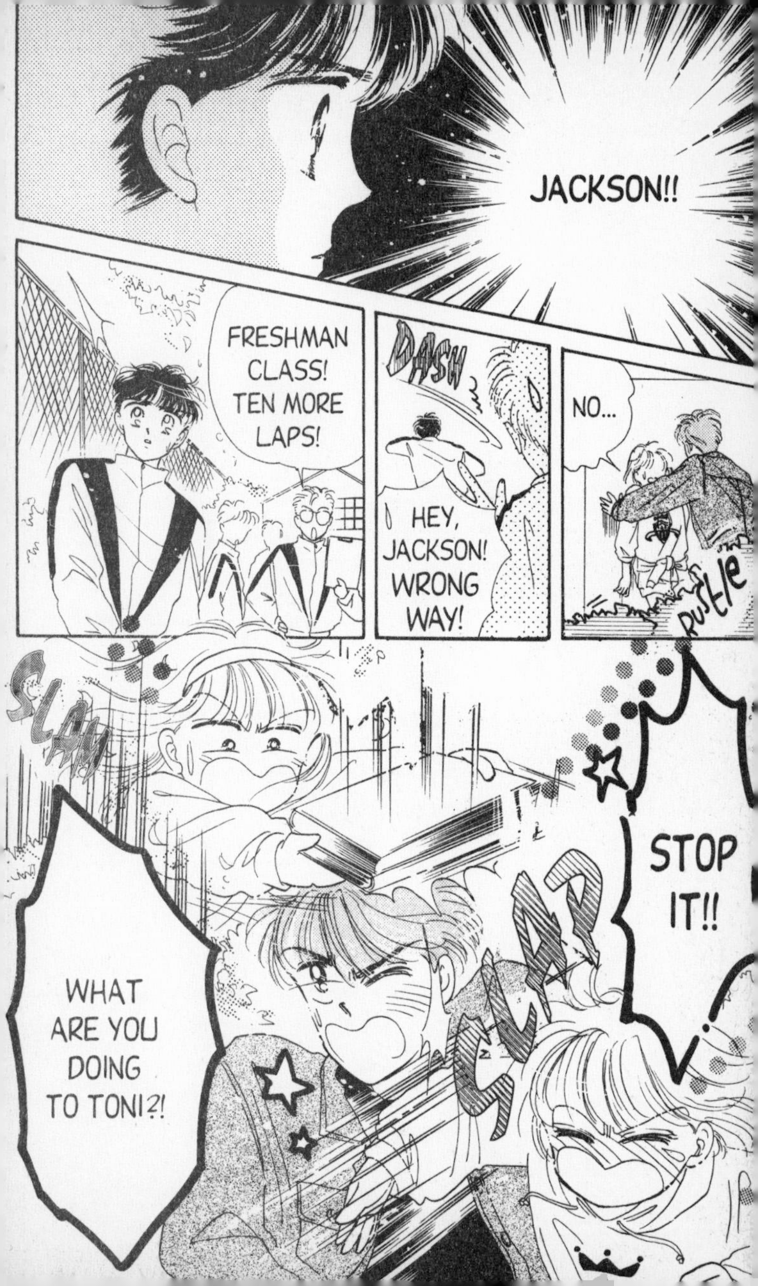
JACKSON!!
FRESHMAN CLASS! TEN MORE LAPS!
DASH
HEY, JACKSON! WRONG WAY!
NO...
RUSTLE
SLAM
STOP IT!!
CLAP
WHAT ARE YOU DOING TO TONI?!

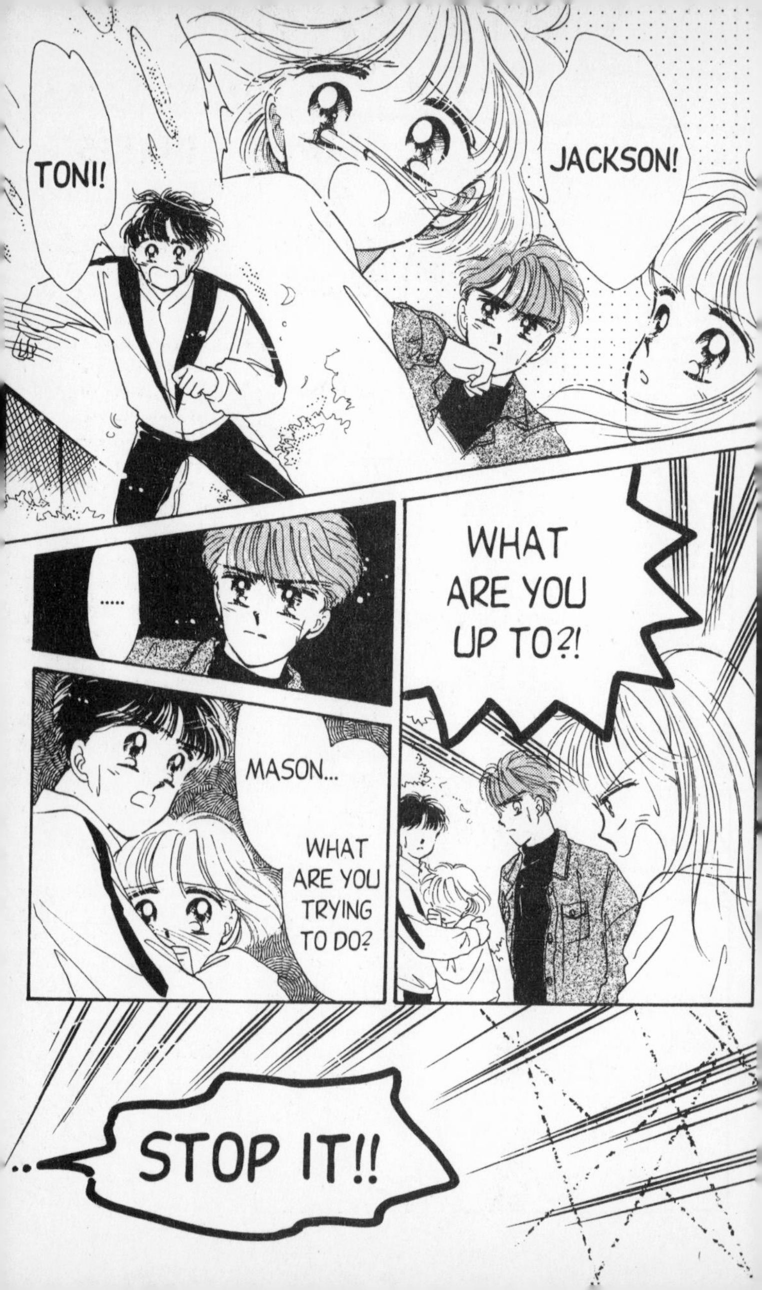

TONI!
JACKSON!
.....
WHAT ARE YOU UP TO?!
MASON...
WHAT ARE YOU TRYING TO DO?
STOP IT!!

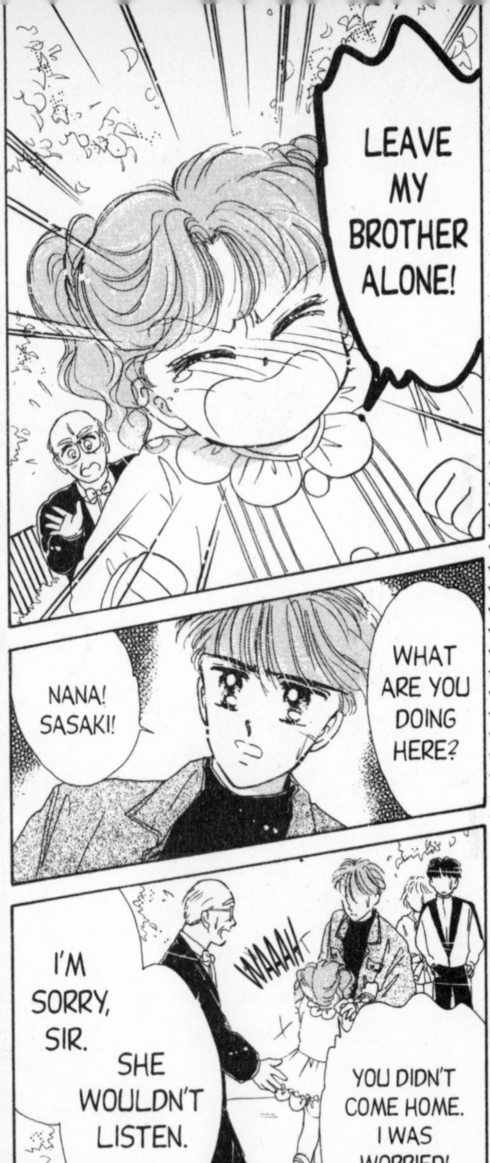
LEAVE MY BROTHER ALONE!
NANA! SASAKI!
WHAT ARE YOU DOING HERE?
I'M SORRY, SIR.
SHE WOULDN'T LISTEN.
WAAAH
YOU DIDN'T COME HOME. I WAS WORRIED!

BONUS

Back at the signing fair, we had a quiz, and one of the questions was: "What is Mason's butler's name?" I didn't think that many people would know, but everyone from Osaka to Tokyo knew the answer. (If you don't know, re-read Book 2, okay?) Another of the questions: Who do you like better, Jackson or Chris? Sadly, there weren't too many Chris fans. Oh well, he's not getting too much to do anyway. I promise to give him a more prominent role in Part 3!

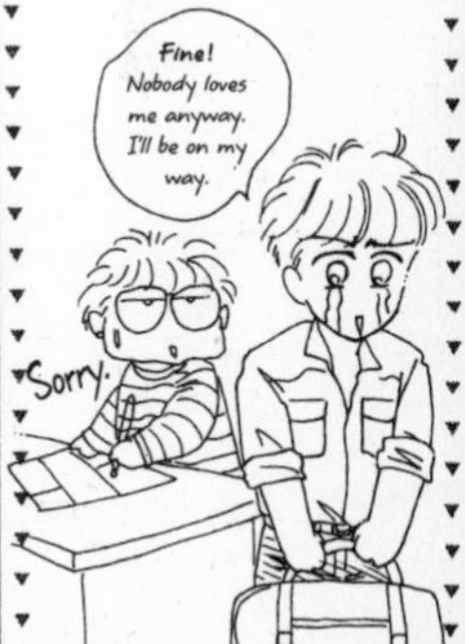
Fine! Nobody loves me anyway. I'll be on my way.
Sorry.

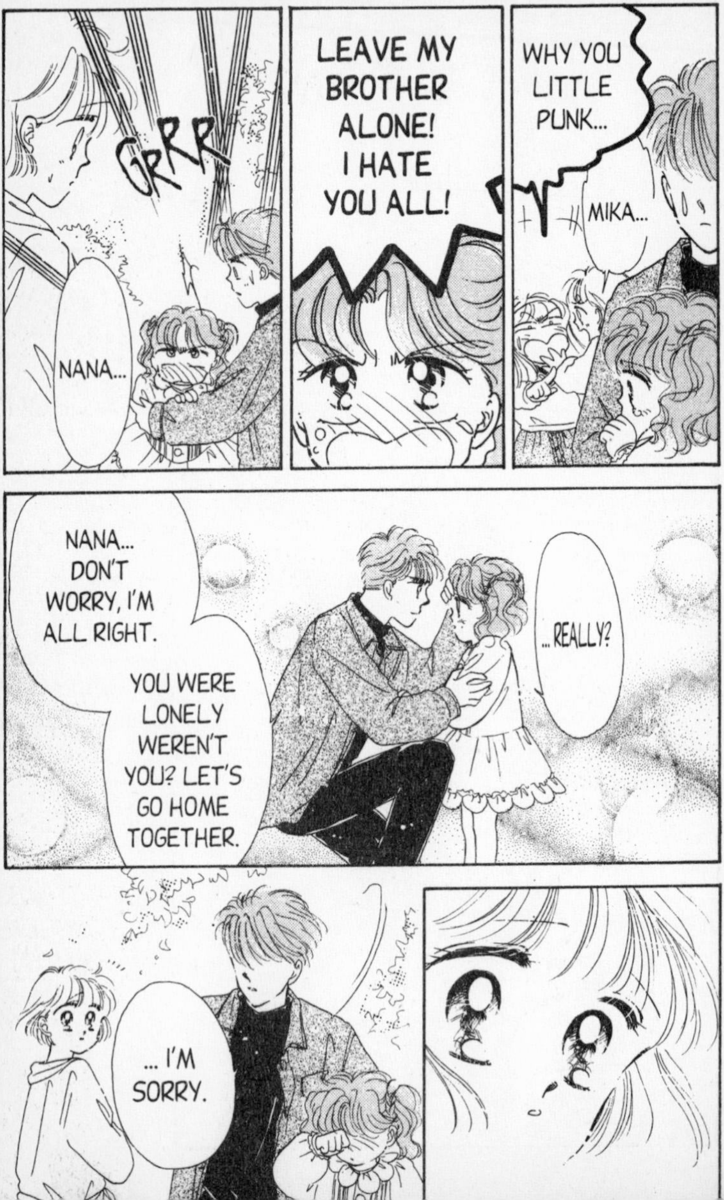
GRRR
NANA...
LEAVE MY BROTHER ALONE! I HATE YOU ALL!
WHY YOU LITTLE PUNK...
MIKA...
NANA... DON'T WORRY, I'M ALL RIGHT.
YOU WERE LONELY WEREN'T YOU? LET'S GO HOME TOGETHER.
...REALLY?
... I'M SORRY.

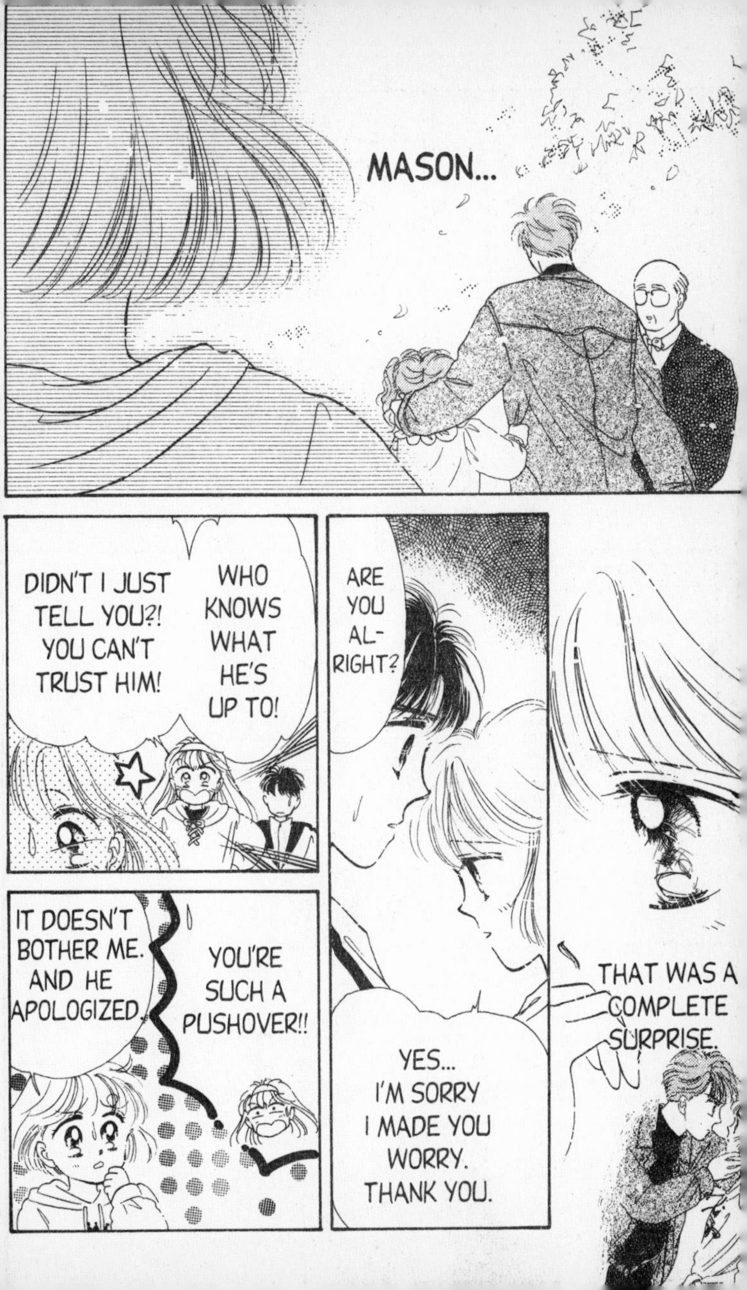
MASON...
DIDN'T I JUST TELL YOU?! YOU CAN'T TRUST HIM!
WHO KNOWS WHAT HE'S UP TO!
IT DOESN'T BOTHER ME. AND HE APOLOGIZED.
YOU'RE SUCH A PUSHOVER!!
ARE YOU AL-RIGHT?
YES... I'M SORRY I MADE YOU WORRY. THANK YOU.
THAT WAS A COMPLETE SURPRISE.

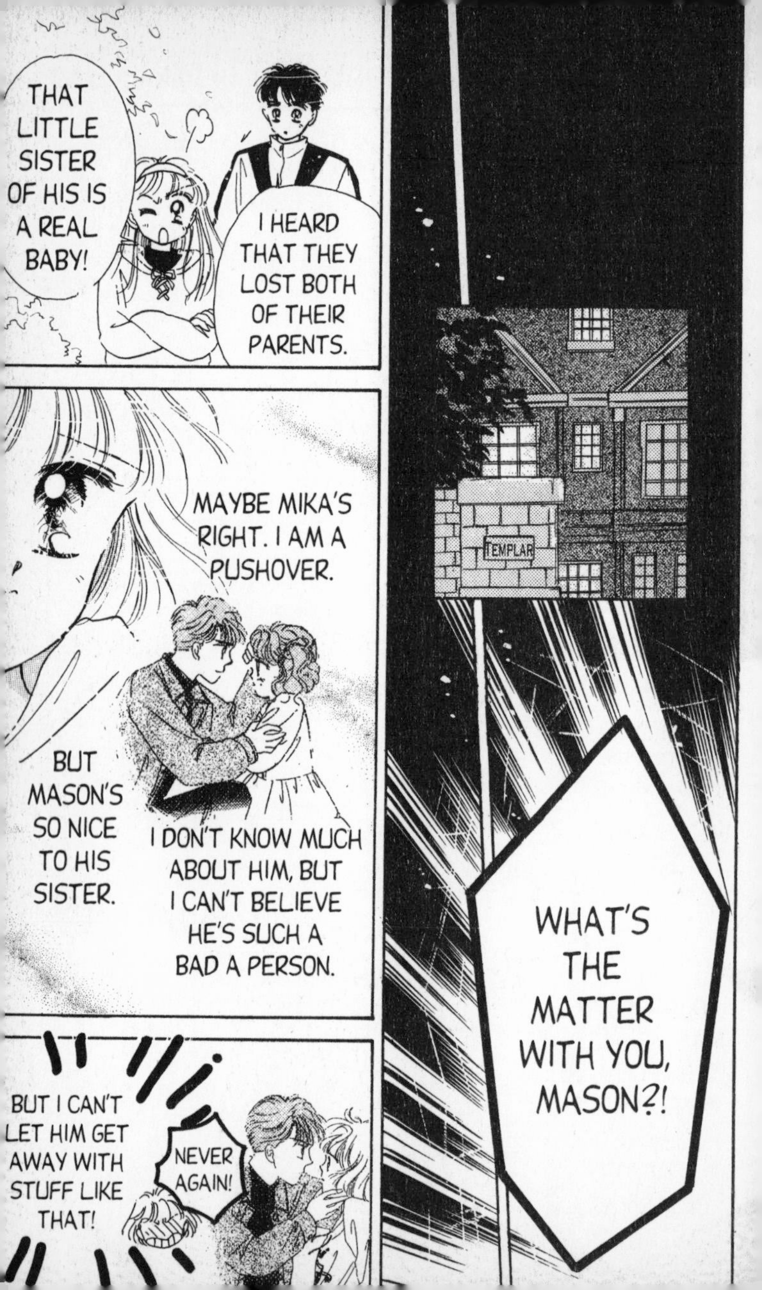
THAT LITTLE SISTER OF HIS IS A REAL BABY!
I HEARD THAT THEY LOST BOTH OF THEIR PARENTS.
MAYBE MIKA'S RIGHT. I AM A PUSHOVER.
BUT MASON'S SO NICE TO HIS SISTER.
I DON'T KNOW MUCH ABOUT HIM, BUT I CAN'T BELIEVE HE'S SUCH A BAD A PERSON.
BUT I CAN'T LET HIM GET AWAY WITH STUFF LIKE THAT!
NEVER AGAIN!
TEMPLAR
WHAT'S THE MATTER WITH YOU, MASON?!

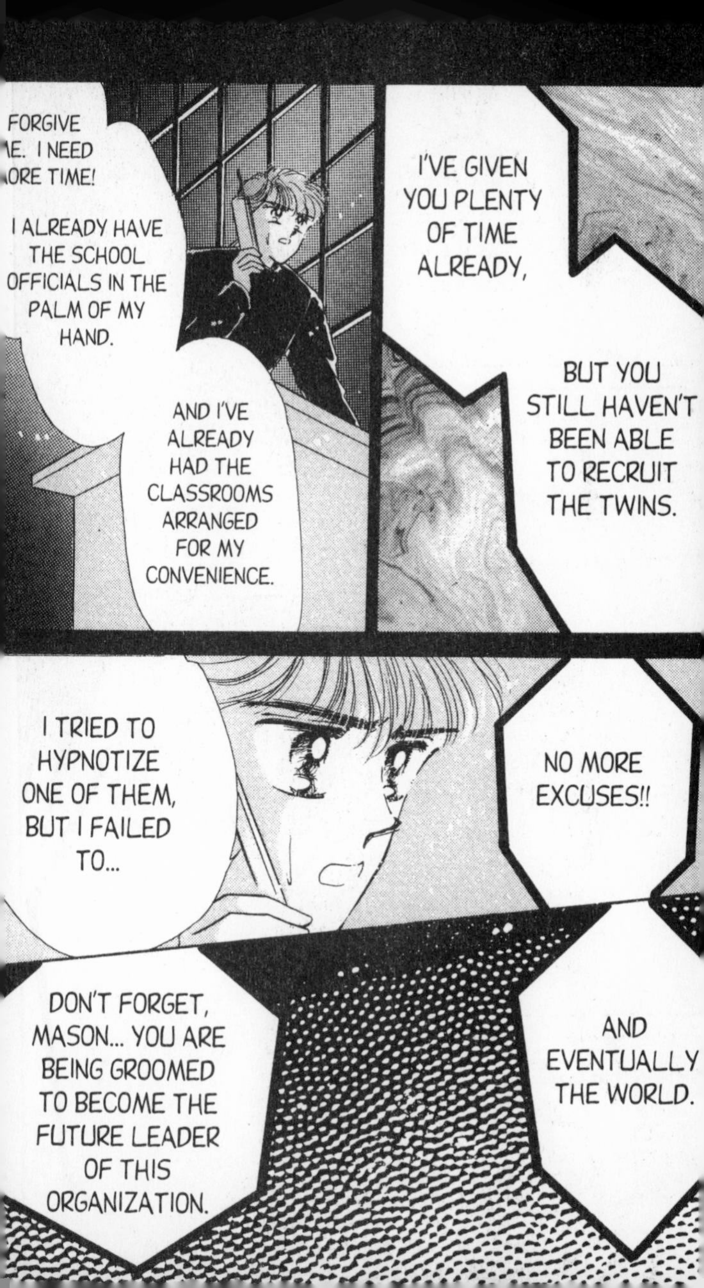
FORGIVE E. I NEED ORE TIME!
I ALREADY HAVE THE SCHOOL OFFICIALS IN THE PALM OF MY HAND.
AND I'VE ALREADY HAD THE CLASSROOMS ARRANGED FOR MY CONVENIENCE.
I'VE GIVEN YOU PLENTY OF TIME ALREADY,
BUT YOU STILL HAVEN'T BEEN ABLE TO RECRUIT THE TWINS.
I TRIED TO HYPNOTIZE ONE OF THEM, BUT I FAILED TO...
NO MORE EXCUSES!!
DON'T FORGET, MASON... YOU ARE BEING GROOMED TO BECOME THE FUTURE LEADER OF THIS ORGANIZATION.
AND EVENTUALLY THE WORLD.

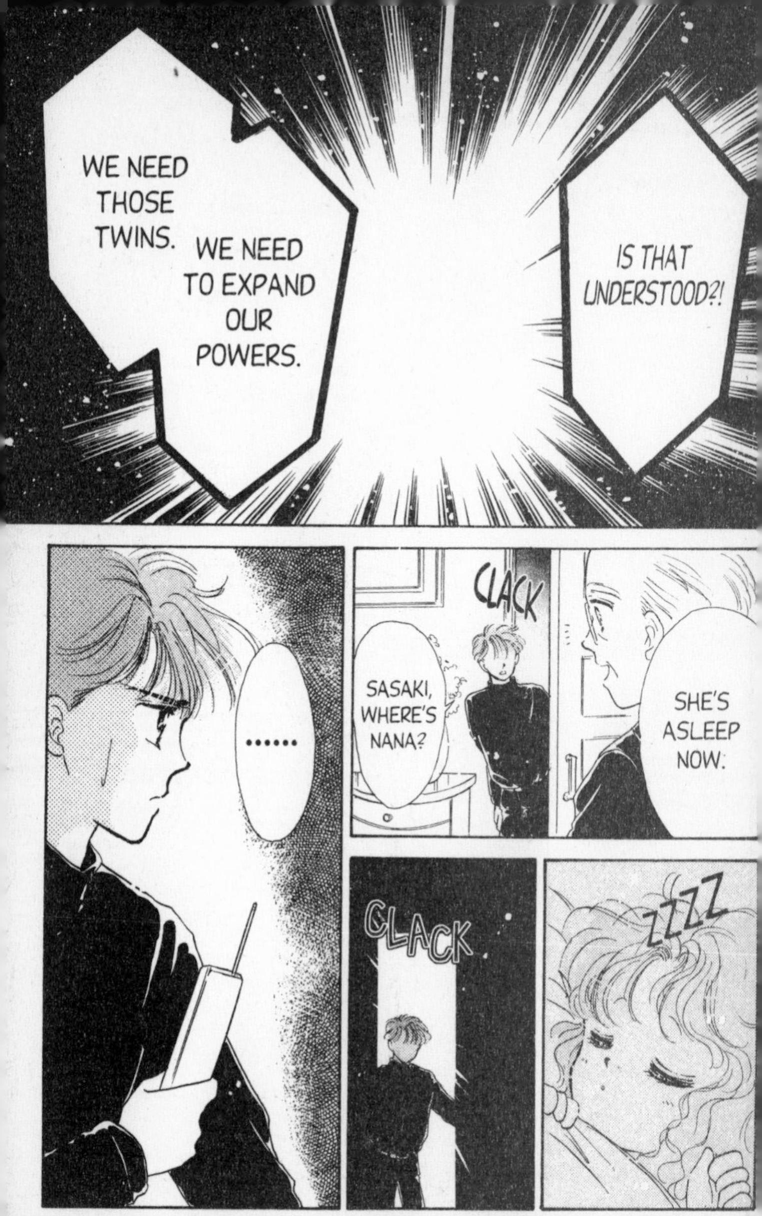
WE NEED THOSE TWINS.
WE NEED TO EXPAND OUR POWERS.
IS THAT UNDERSTOOD?!
......
CLACK
SASAKI, WHERE'S NANA?
SHE'S ASLEEP NOW.
CLACK
ZZZZ

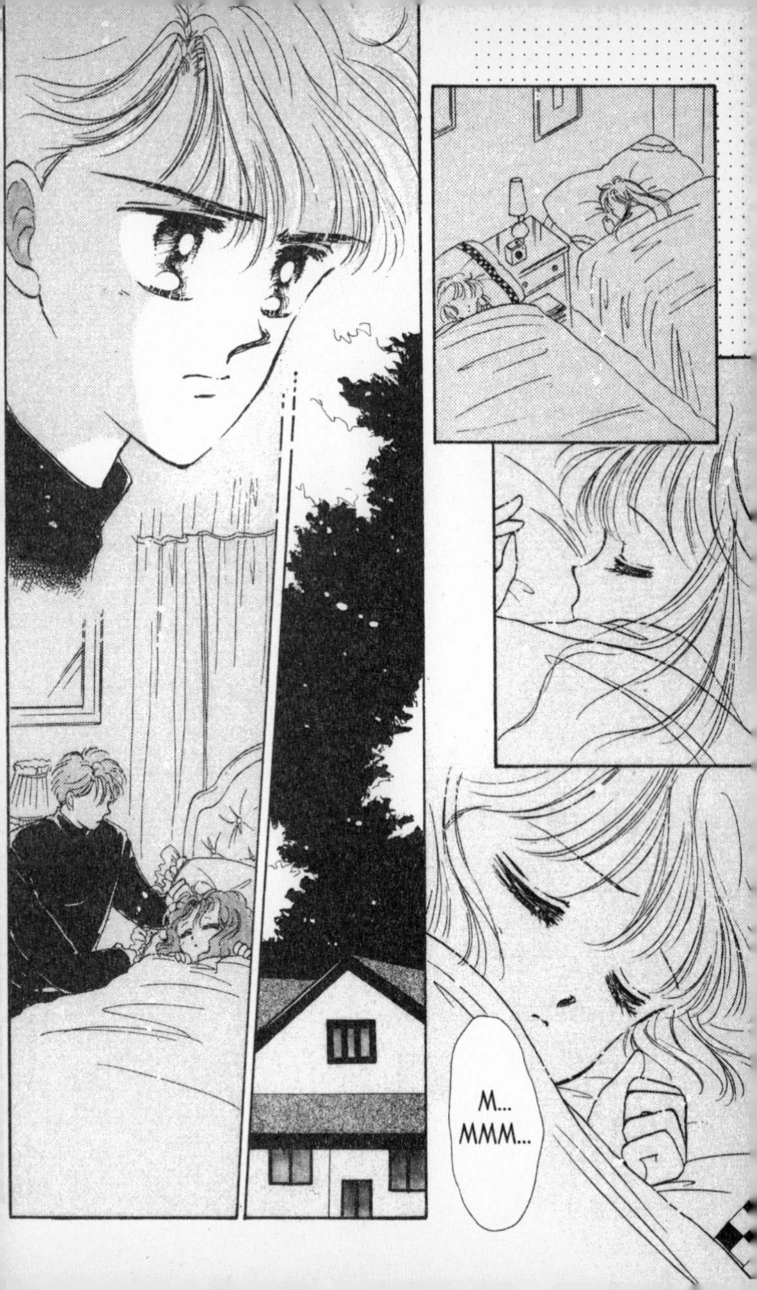
M... MMM...

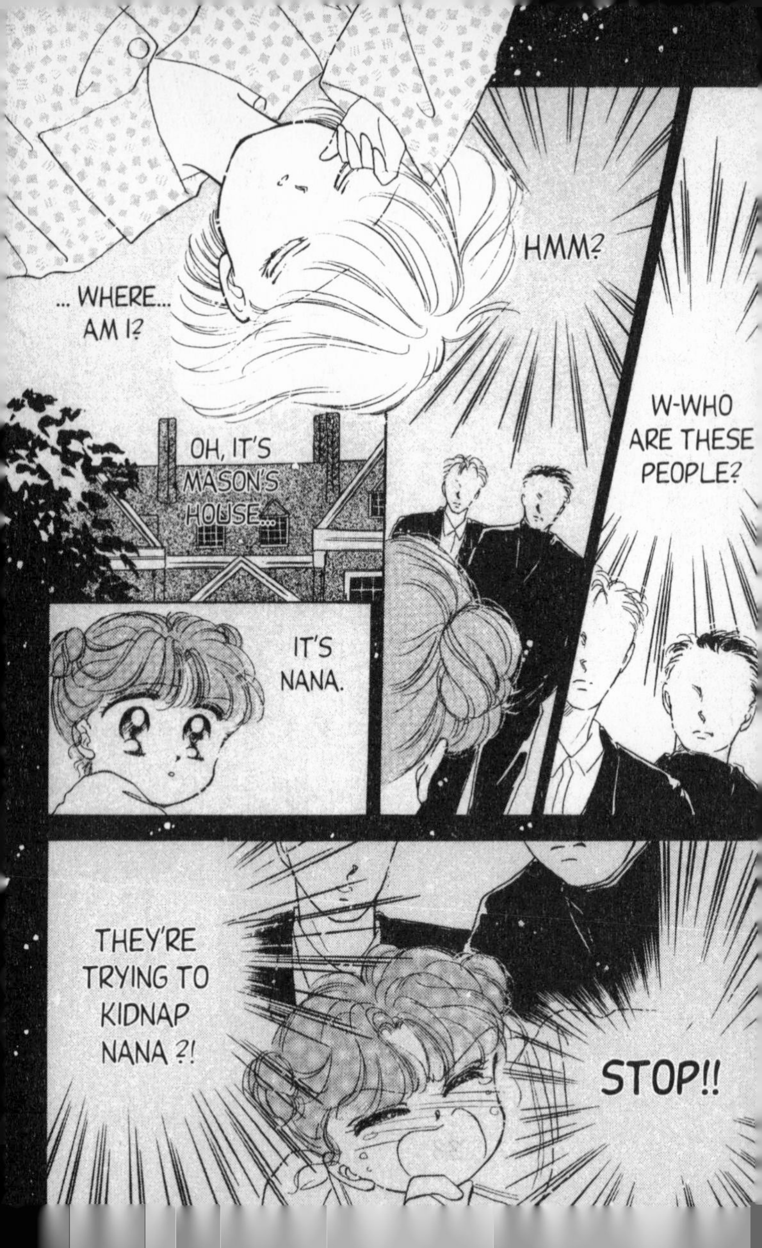
... WHERE... AM I?
OH, IT'S MASON'S HOUSE...
IT'S NANA.
HMM?
W-WHO ARE THESE PEOPLE?
THEY'RE TRYING TO KIDNAP NANA ?!
STOP!!

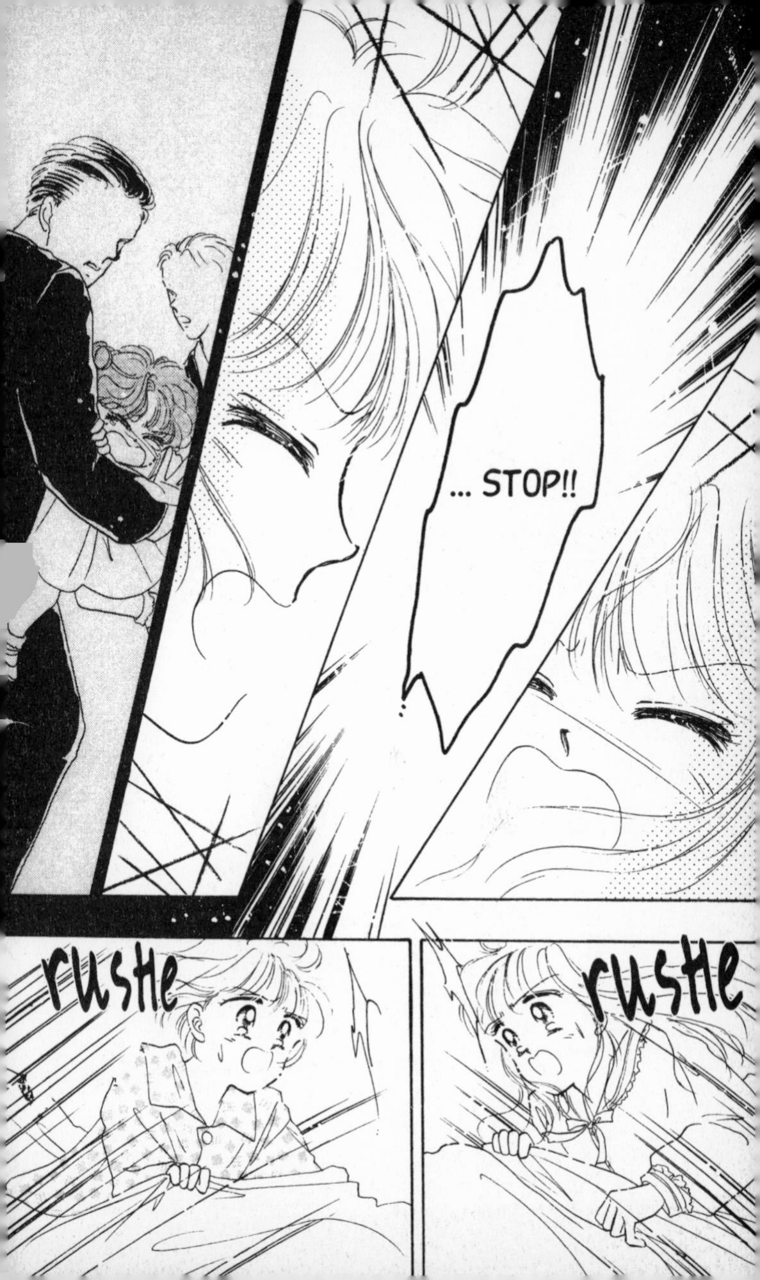
... STOP!!
rustle
rustle

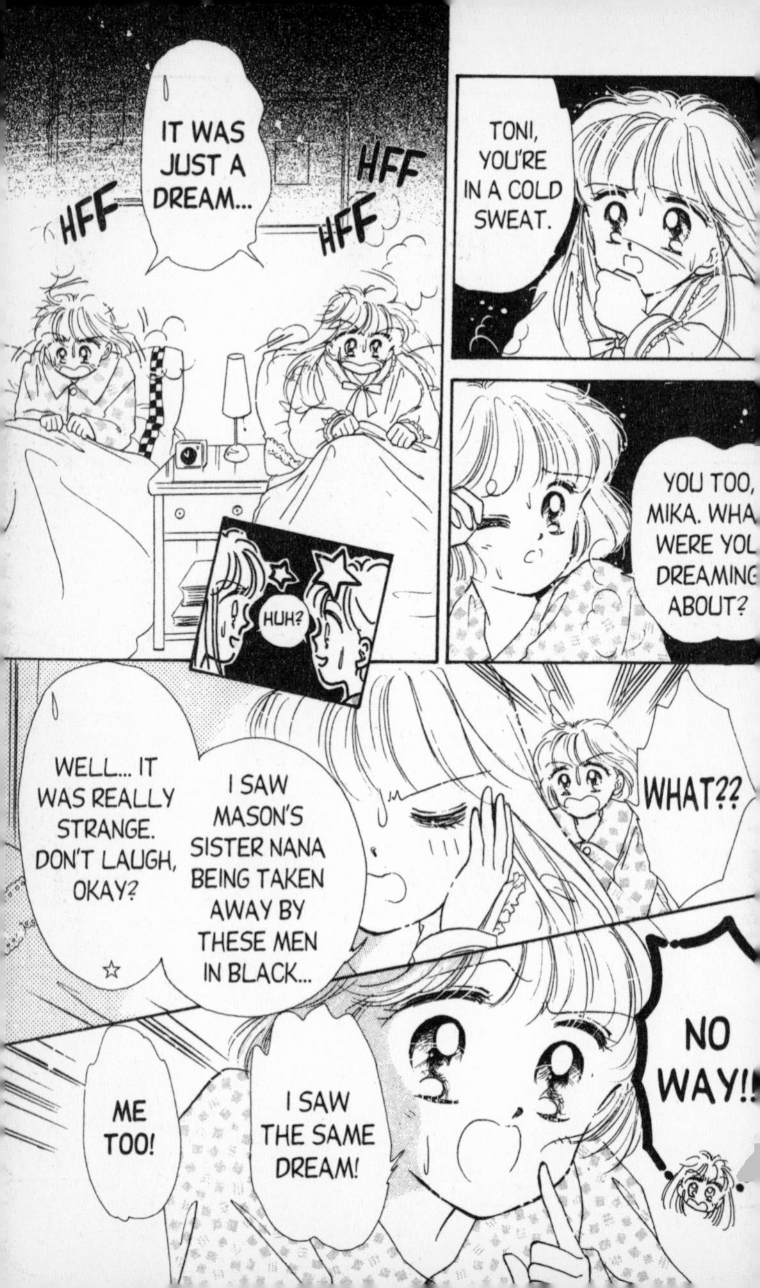
HFF
IT WAS JUST A DREAM...
HFF
HFF
HUH?
TONI, YOU'RE IN A COLD SWEAT.
YOU TOO, MIKA. WHA WERE YO DREAMING ABOUT?
WELL... IT WAS REALLY STRANGE. DON'T LAUGH, OKAY?
I SAW MASON'S SISTER NANA BEING TAKEN AWAY BY THESE MEN IN BLACK...
WHAT??
ME TOO!
I SAW THE SAME DREAM!
NO WAY!!

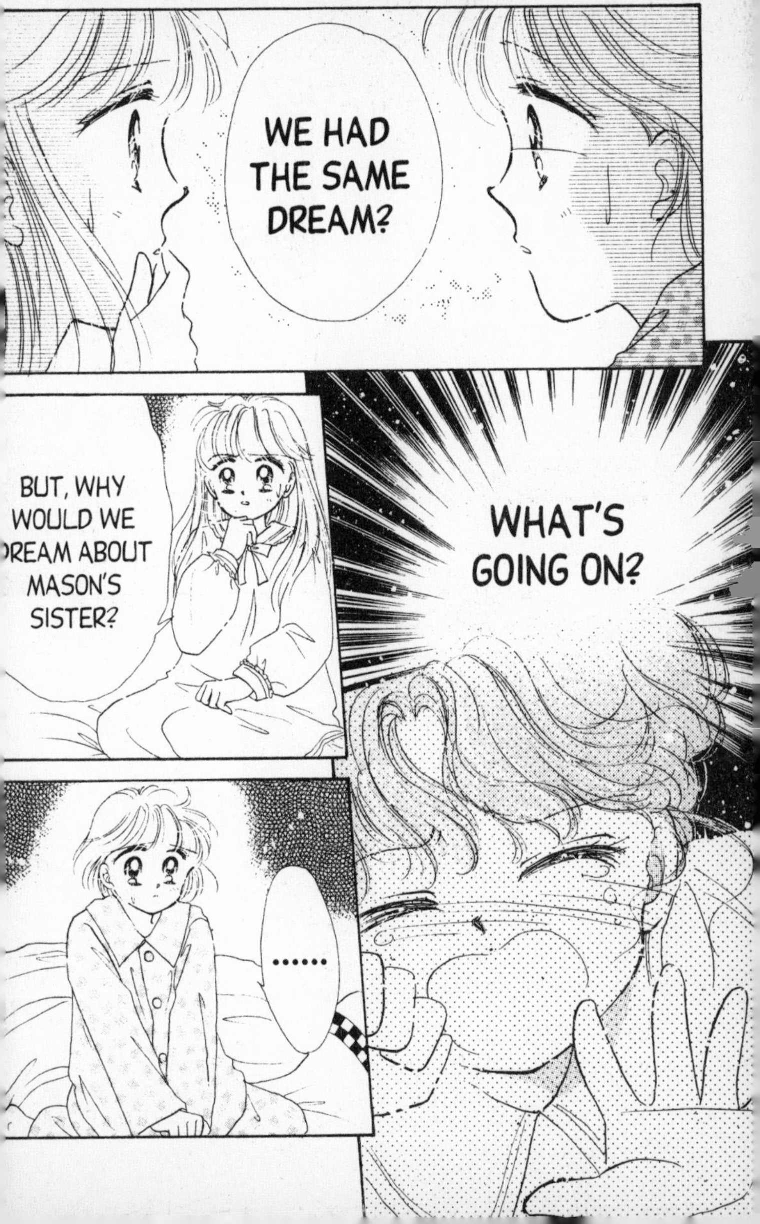
WE HAD THE SAME DREAM?
BUT, WHY WOULD WE DREAM ABOUT MASON'S SISTER?
WHAT'S GOING ON?
......

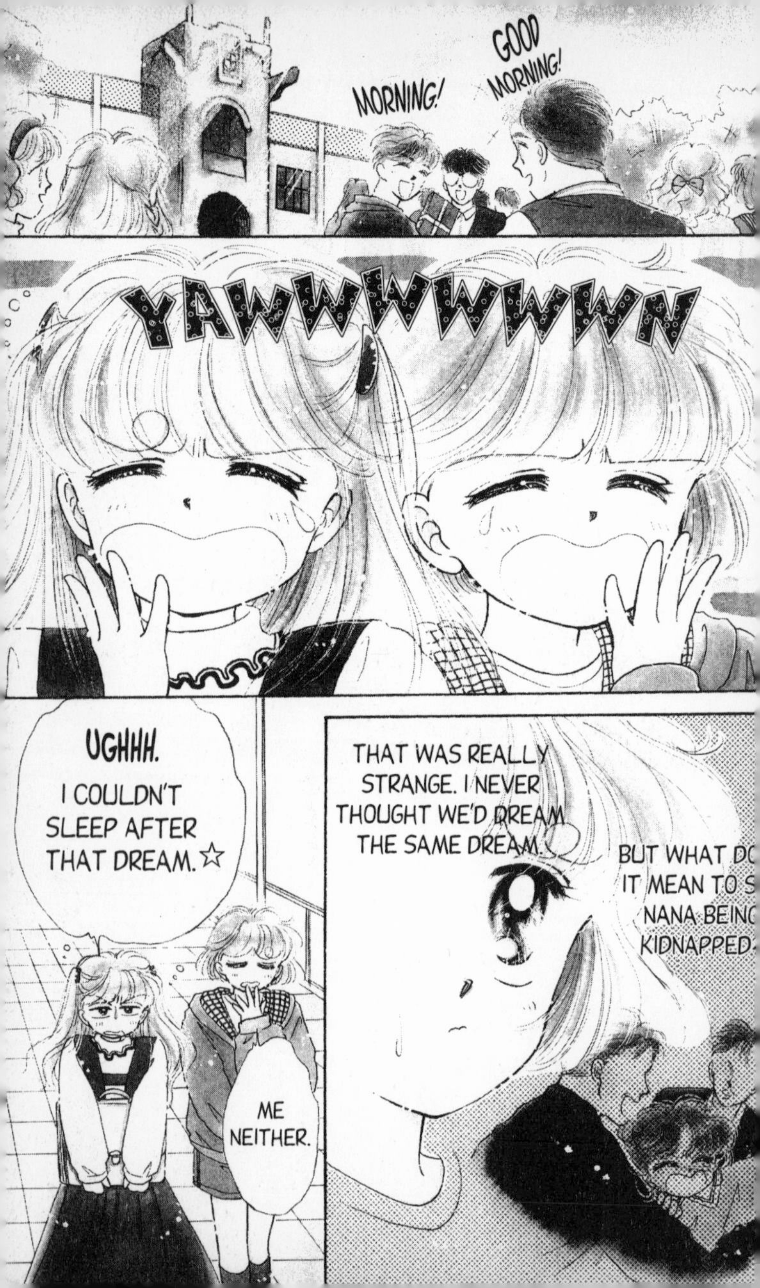
MORNING!
GOOD MORNING!
YAWWWWWWN
UGHHH. I COULDN'T SLEEP AFTER THAT DREAM. ☆
ME NEITHER.
THAT WAS REALLY STRANGE. I NEVER THOUGHT WE'D DREAM THE SAME DREAM.
BUT WHAT DO IT MEAN TO S NANA BEING KIDNAPPED

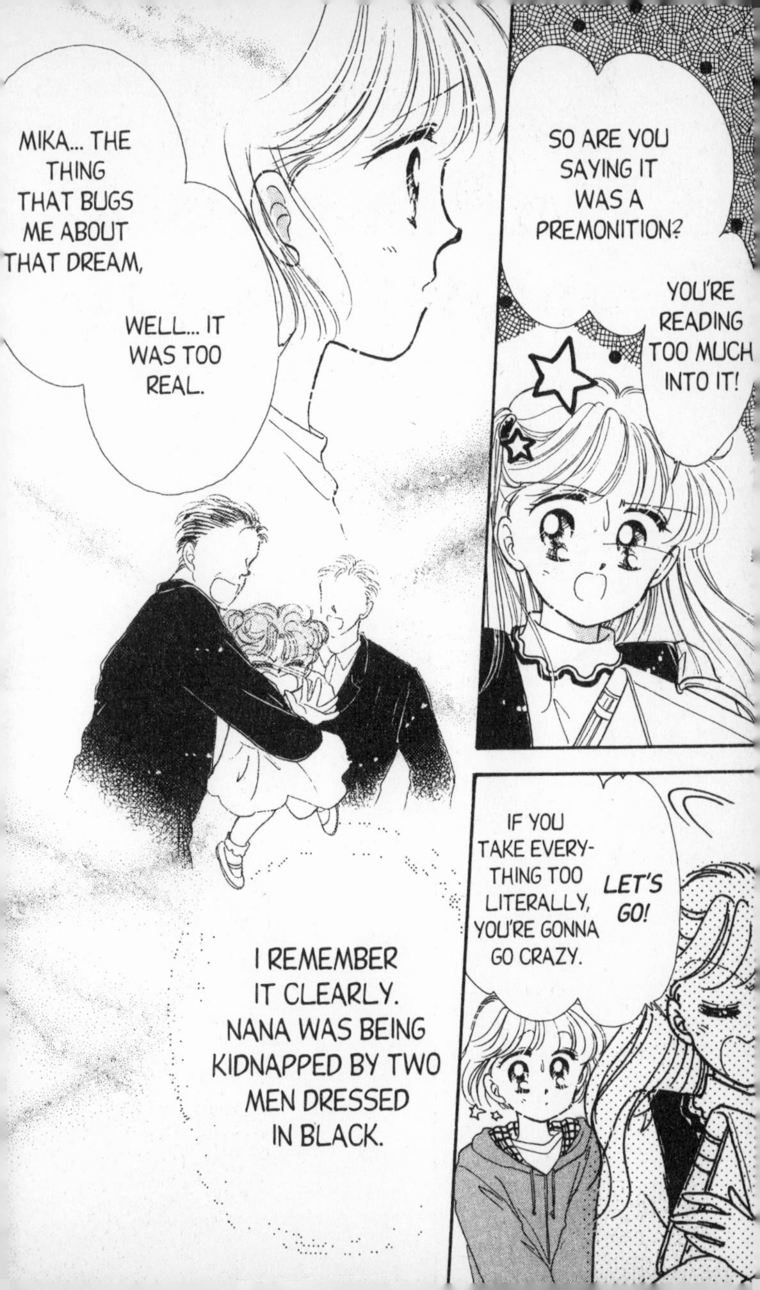
MIKA... THE THING THAT BUGS ME ABOUT THAT DREAM,
WELL... IT WAS TOO REAL.
I REMEMBER IT CLEARLY. NANA WAS BEING KIDNAPPED BY TWO MEN DRESSED IN BLACK.
SO ARE YOU SAYING IT WAS A PREMONITION?
YOU'RE READING TOO MUCH INTO IT!
IF YOU TAKE EVERY-THING TOO LITERALLY, YOU'RE GONNA GO CRAZY.
LET'S GO!

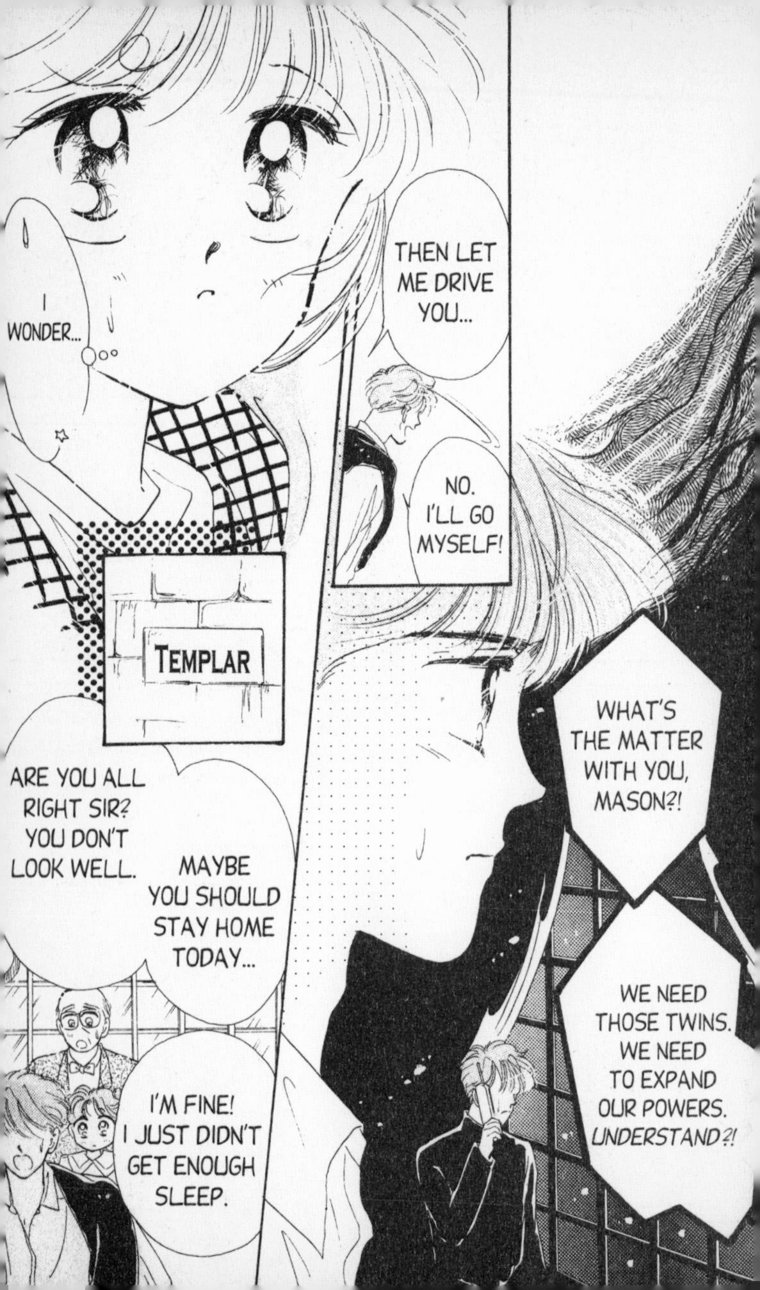
I WONDER...
THEN LET ME DRIVE YOU...
NO. I'LL GO MYSELF!
TEMPLAR
ARE YOU ALL RIGHT SIR? YOU DON'T LOOK WELL.
MAYBE YOU SHOULD STAY HOME TODAY...
I'M FINE! I JUST DIDN'T GET ENOUGH SLEEP.
WHAT'S THE MATTER WITH YOU, MASON?!
WE NEED THOSE TWINS. WE NEED TO EXPAND OUR POWERS. UNDERSTAND?!

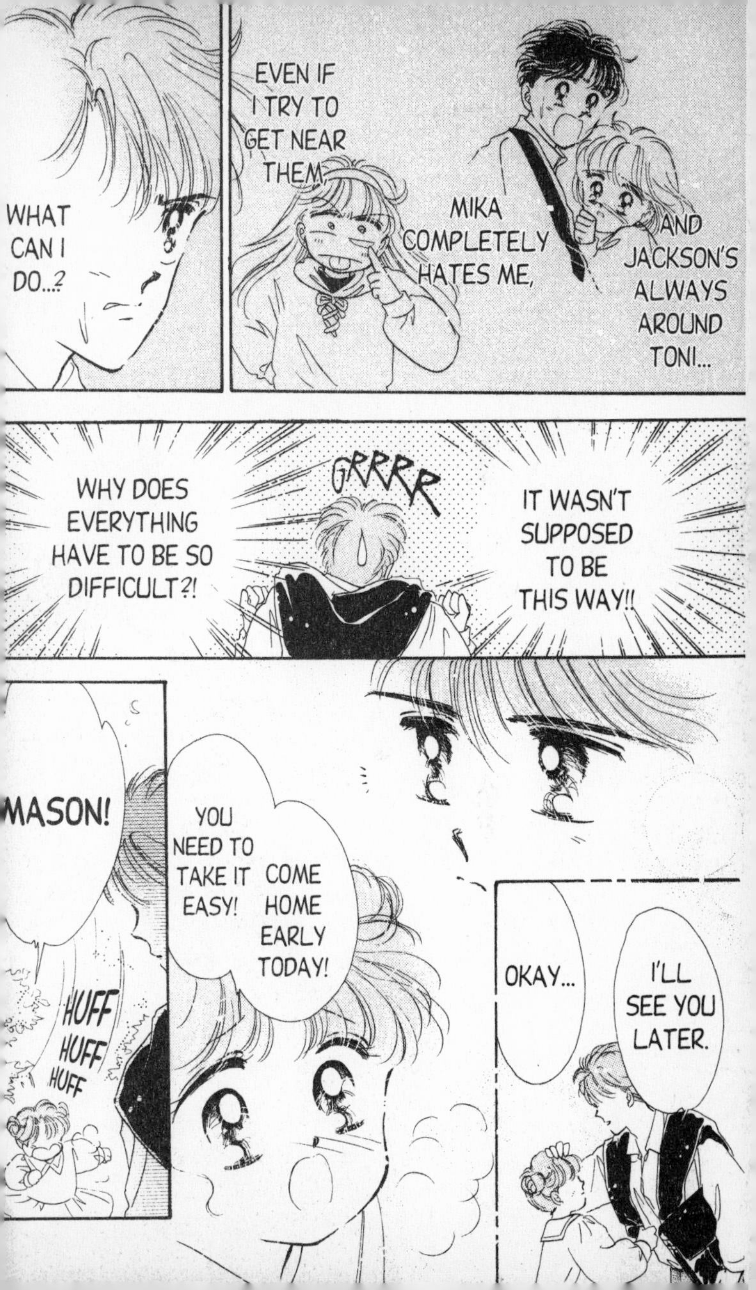
WHAT CAN I DO...?
EVEN IF I TRY TO GET NEAR THEM,
MIKA COMPLETELY HATES ME,
AND JACKSON'S ALWAYS AROUND TONI...
WHY DOES EVERYTHING HAVE TO BE SO DIFFICULT?!
GRRRR
IT WASN'T SUPPOSED TO BE THIS WAY!!
MASON!
HUFF HUFF HUFF
YOU NEED TO TAKE IT EASY!
COME HOME EARLY TODAY!
OKAY...
I'LL SEE YOU LATER.

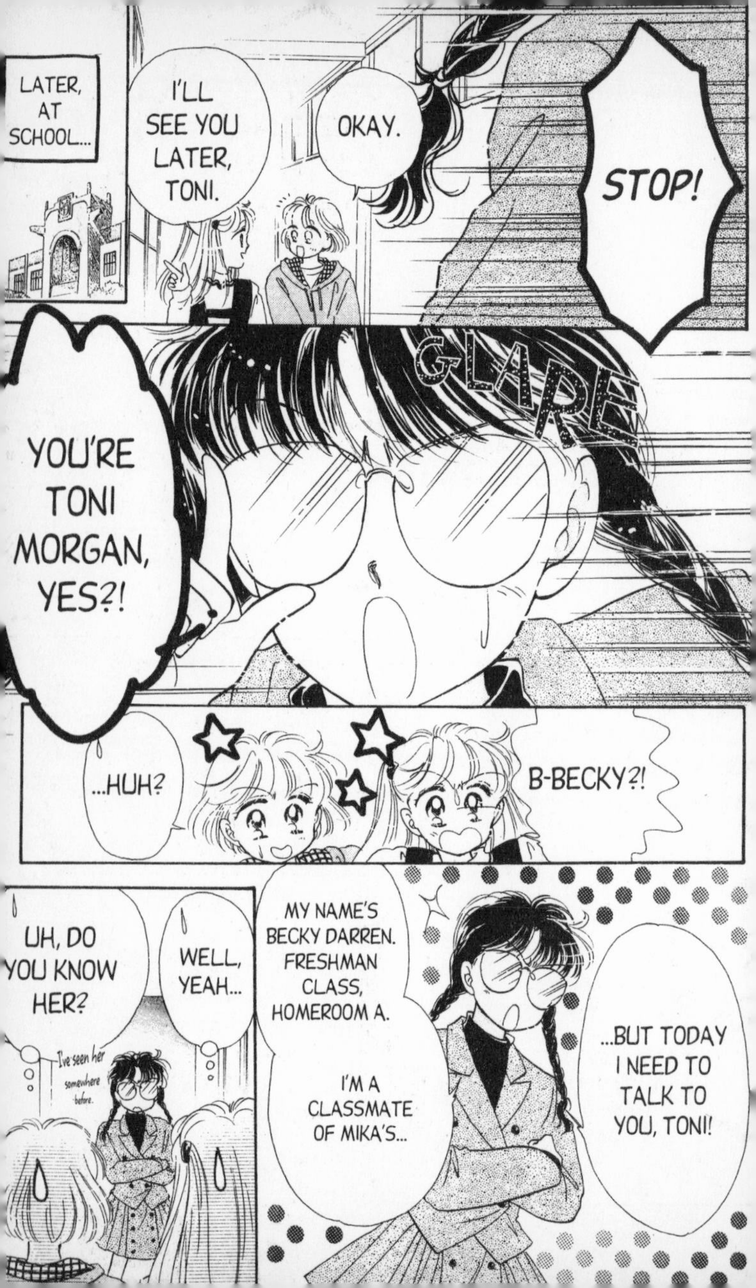

LATER, AT SCHOOL...
I'LL SEE YOU LATER, TONI.
OKAY.
STOP!
YOU'RE TONI MORGAN, YES?!
GLARE
...HUH?
B-BECKY?!
UH, DO YOU KNOW HER?
WELL, YEAH...
I've seen her somewhere before.
MY NAME'S BECKY DARREN. FRESHMAN CLASS, HOMEROOM A.
I'M A CLASSMATE OF MIKA'S...
...BUT TODAY I NEED TO TALK TO YOU, TONI!

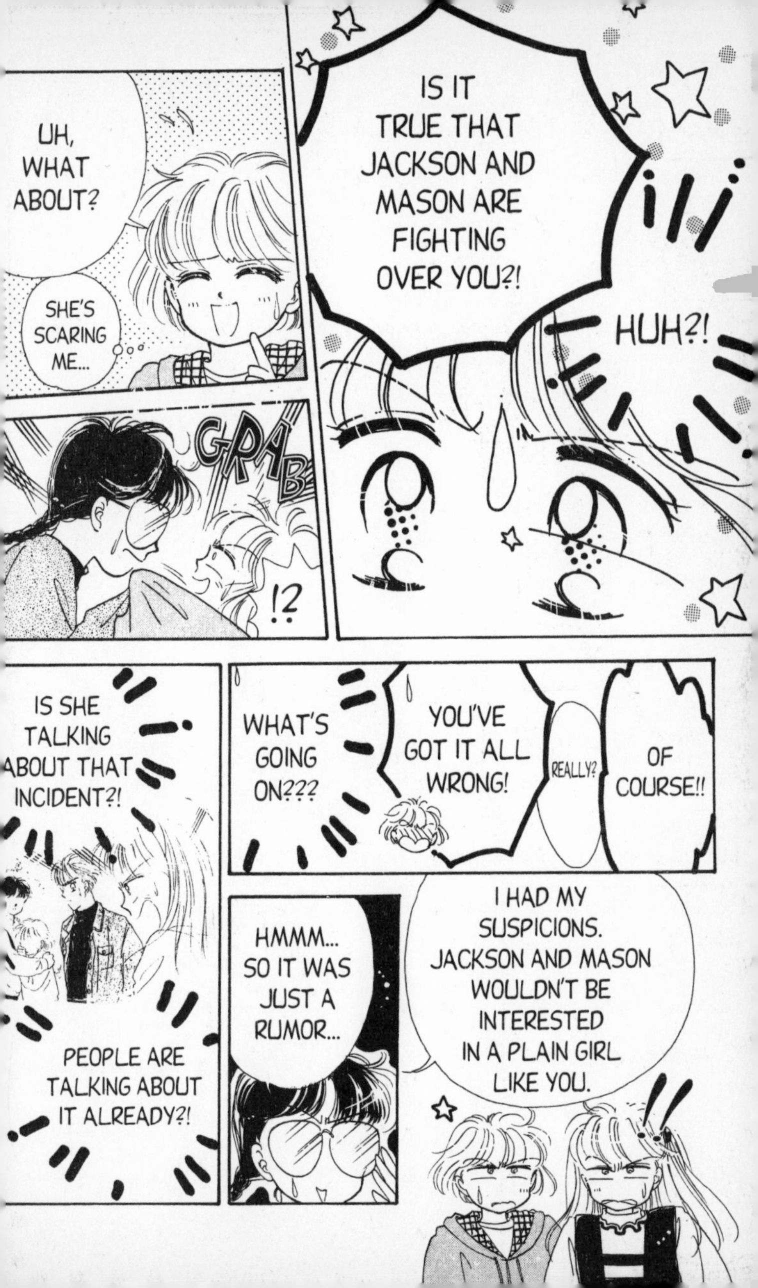

UH, WHAT ABOUT?
SHE'S SCARING ME...
GRAB
!?
IS IT TRUE THAT JACKSON AND MASON ARE FIGHTING OVER YOU?!
HUH?!
IS SHE TALKING ABOUT THAT INCIDENT?!
PEOPLE ARE TALKING ABOUT IT ALREADY?!
WHAT'S GOING ON???
YOU'VE GOT IT ALL WRONG!
REALLY?
OF COURSE!!
HMMM... SO IT WAS JUST A RUMOR...
I HAD MY SUSPICIONS. JACKSON AND MASON WOULDN'T BE INTERESTED IN A PLAIN GIRL LIKE YOU.
!!

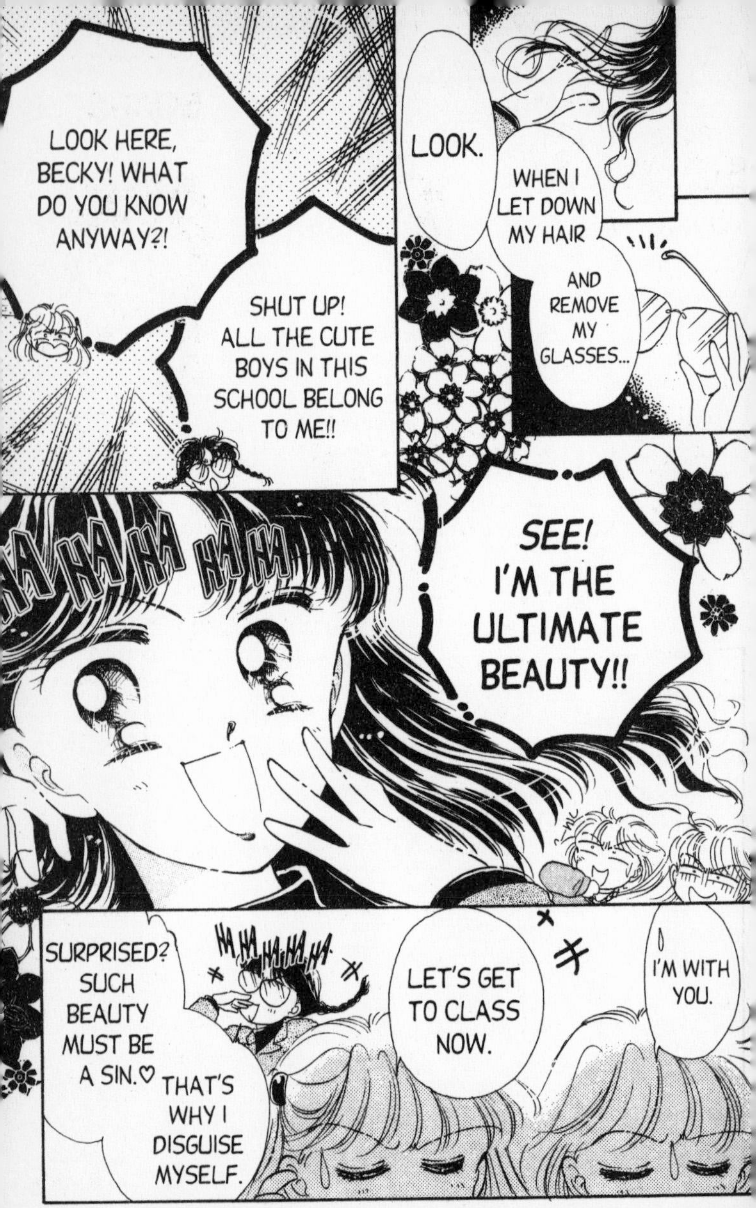
LOOK HERE, BECKY! WHAT DO YOU KNOW ANYWAY?!
SHUT UP! ALL THE CUTE BOYS IN THIS SCHOOL BELONG TO ME!!
LOOK.
WHEN I LET DOWN MY HAIR
AND REMOVE MY GLASSES...
HA HA HA HA HA HA
SEE! I'M THE ULTIMATE BEAUTY!!
SURPRISED? SUCH BEAUTY MUST BE A SIN.♡
HA HA HA HA HA
THAT'S WHY I DISGUISE MYSELF.
LET'S GET TO CLASS NOW.
I'M WITH YOU.

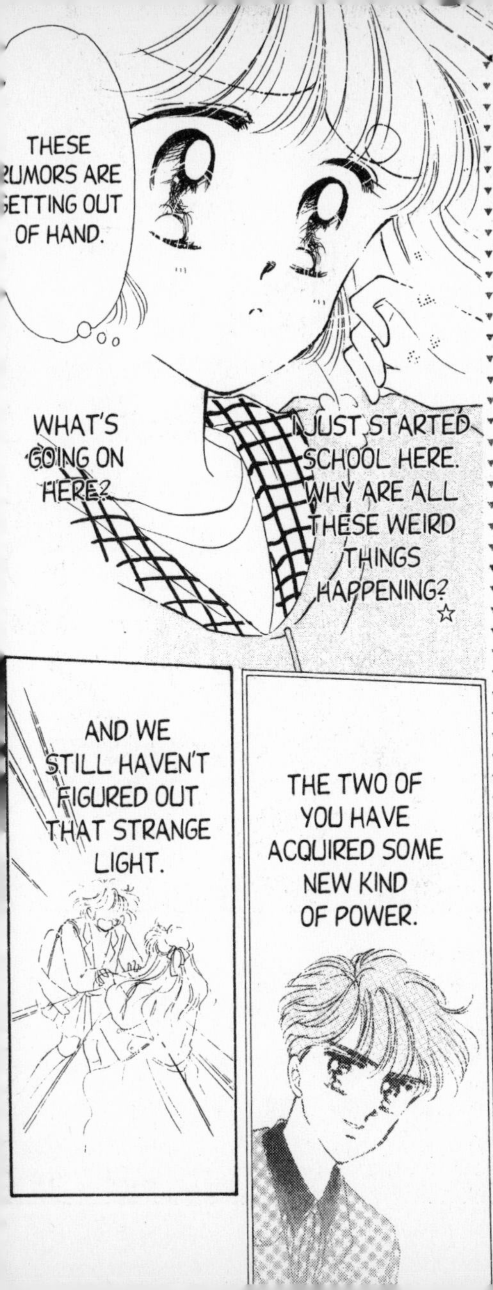

THESE RUMORS ARE GETTING OUT OF HAND.
WHAT'S GOING ON HERE?
I JUST STARTED SCHOOL HERE. WHY ARE ALL THESE WEIRD THINGS HAPPENING? ☆
AND WE STILL HAVEN'T FIGURED OUT THAT STRANGE LIGHT.
THE TWO OF YOU HAVE ACQUIRED SOME NEW KIND OF POWER.

BONUS

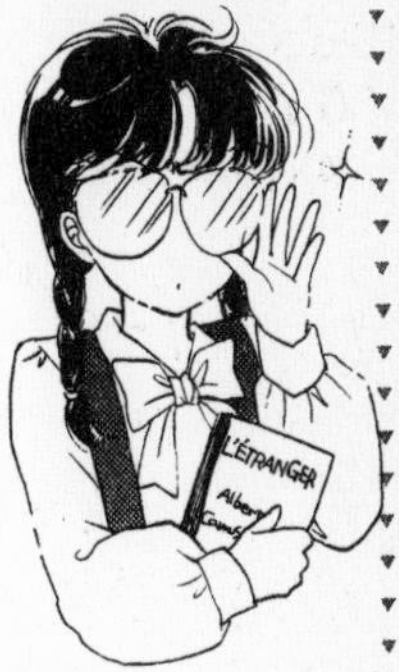

L'ÉTRANGER
Albert Camus

Becky Darren has appeared here and there in Part One as a minor character. But I plan to feature her more in Part Three. I'm getting good at drawing her now. I actually had planned on the idea of introducing her as a beauty in disguise in Part One. But I ended up waiting until Part Two... Well, who cares, right?

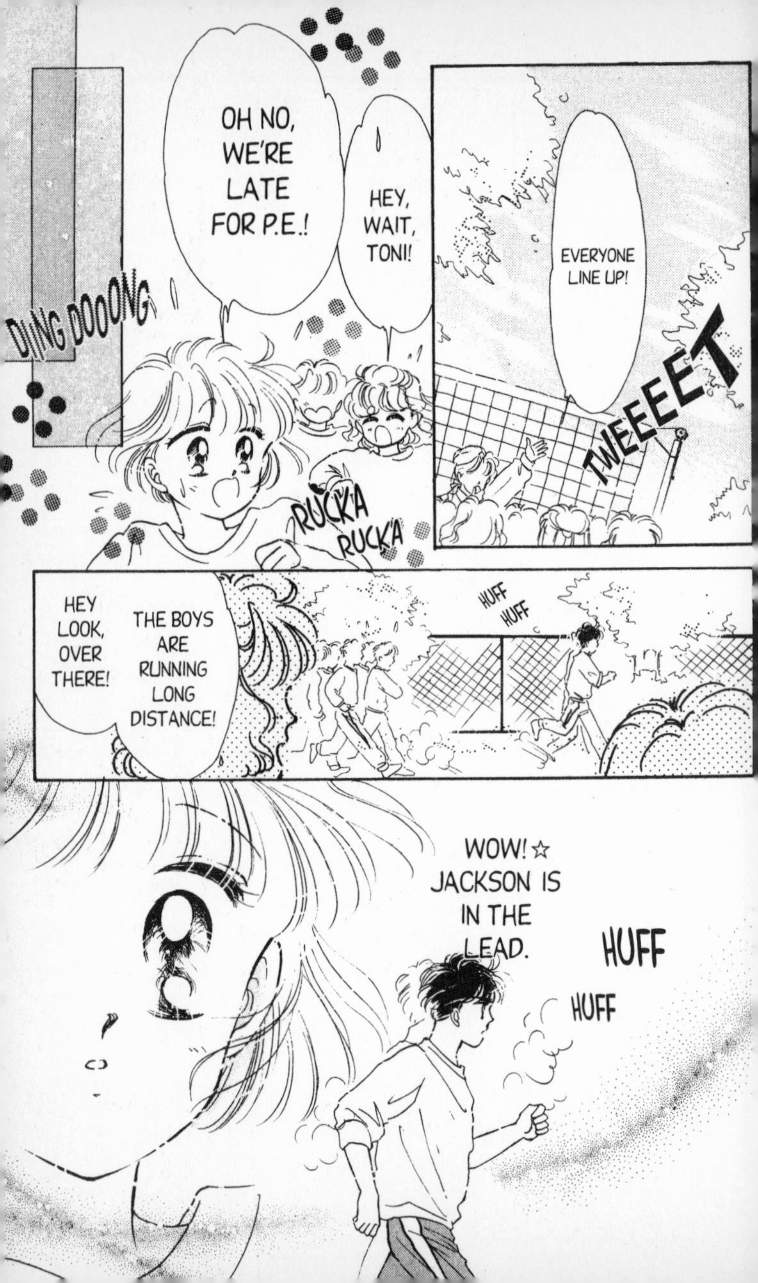
DIIING DOOONG
OH NO, WE'RE LATE FOR P.E.!
HEY, WAIT, TONI!
RUCK'A RUCK'A
EVERYONE LINE UP!
TWEEEET
HEY LOOK, OVER THERE!
THE BOYS ARE RUNNING LONG DISTANCE!
HUFF HUFF
WOW! ☆ JACKSON IS IN THE LEAD.
HUFF
HUFF

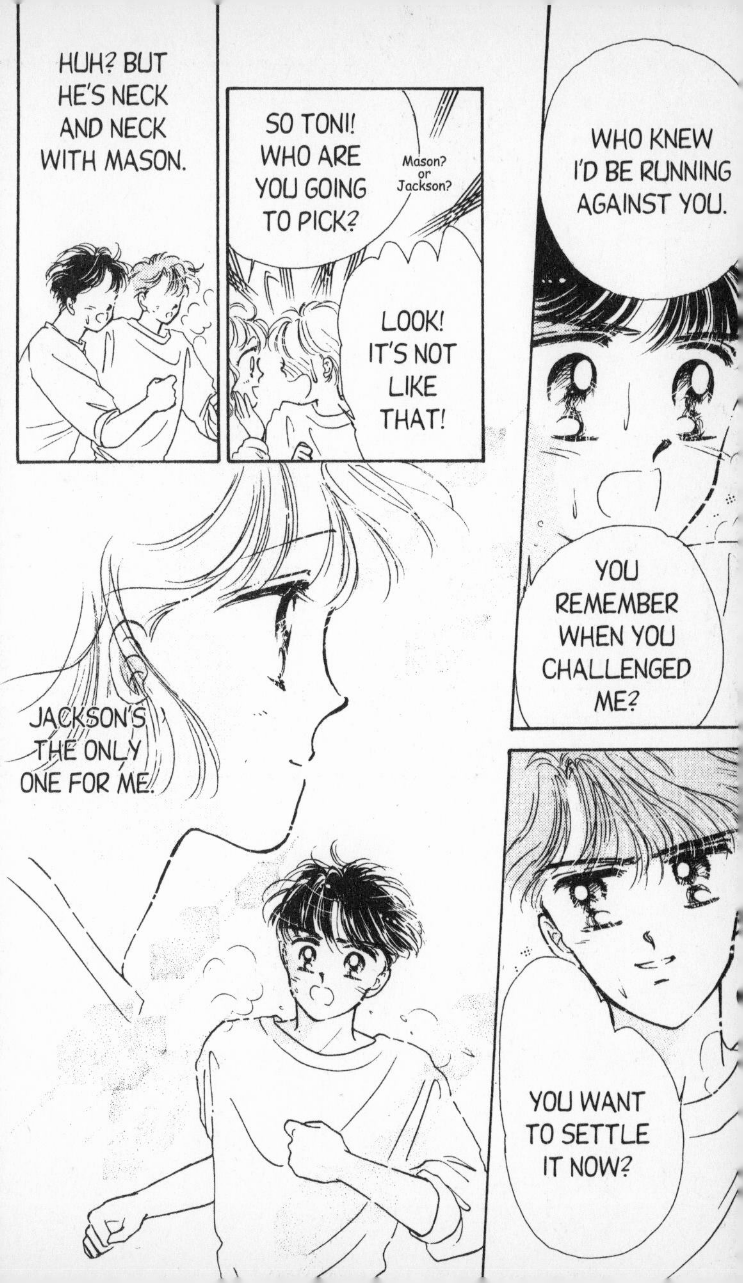
HUH? BUT HE'S NECK AND NECK WITH MASON.
SO TONI! WHO ARE YOU GOING TO PICK?
Mason? or Jackson?
LOOK! IT'S NOT LIKE THAT!
JACKSON'S THE ONLY ONE FOR ME.
WHO KNEW I'D BE RUNNING AGAINST YOU.
YOU REMEMBER WHEN YOU CHALLENGED ME?
YOU WANT TO SETTLE IT NOW?

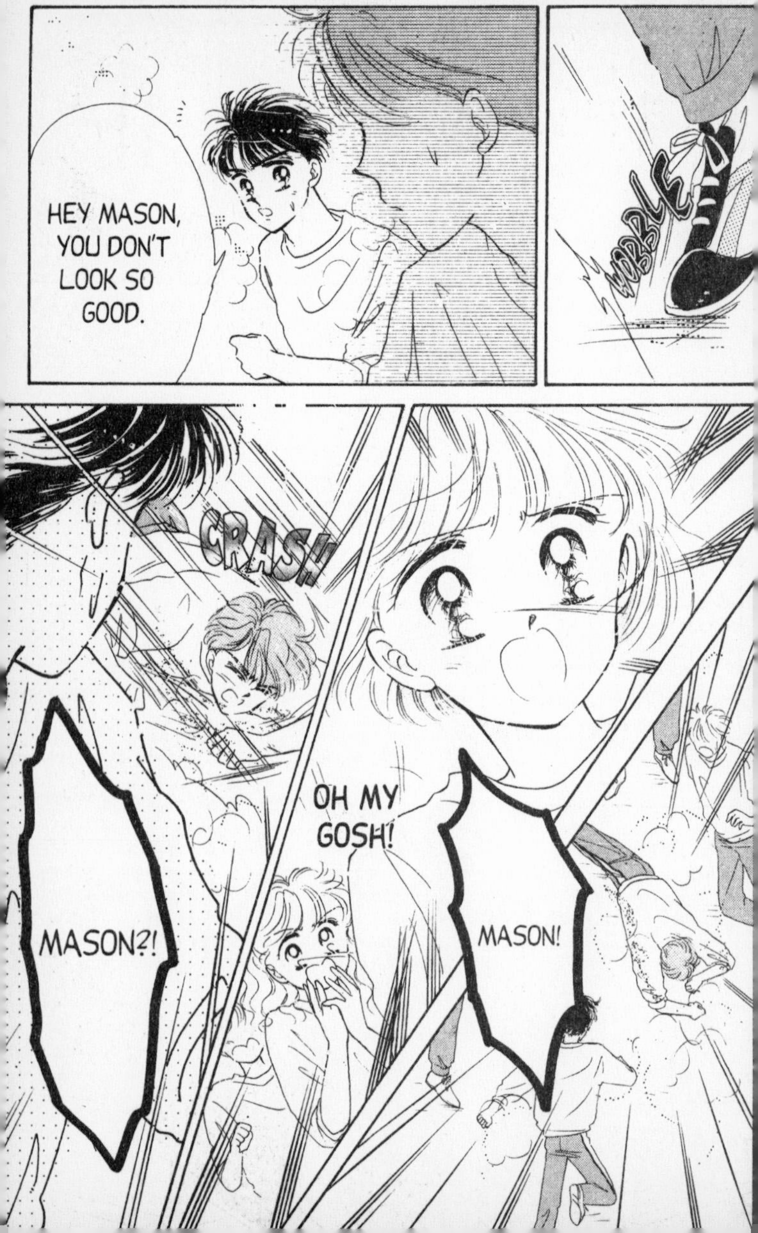
HEY MASON, YOU DON'T LOOK SO GOOD.
WOBBLE
CRASH
MASON?!
OH MY GOSH!
MASON!

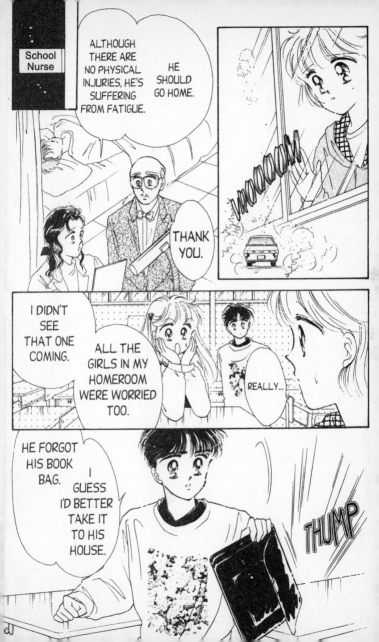

School Nurse

ALTHOUGH THERE ARE NO PHYSICAL INJURIES, HE'S SUFFERING FROM FATIGUE.

HE SHOULD GO HOME.

THANK YOU.

VROOOOM

I DIDN'T SEE THAT ONE COMING.

ALL THE GIRLS IN MY HOMEROOM WERE WORRIED TOO.

REALLY...

HE FORGOT HIS BOOK BAG. I GUESS I'D BETTER TAKE IT TO HIS HOUSE.

THUMP

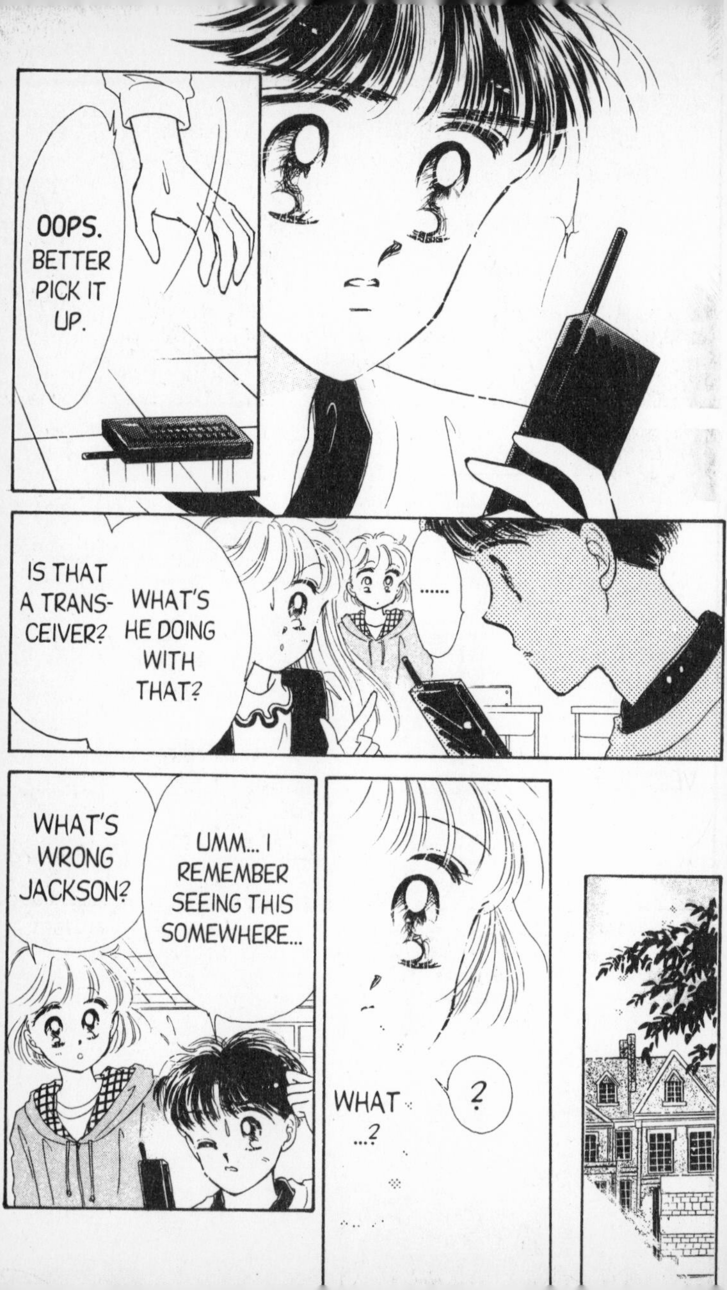
OOPS. BETTER PICK IT UP.
IS THAT A TRANS-CEIVER?
WHAT'S HE DOING WITH THAT?
......
WHAT'S WRONG JACKSON?
UMM... I REMEMBER SEEING THIS SOMEWHERE...
WHAT ...?
?

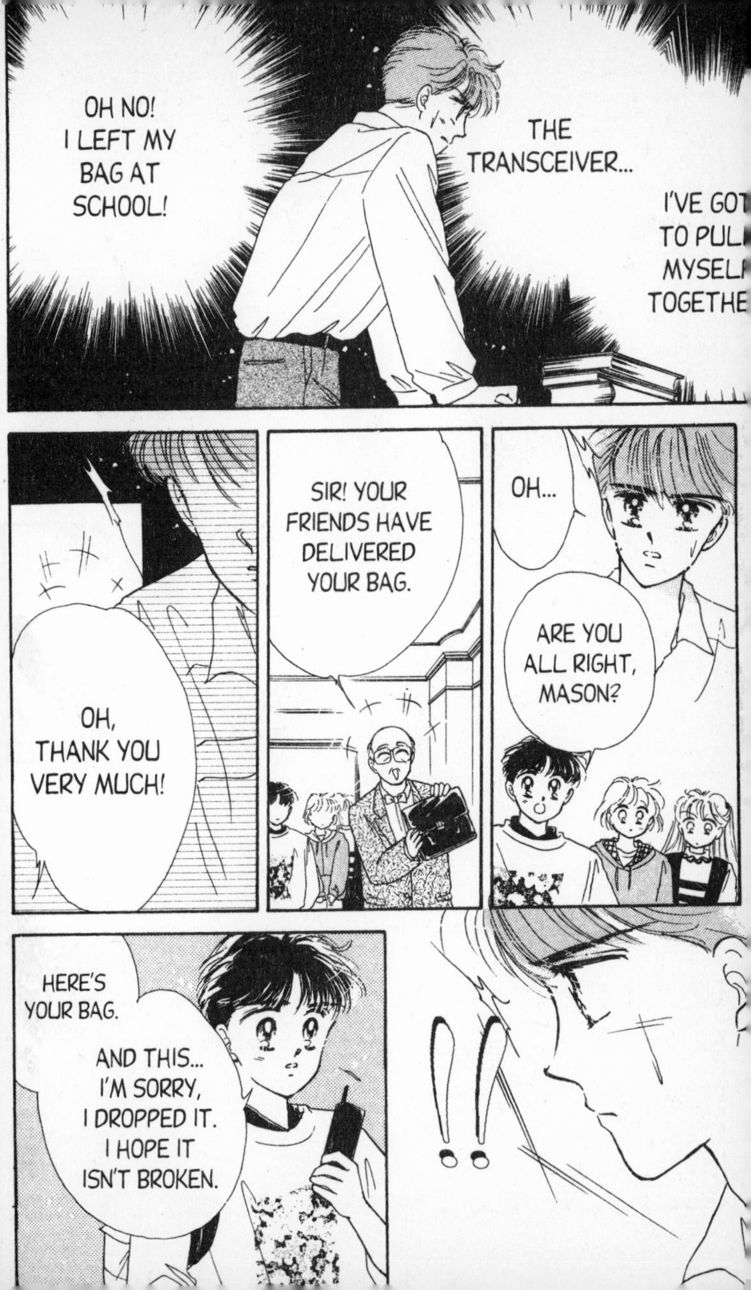
OH NO! I LEFT MY BAG AT SCHOOL!
THE TRANSCEIVER...
I'VE GOT TO PUL MYSEL TOGETHE
OH, THANK YOU VERY MUCH!
SIR! YOUR FRIENDS HAVE DELIVERED YOUR BAG.
OH...
ARE YOU ALL RIGHT, MASON?
HERE'S YOUR BAG.
AND THIS... I'M SORRY, I DROPPED IT. I HOPE IT ISN'T BROKEN.
!!

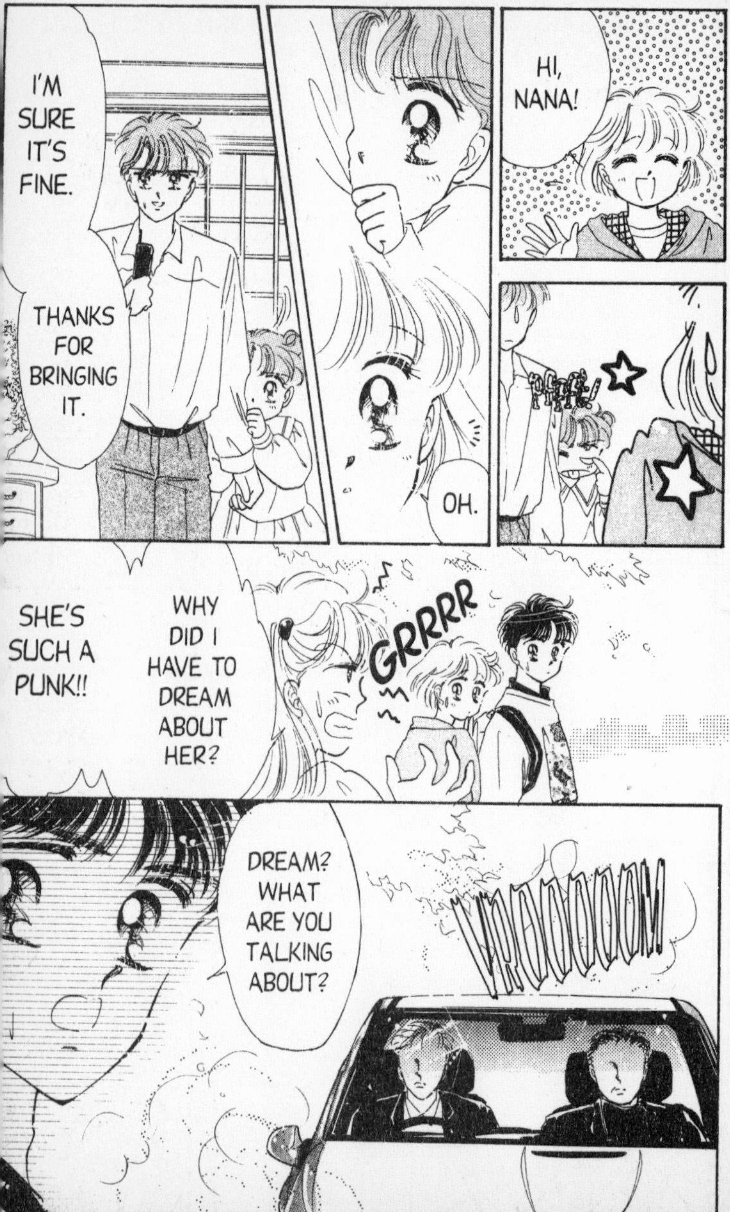
I'M SURE IT'S FINE.
THANKS FOR BRINGING IT.
OH.
HI, NANA!
SHE'S SUCH A PUNK!!
WHY DID I HAVE TO DREAM ABOUT HER?
GRRRR
DREAM? WHAT ARE YOU TALKING ABOUT?
VROOOOOOM

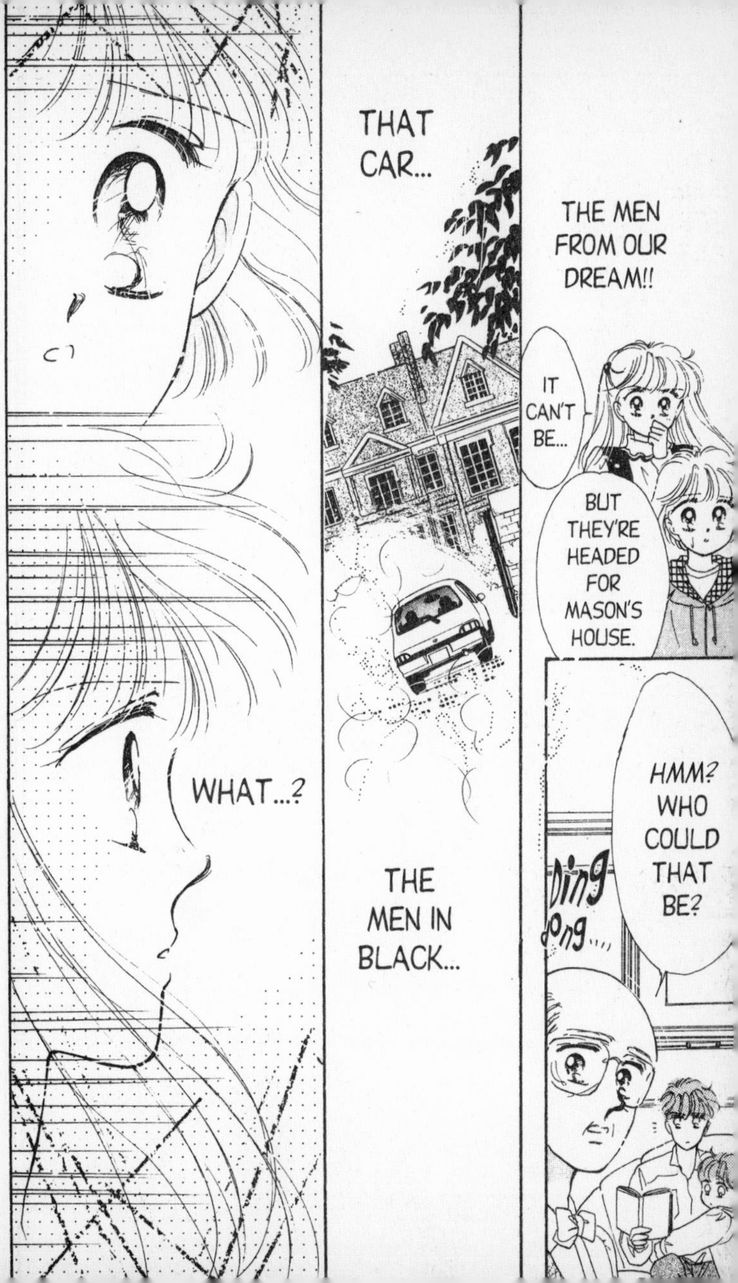
WHAT...?
THAT CAR...
THE MEN IN BLACK...
THE MEN FROM OUR DREAM!!
IT CAN'T BE...
BUT THEY'RE HEADED FOR MASON'S HOUSE.
Ding dong...
HMM? WHO COULD THAT BE?

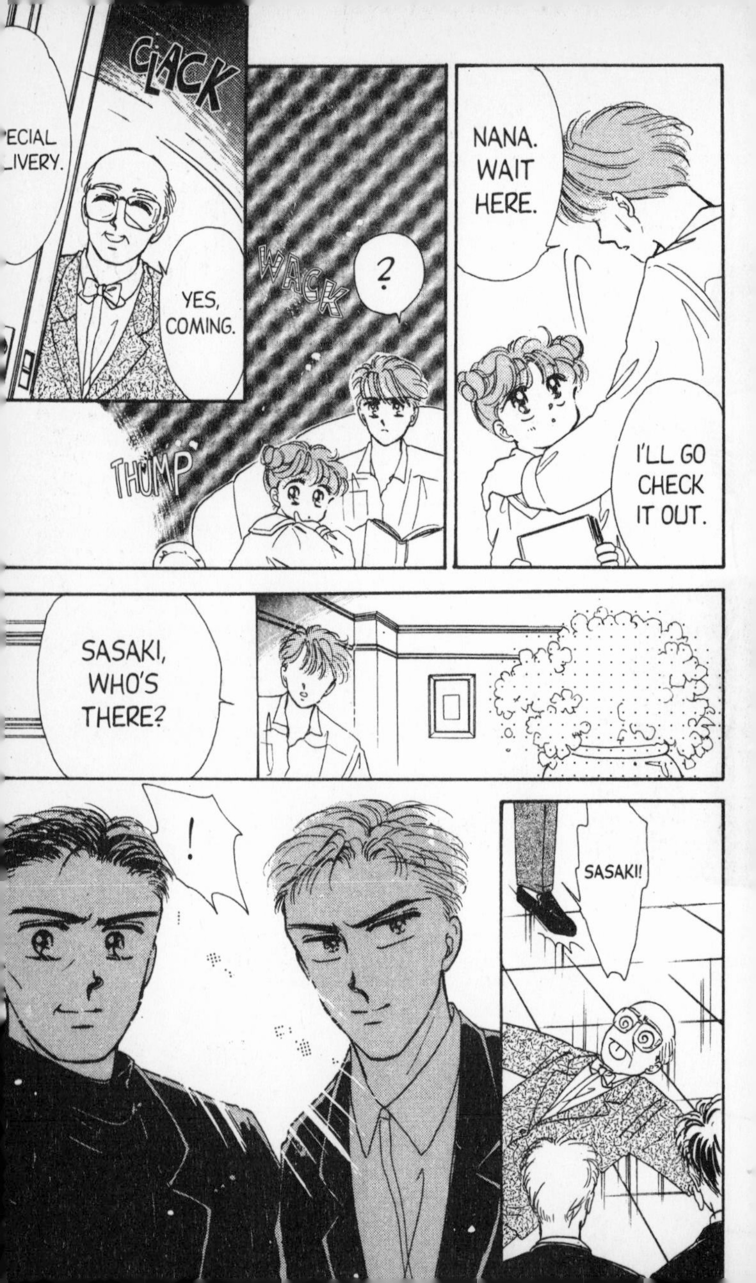

ECIAL
LIVERY.
CLACK
YES, COMING.
WACK
?
THUMP
NANA. WAIT HERE.
I'LL GO CHECK IT OUT.
SASAKI, WHO'S THERE?
!
SASAKI!

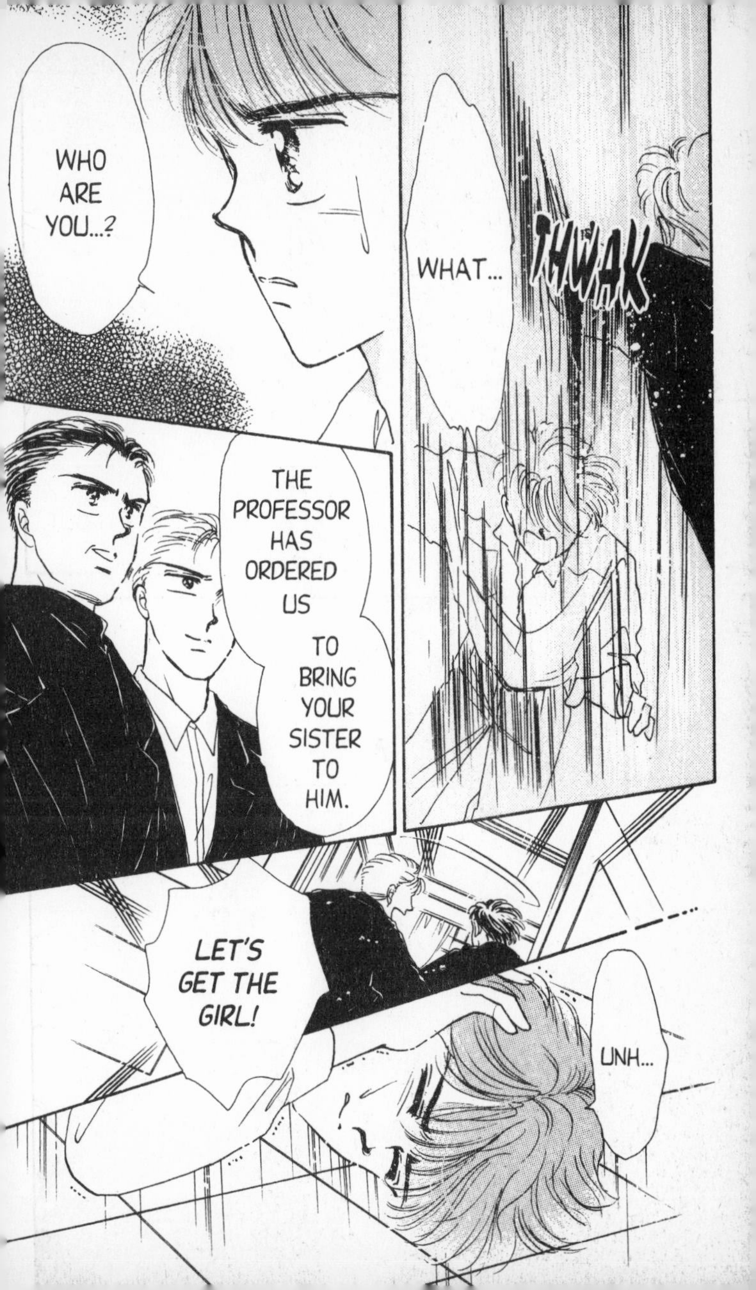
WHO ARE YOU...?
WHAT...
THWAK
THE PROFESSOR HAS ORDERED US
TO BRING YOUR SISTER TO HIM.
LET'S GET THE GIRL!
UNH...

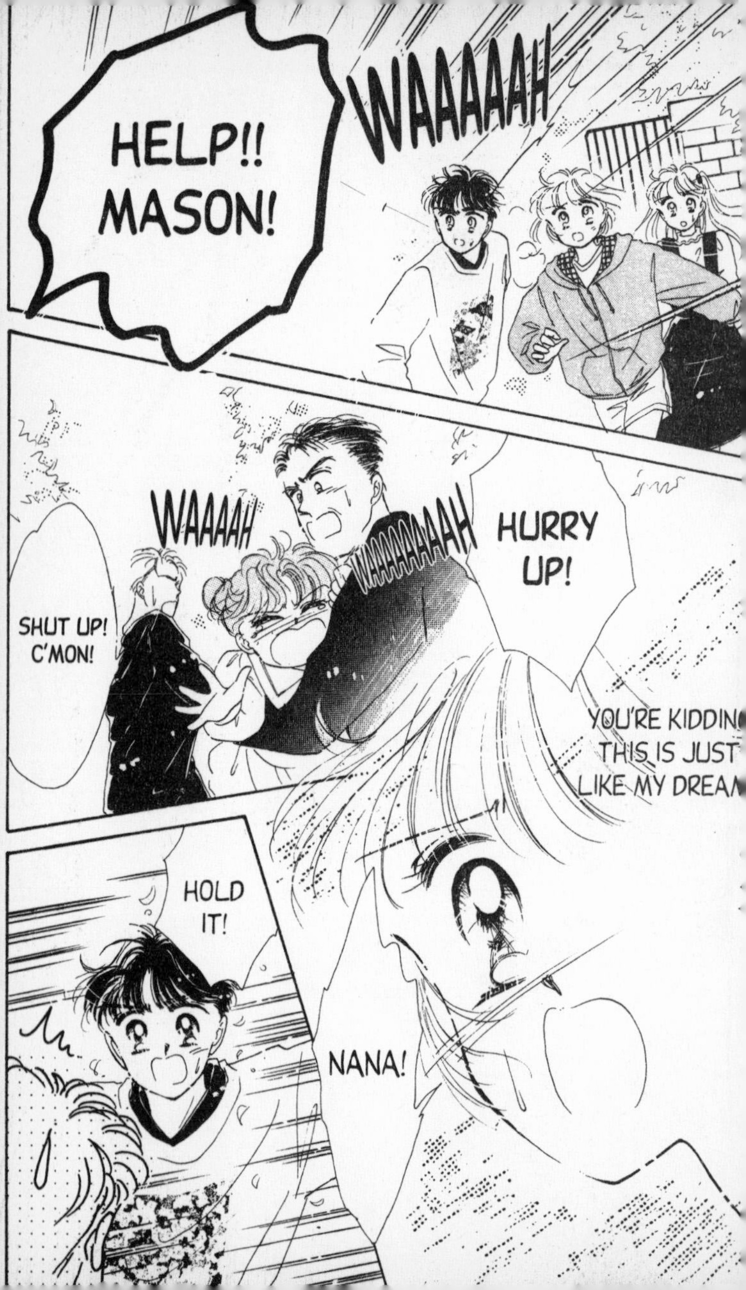
HELP!! MASON!
WAAAAAH
SHUT UP! C'MON!
WAAAAH
WAAAAAAAAH
HURRY UP!
YOU'RE KIDDIN
THIS IS JUST
LIKE MY DREA
HOLD IT!
NANA!

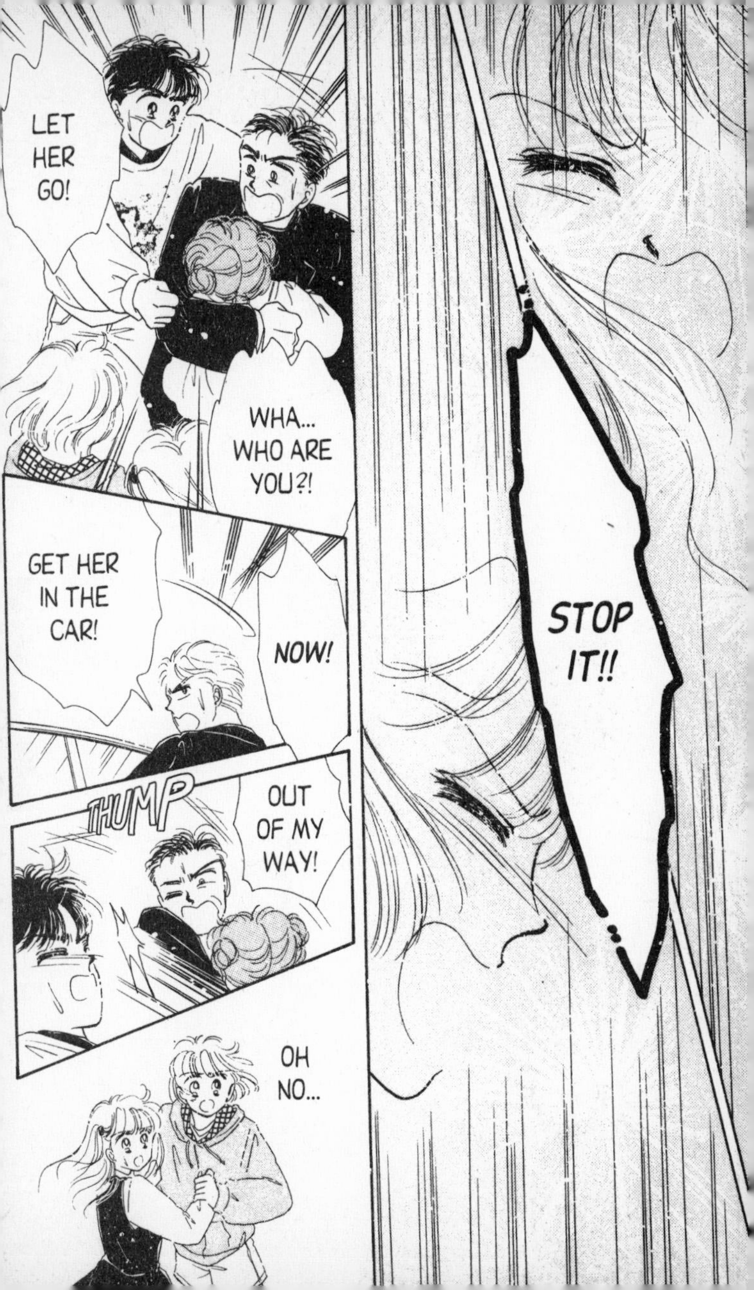
LET HER GO!
WHA... WHO ARE YOU?!
GET HER IN THE CAR!
NOW!
THUMP
OUT OF MY WAY!
OH NO...
STOP IT!!

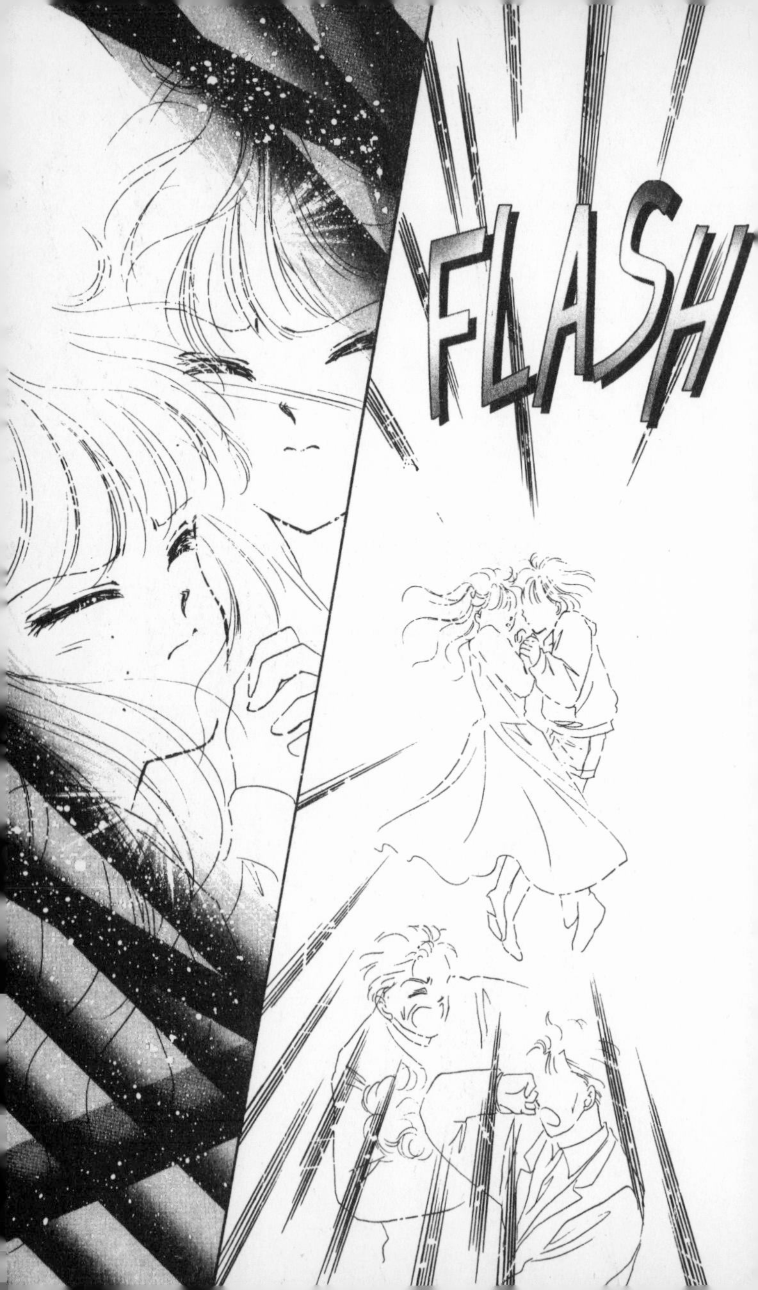
FLASH

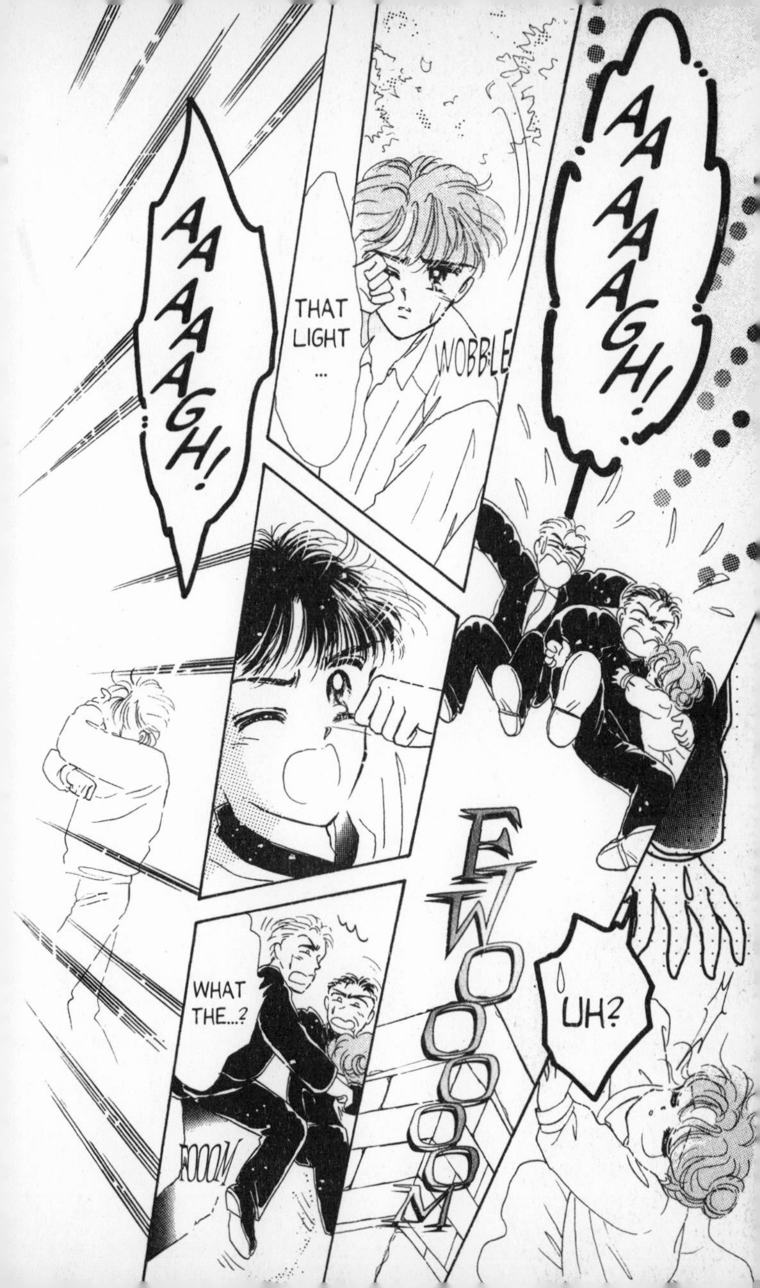
AAAAAAGH!
THAT LIGHT ...
WOBBLE
AAAAAGH!
UH?
EFWOOOOOM
WHAT THE...?
FOOOM

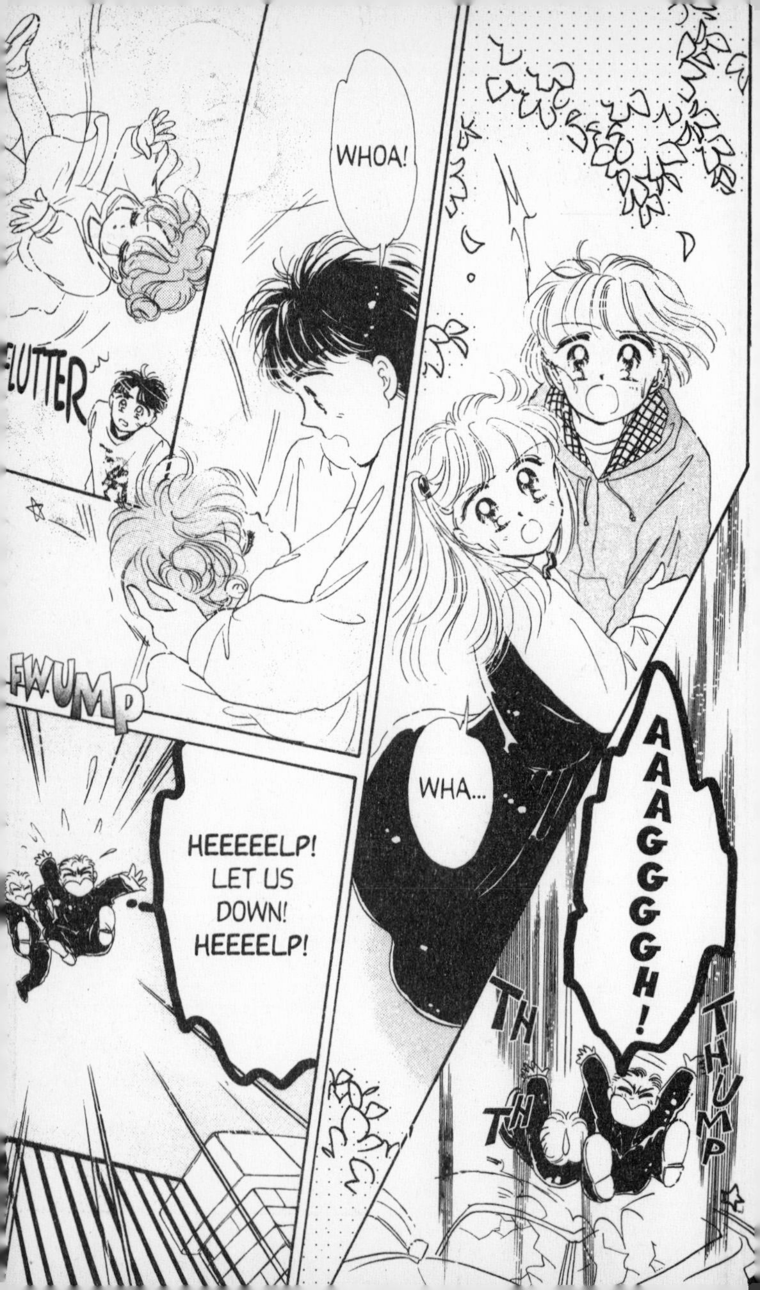
FLUTTER
FWUMP
WHOA!
HEEEEELP! LET US DOWN! HEEEELP!
WHA...
AAAAGGGGGH!
TH
TH
THUMP

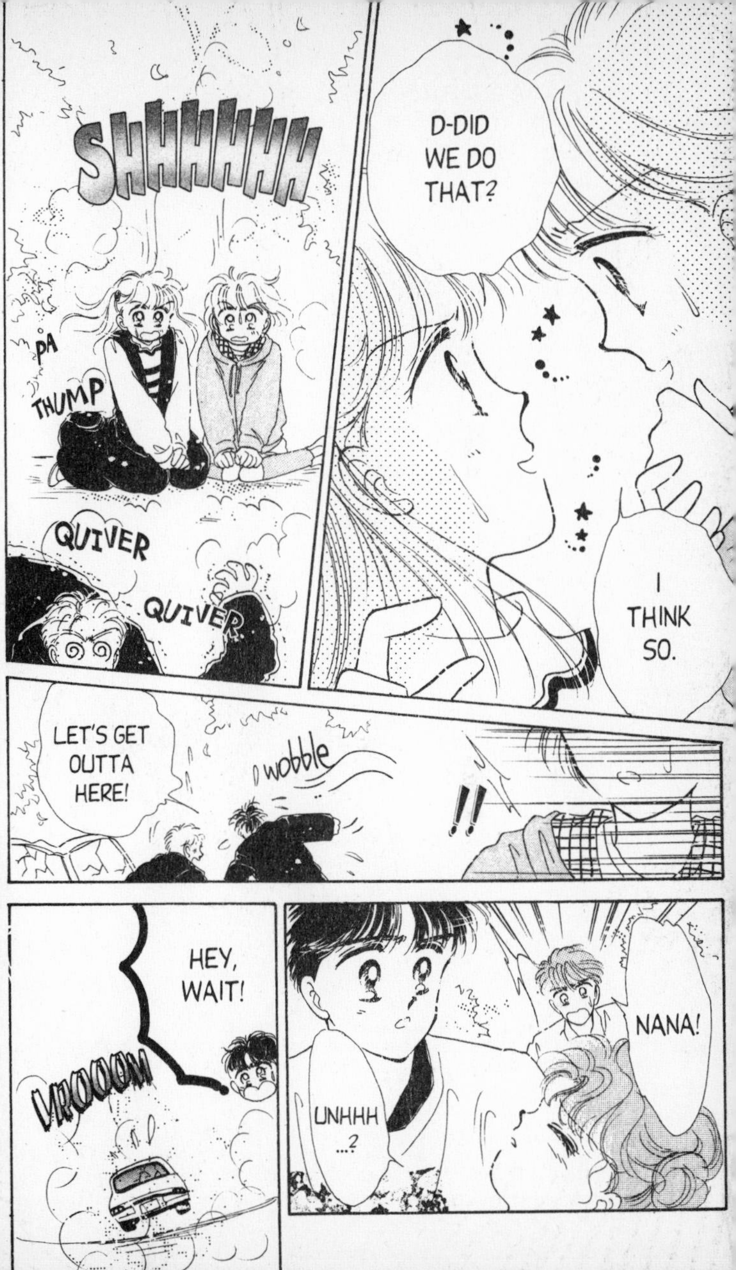
SHHHHHHH
PA
THUMP
QUIVER
QUIVER
D-DID WE DO THAT?
I THINK SO.
LET'S GET OUTTA HERE!
wobble
!!
HEY, WAIT!
VROOOM
NANA!
UNHHH ...?

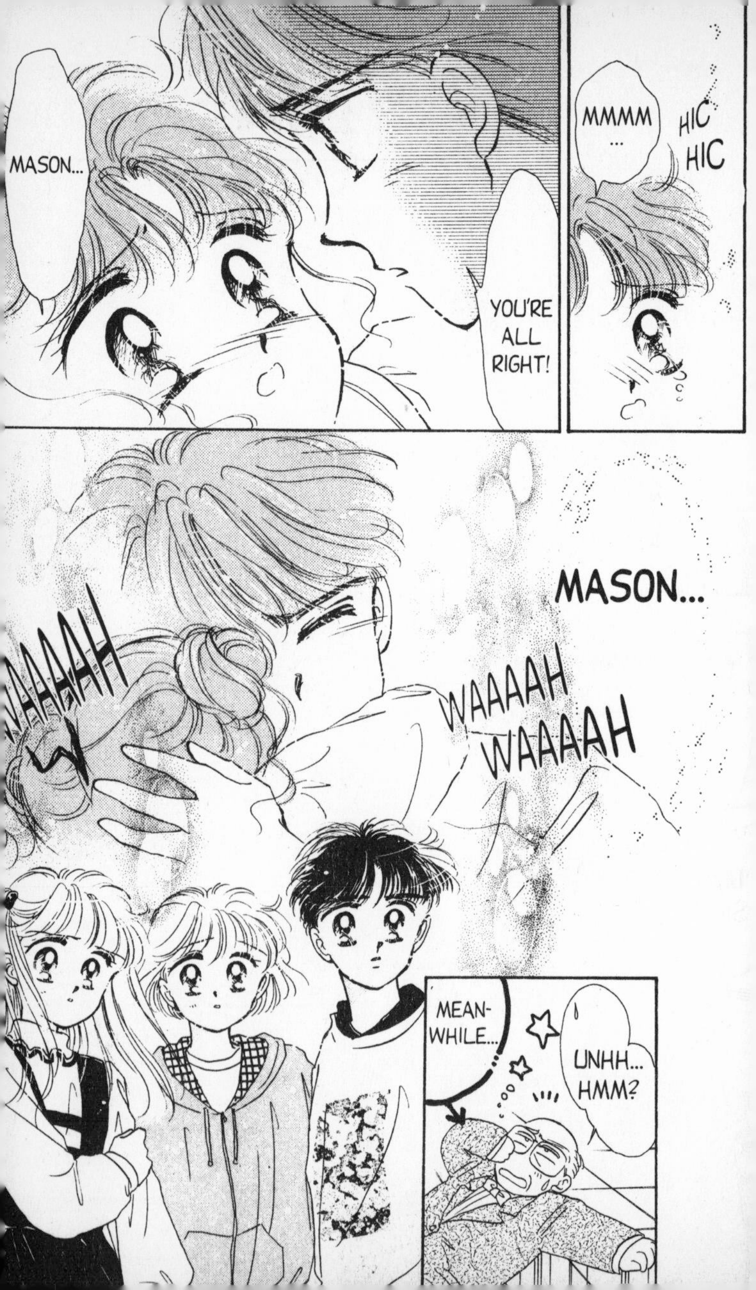

MASON...
YOU'RE ALL RIGHT!
MMMM ...
HIC HIC
WAAAAH
MASON...
WAAAAH WAAAAH
MEAN-WHILE...
UNHH... HMM?

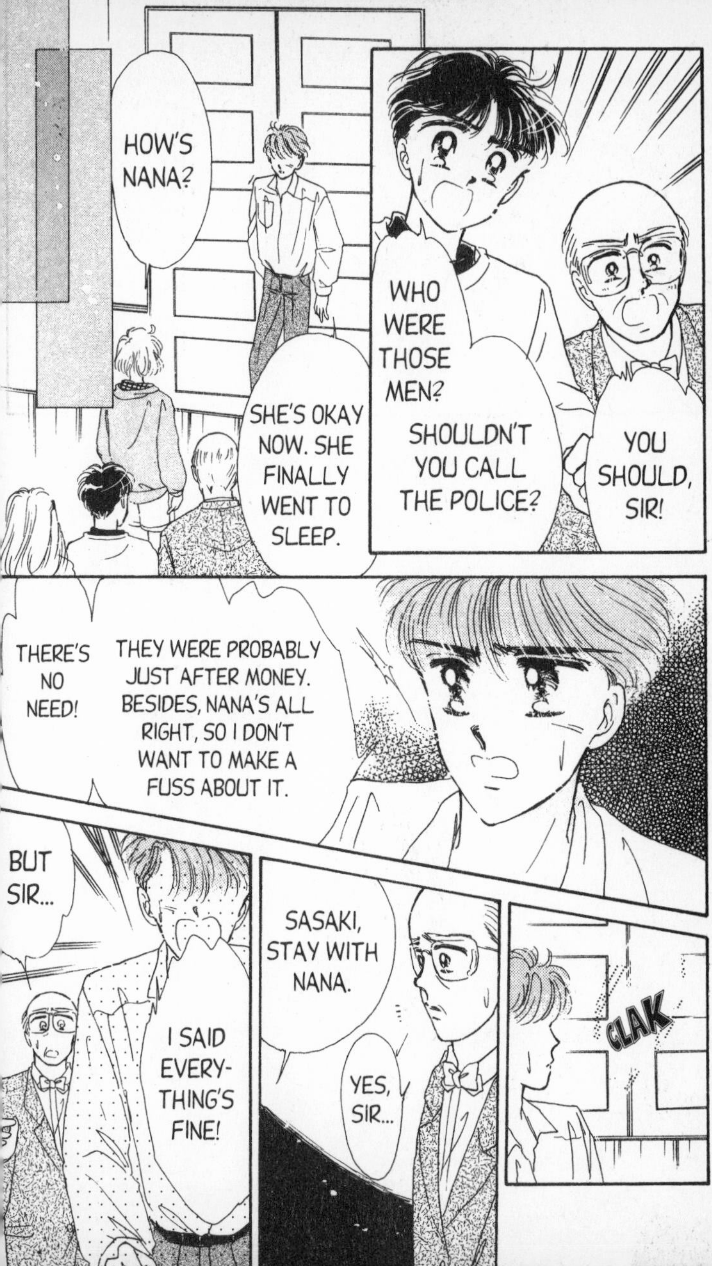
HOW'S NANA?
SHE'S OKAY NOW. SHE FINALLY WENT TO SLEEP.
WHO WERE THOSE MEN?
SHOULDN'T YOU CALL THE POLICE?
YOU SHOULD, SIR!
THERE'S NO NEED!
THEY WERE PROBABLY JUST AFTER MONEY. BESIDES, NANA'S ALL RIGHT, SO I DON'T WANT TO MAKE A FUSS ABOUT IT.
BUT SIR...
I SAID EVERY-THING'S FINE!
SASAKI, STAY WITH NANA.
YES, SIR...
CLAK

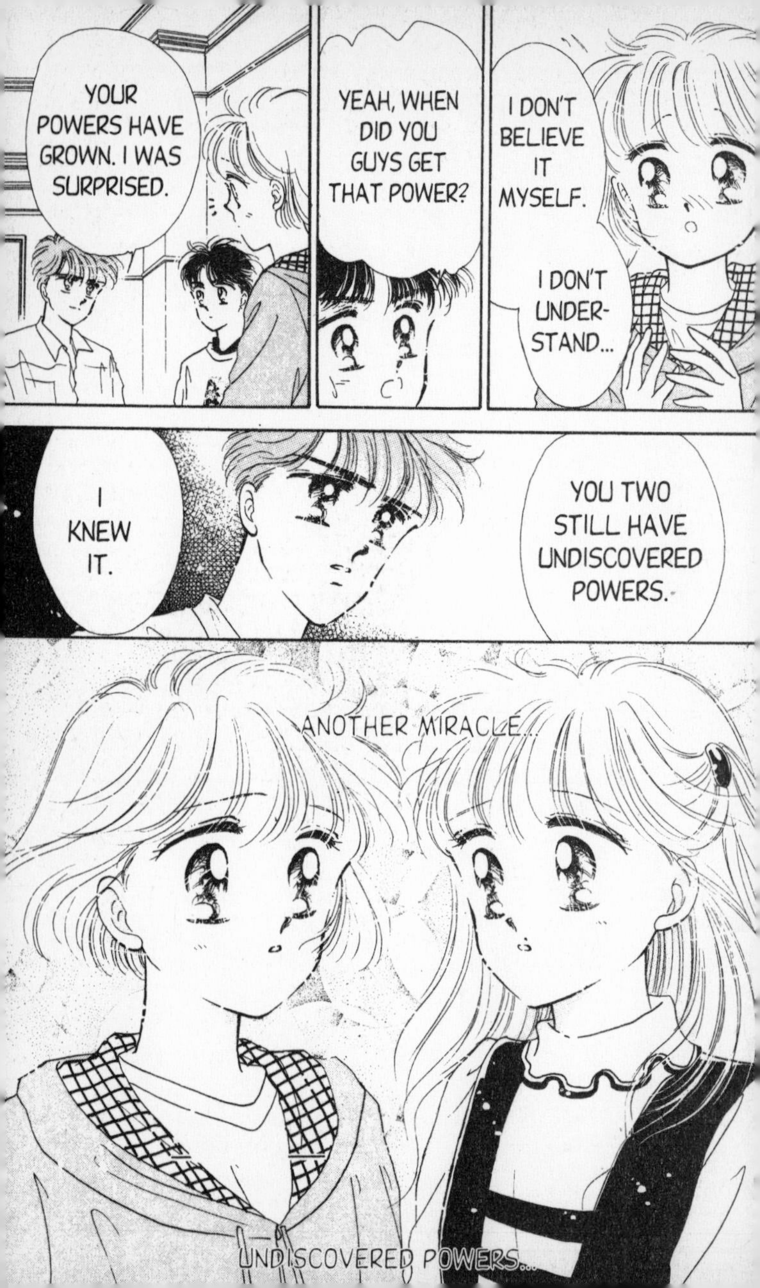
YOUR POWERS HAVE GROWN. I WAS SURPRISED.
YEAH, WHEN DID YOU GUYS GET THAT POWER?
I DON'T BELIEVE IT MYSELF.
I DON'T UNDER-STAND...
I KNEW IT.
YOU TWO STILL HAVE UNDISCOVERED POWERS.
ANOTHER MIRACLE...
UNDISCOVERED POWERS...

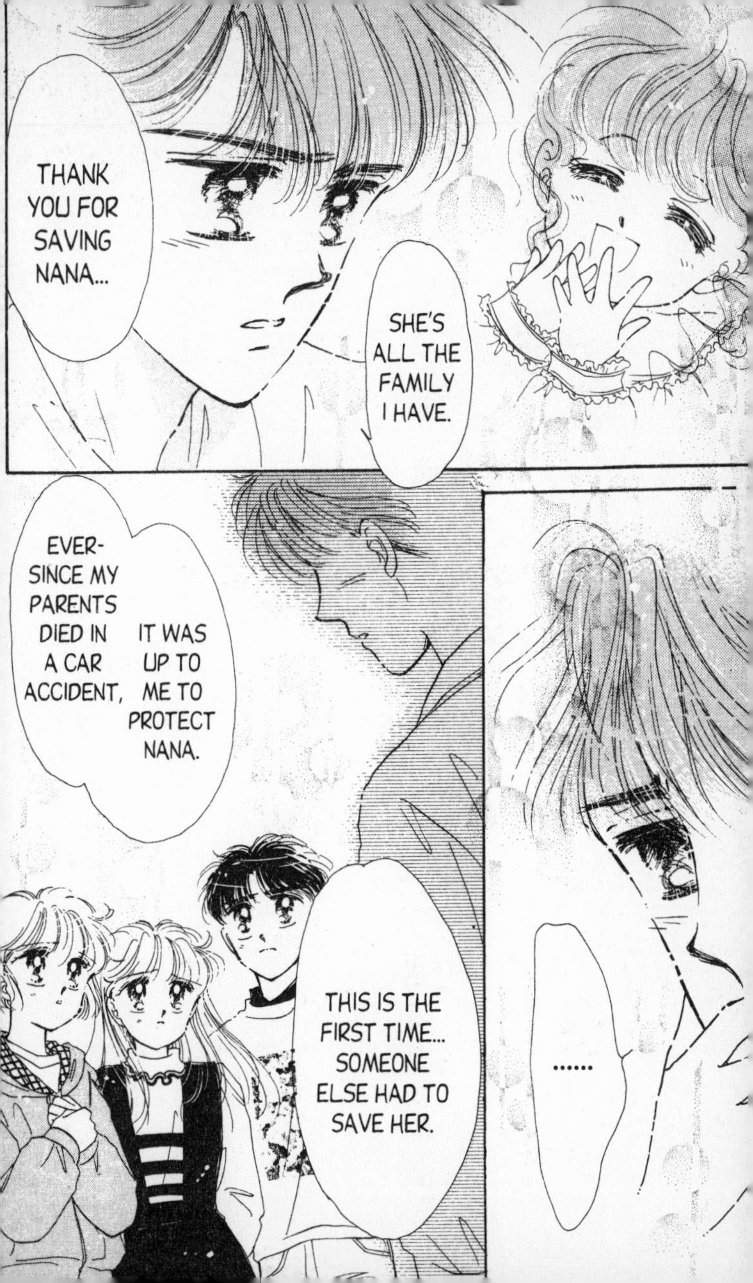
THANK YOU FOR SAVING NANA...
SHE'S ALL THE FAMILY I HAVE.
EVER-SINCE MY PARENTS DIED IN A CAR ACCIDENT,
IT WAS UP TO ME TO PROTECT NANA.
THIS IS THE FIRST TIME... SOMEONE ELSE HAD TO SAVE HER.
......

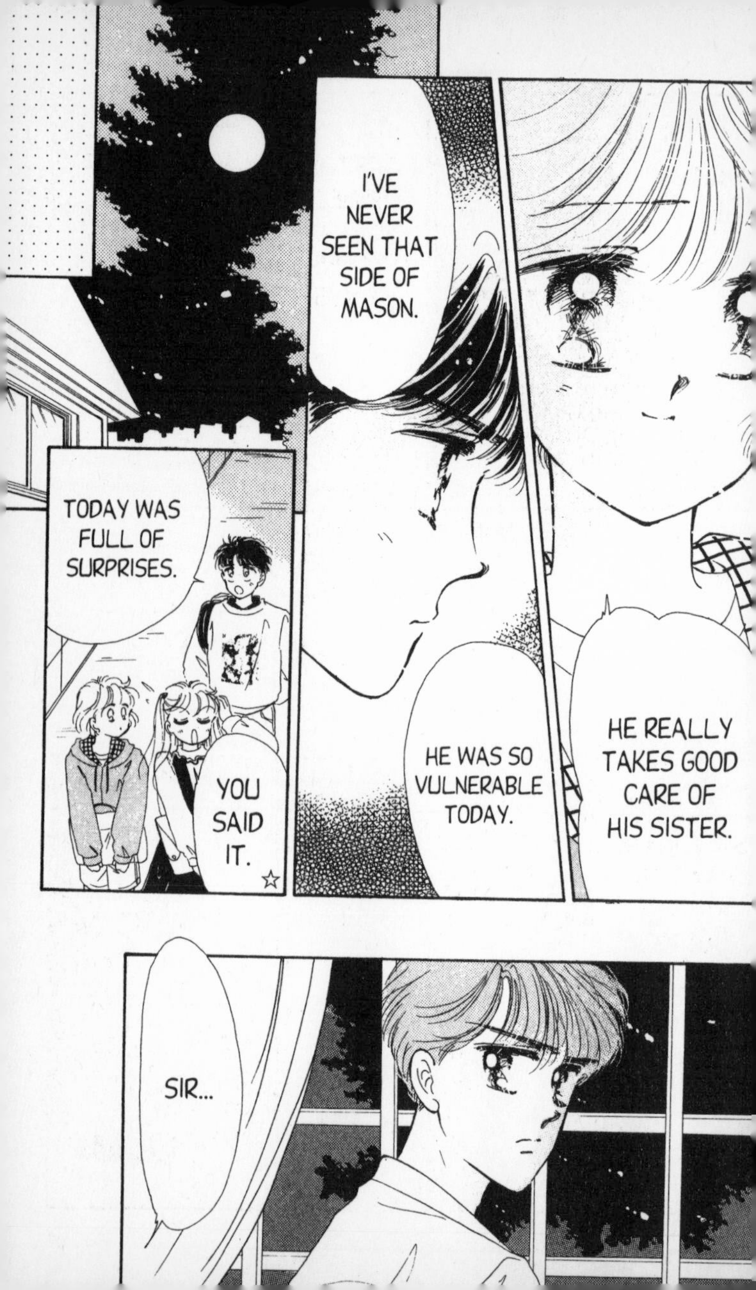
TODAY WAS FULL OF SURPRISES.
YOU SAID IT. ☆
I'VE NEVER SEEN THAT SIDE OF MASON.
HE WAS SO VULNERABLE TODAY.
HE REALLY TAKES GOOD CARE OF HIS SISTER.
SIR...

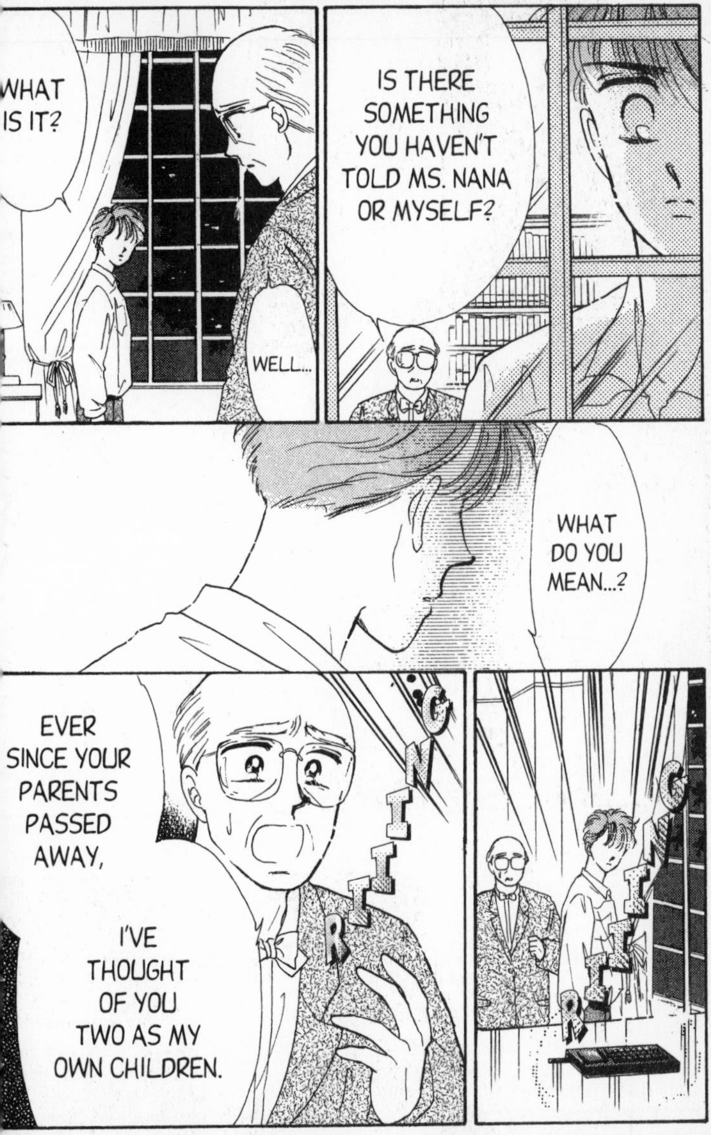
WHAT IS IT?
WELL...
IS THERE SOMETHING YOU HAVEN'T TOLD MS. NANA OR MYSELF?
WHAT DO YOU MEAN...?
EVER SINCE YOUR PARENTS PASSED AWAY,
I'VE THOUGHT OF YOU TWO AS MY OWN CHILDREN.
RIIING
RIIING

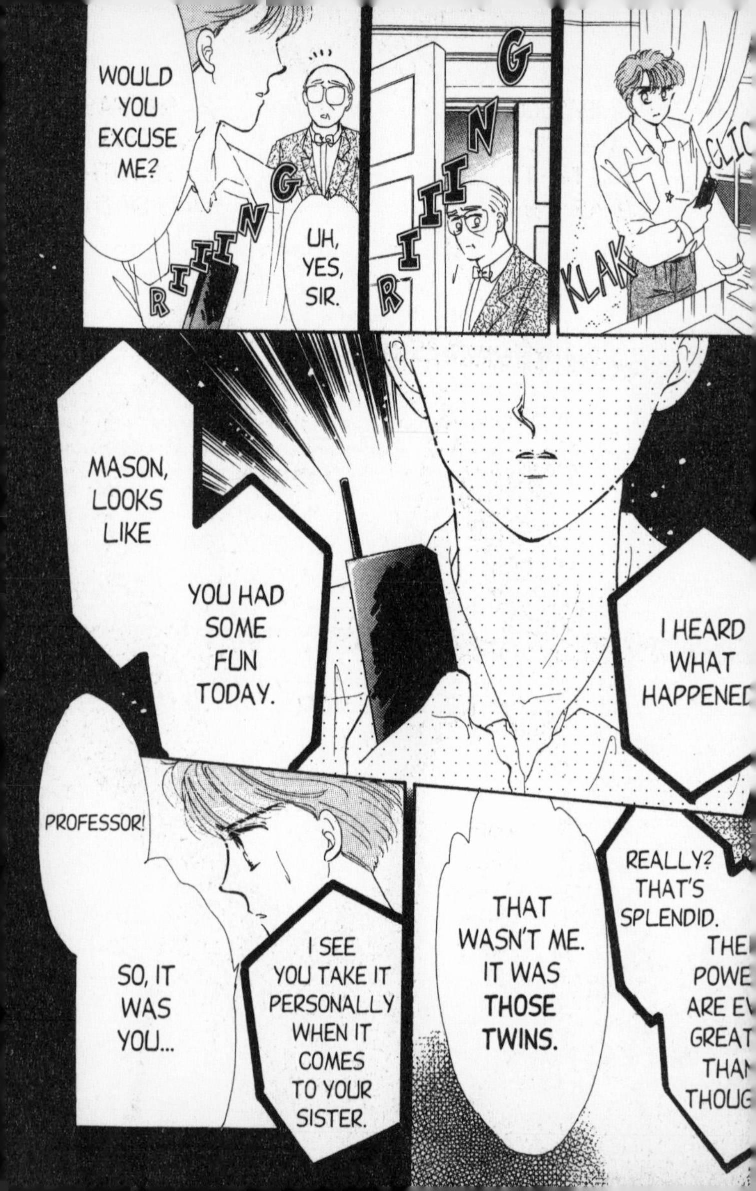
WOULD YOU EXCUSE ME?
RIIING
UH, YES, SIR.
RIIING
KLAK
CLIC
MASON, LOOKS LIKE
YOU HAD SOME FUN TODAY.
I HEARD WHAT HAPPENED
PROFESSOR!
SO, IT WAS YOU...
I SEE YOU TAKE IT PERSONALLY WHEN IT COMES TO YOUR SISTER.
THAT WASN'T ME. IT WAS THOSE TWINS.
REALLY? THAT'S SPLENDID.
THE POWE ARE EV GREAT THAN THOUG

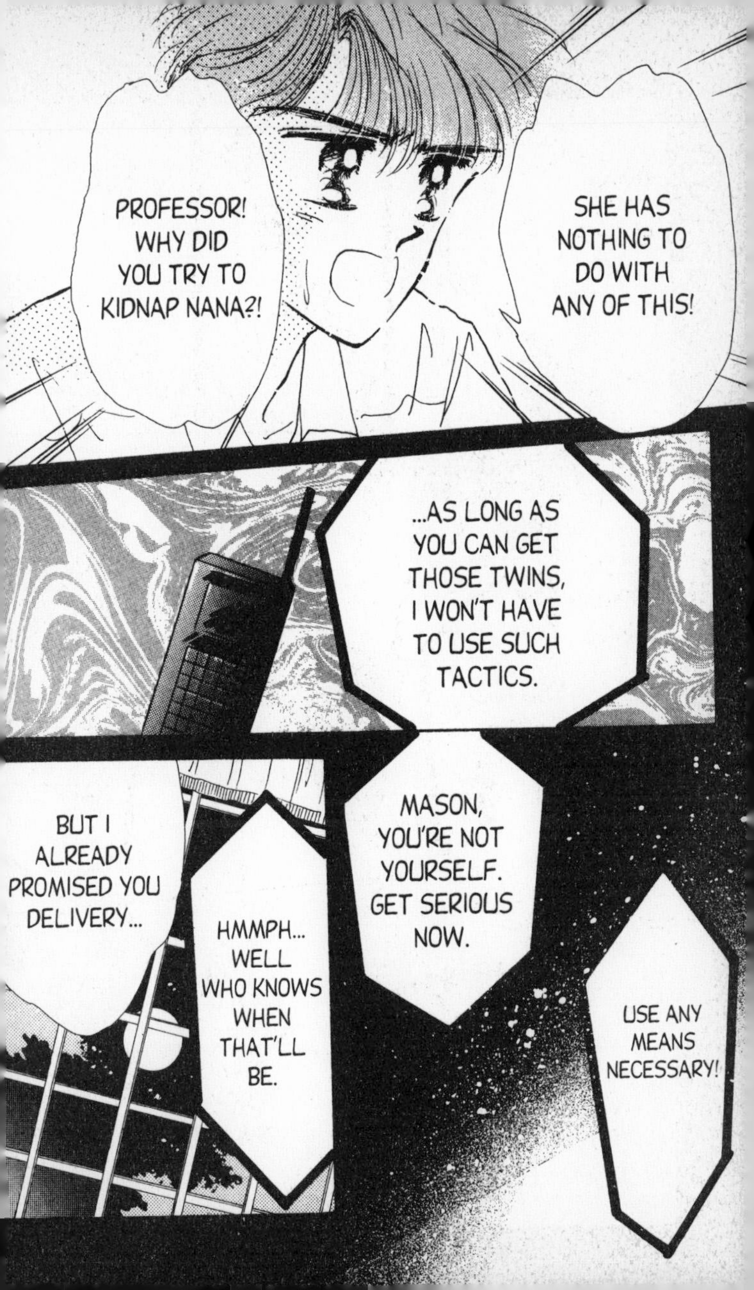
PROFESSOR! WHY DID YOU TRY TO KIDNAP NANA?!
SHE HAS NOTHING TO DO WITH ANY OF THIS!
...AS LONG AS YOU CAN GET THOSE TWINS, I WON'T HAVE TO USE SUCH TACTICS.
BUT I ALREADY PROMISED YOU DELIVERY...
HMMPH... WELL WHO KNOWS WHEN THAT'LL BE.
MASON, YOU'RE NOT YOURSELF. GET SERIOUS NOW.
USE ANY MEANS NECESSARY!

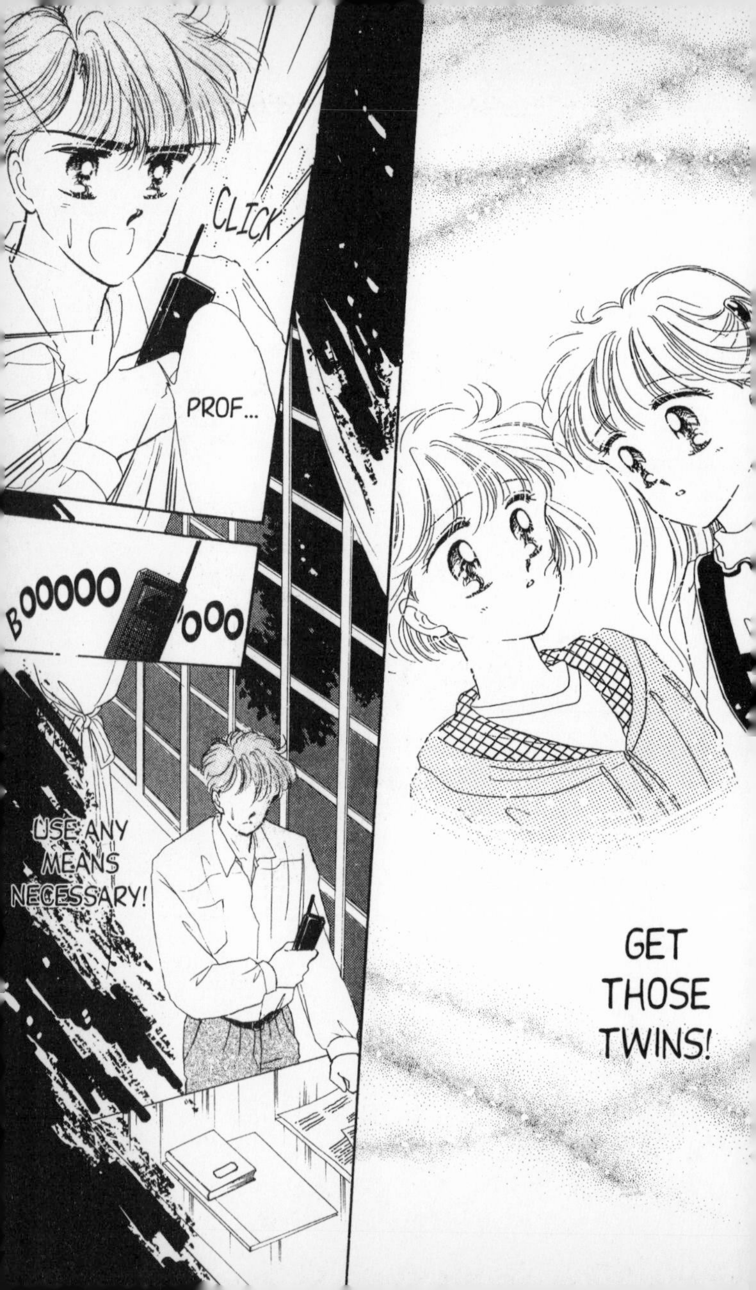
CLICK
PROF...
BOOOOO
OOO
USE ANY MEANS NECESSARY!
GET THOSE TWINS!

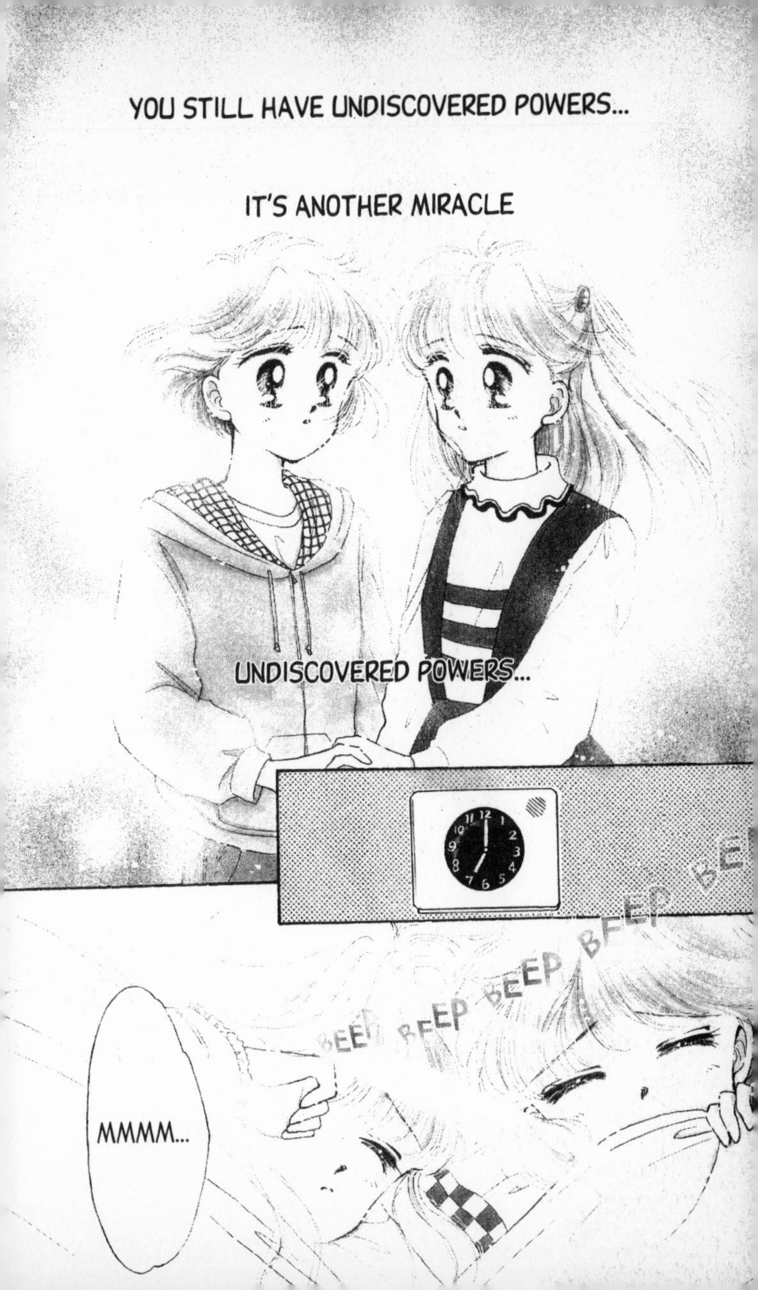
YOU STILL HAVE UNDISCOVERED POWERS...
IT'S ANOTHER MIRACLE
UNDISCOVERED POWERS...
MMMM...
BEEP BEEP BEEP BEEP BEEP BEE

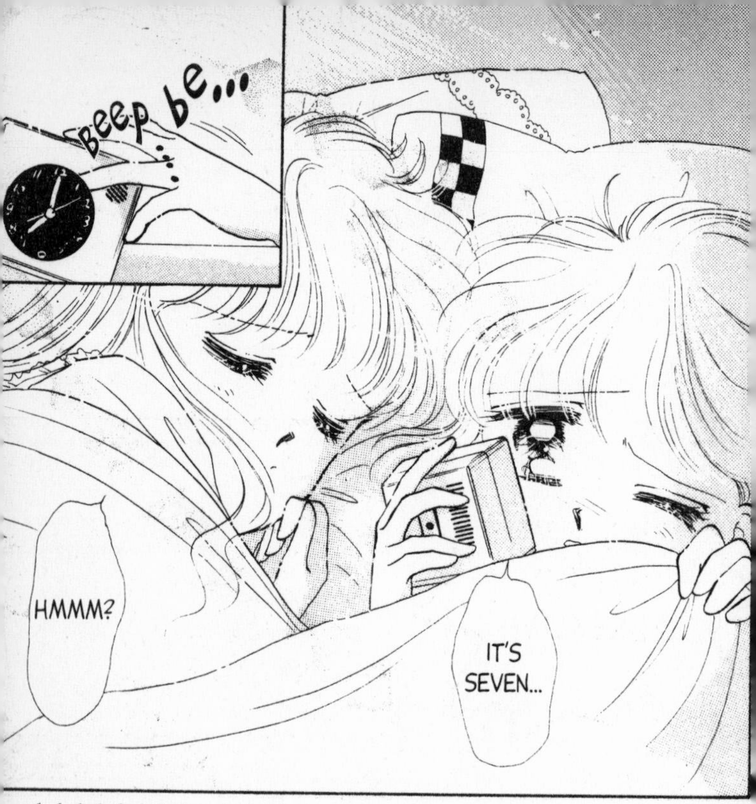

Beep be...
HMMM?
IT'S SEVEN...

BONUS

I love to travel! And I especially love to fly!
But I've been so busy lately
that I haven't found time to take a vacation. But!!
I forced myself to take a break and went to Milan
and Paris from 9/3 to 9/11. Before that, I went to
New York two years ago, so it's been a long time! I had
to go to Narita Airport in July for some research, but I wish
I could have hopped on one of the planes somewhere!
Anyway, let me talk about my trip to Milan and Paris.

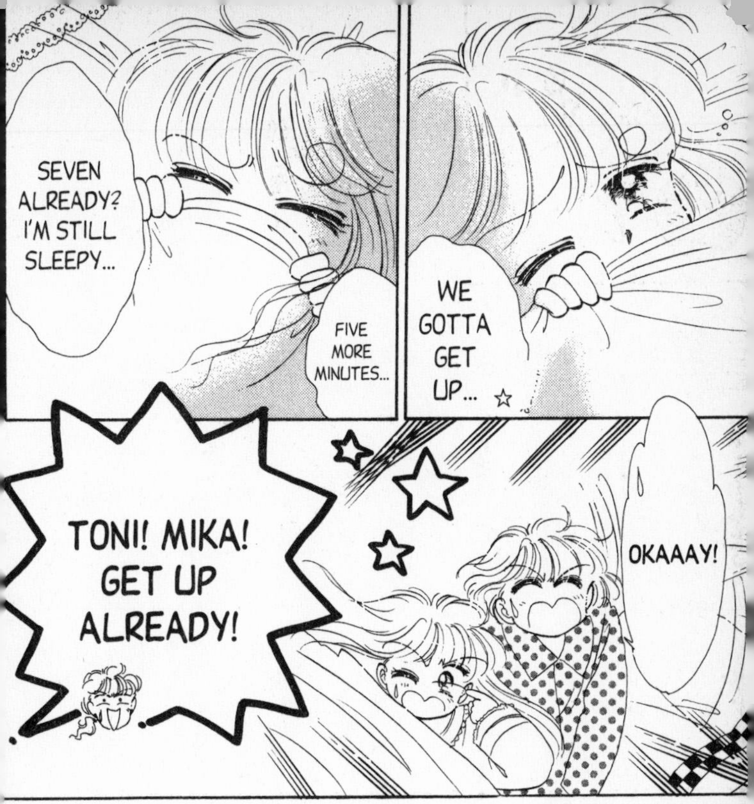
SEVEN ALREADY? I'M STILL SLEEPY...
FIVE MORE MINUTES...
WE GOTTA GET UP... ☆
TONI! MIKA! GET UP ALREADY!
OKAAAY!

I really intended to take an official vacation, but I ended up working on Part 3 right after Part 2, so I had to jump through hoops to make this trip happen... I guess I didn't have to go through that much trouble, but I NEED MY SUMMER VACATION! I never really plan these things. I just go with my gut. Well, actually, I booked a tour this time, so it wasn't that thrilling. But still I found time to panic. I'll tell you more in the next Bonus section...

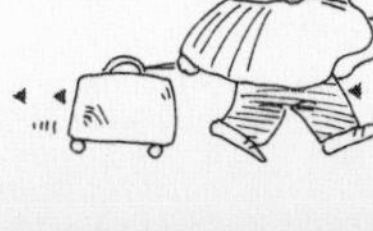

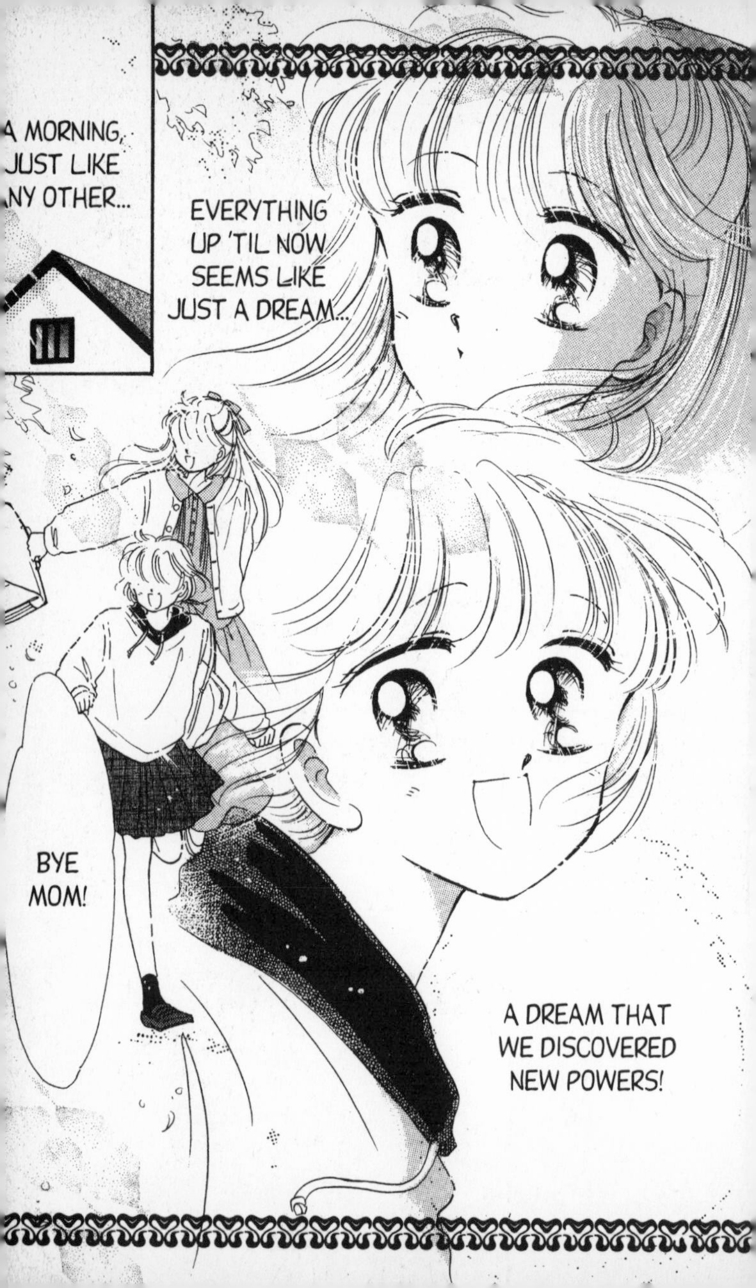

A MORNING, JUST LIKE ANY OTHER...
EVERYTHING UP 'TIL NOW SEEMS LIKE JUST A DREAM...
BYE MOM!
A DREAM THAT WE DISCOVERED NEW POWERS!

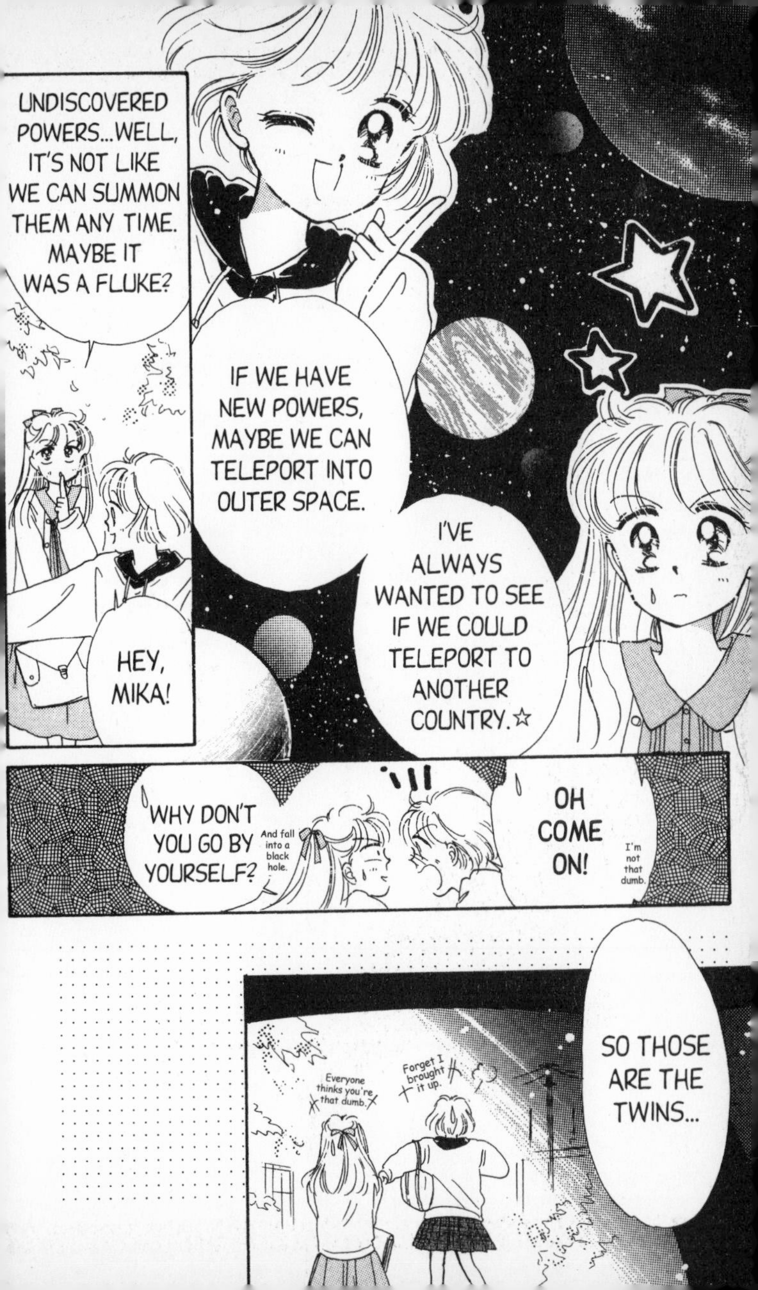
UNDISCOVERED POWERS...WELL, IT'S NOT LIKE WE CAN SUMMON THEM ANY TIME. MAYBE IT WAS A FLUKE?
HEY, MIKA!
IF WE HAVE NEW POWERS, MAYBE WE CAN TELEPORT INTO OUTER SPACE.
I'VE ALWAYS WANTED TO SEE IF WE COULD TELEPORT TO ANOTHER COUNTRY.☆
WHY DON'T YOU GO BY YOURSELF?
And fall into a black hole.
OH COME ON!
I'm not that dumb.
Everyone thinks you're that dumb.
Forget I brought it up.
SO THOSE ARE THE TWINS...

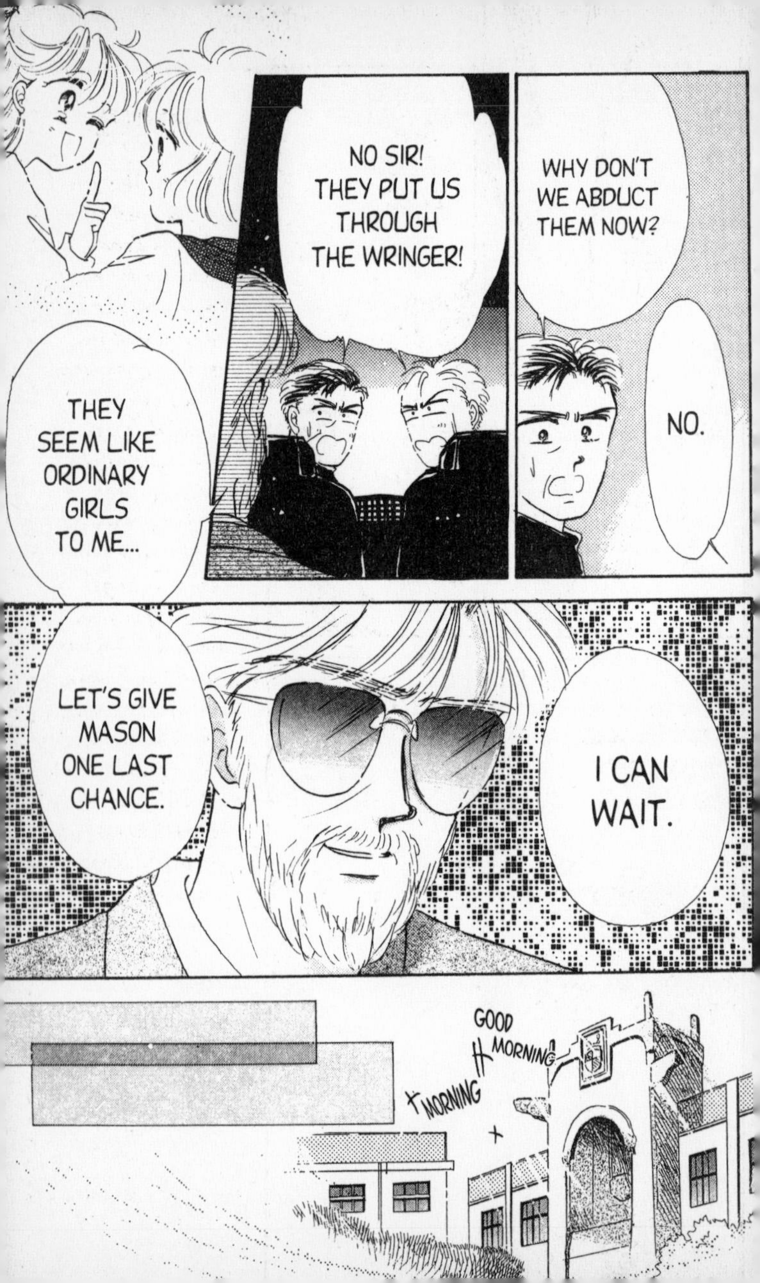
THEY SEEM LIKE ORDINARY GIRLS TO ME...
NO SIR! THEY PUT US THROUGH THE WRINGER!
WHY DON'T WE ABDUCT THEM NOW?
NO.
LET'S GIVE MASON ONE LAST CHANCE.
I CAN WAIT.
GOOD MORNING
MORNING

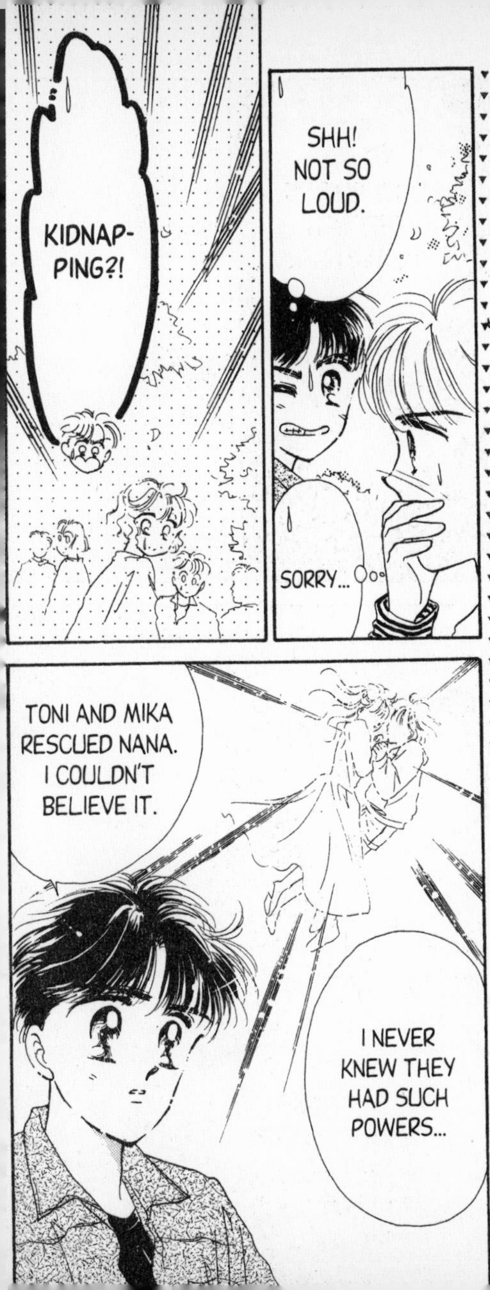
KIDNAP-PING?!
SHH! NOT SO LOUD.
SORRY...
TONI AND MIKA RESCUED NANA. I COULDN'T BELIEVE IT.
I NEVER KNEW THEY HAD SUCH POWERS...

BONUS

My trip: This one was a hard one. I had a deadline waiting for me when I got back, and it was my first tour group trip. I was so nervous I couldn't sleep the night before. I always used to leave from Yokohama City Terminal to get to the airport, but this time I had to leave from Tokyo, and on a weekday, so who knows when I'll get there! I didn't know you had to reserve the Narita Express train one month in advance! Jeeez! Well, I made it anyway!

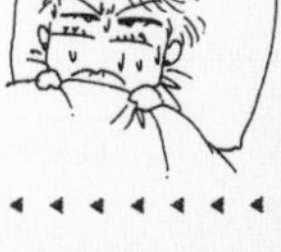

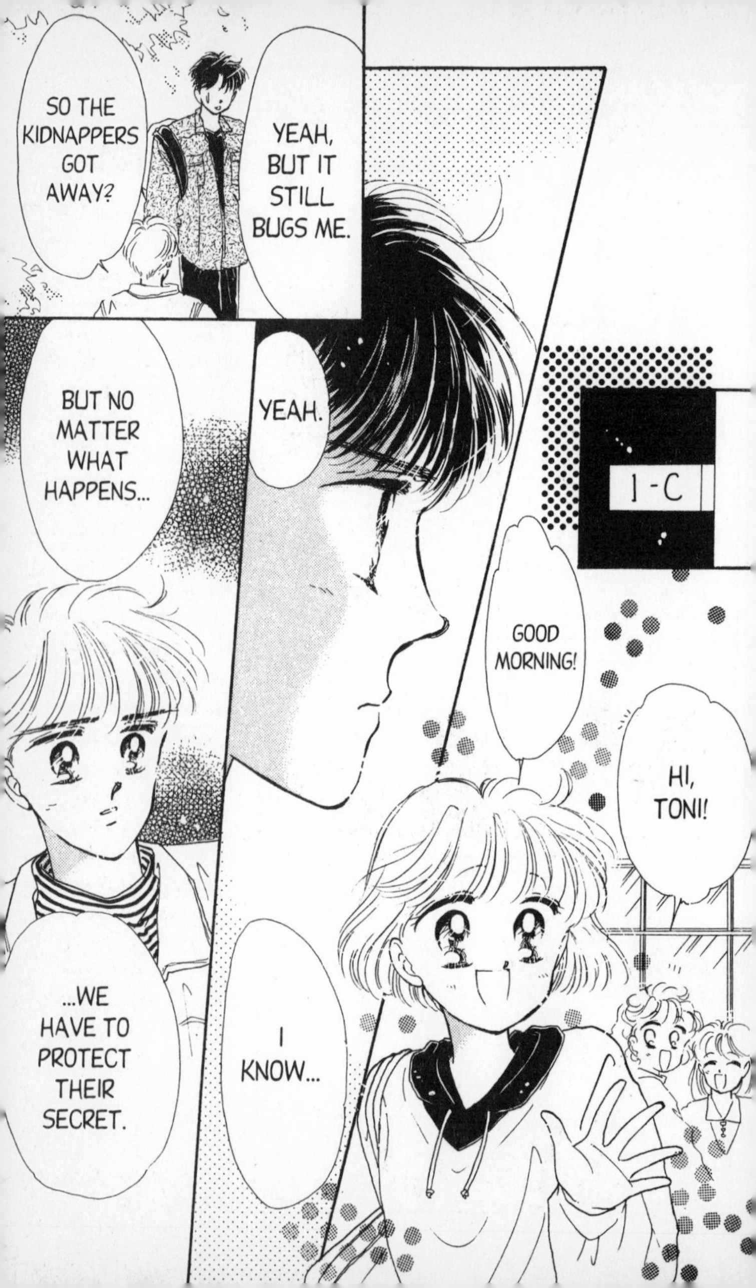
SO THE KIDNAPPERS GOT AWAY?
YEAH, BUT IT STILL BUGS ME.
BUT NO MATTER WHAT HAPPENS...
...WE HAVE TO PROTECT THEIR SECRET.
YEAH.
I KNOW...
1-C
GOOD MORNING!
HI, TONI!

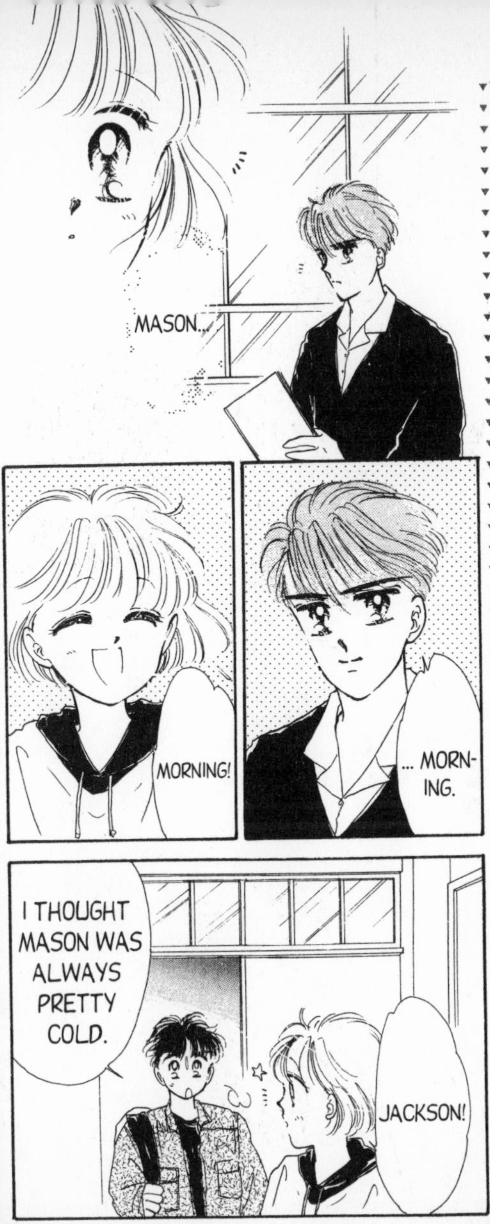
MASON...
MORNING!
... MORN-ING.
I THOUGHT MASON WAS ALWAYS PRETTY COLD.
JACKSON!

BONUS

Inside the plane: Well, somehow I made it to Narita (I got up at 4:00 AM to make it there at 9:00). Usually I can fall fast asleep in the plane, but I was worried about my deadlines this time. I tried to work during the flight, but the passenger next to me was playing video games the whole time! So instead, I tried learning Italian from my guidebook, but I couldn't get anything into my head. Finally, the steward came by and asked me, "Are you enjoying your flight?"

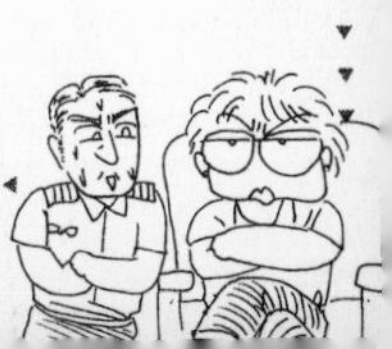

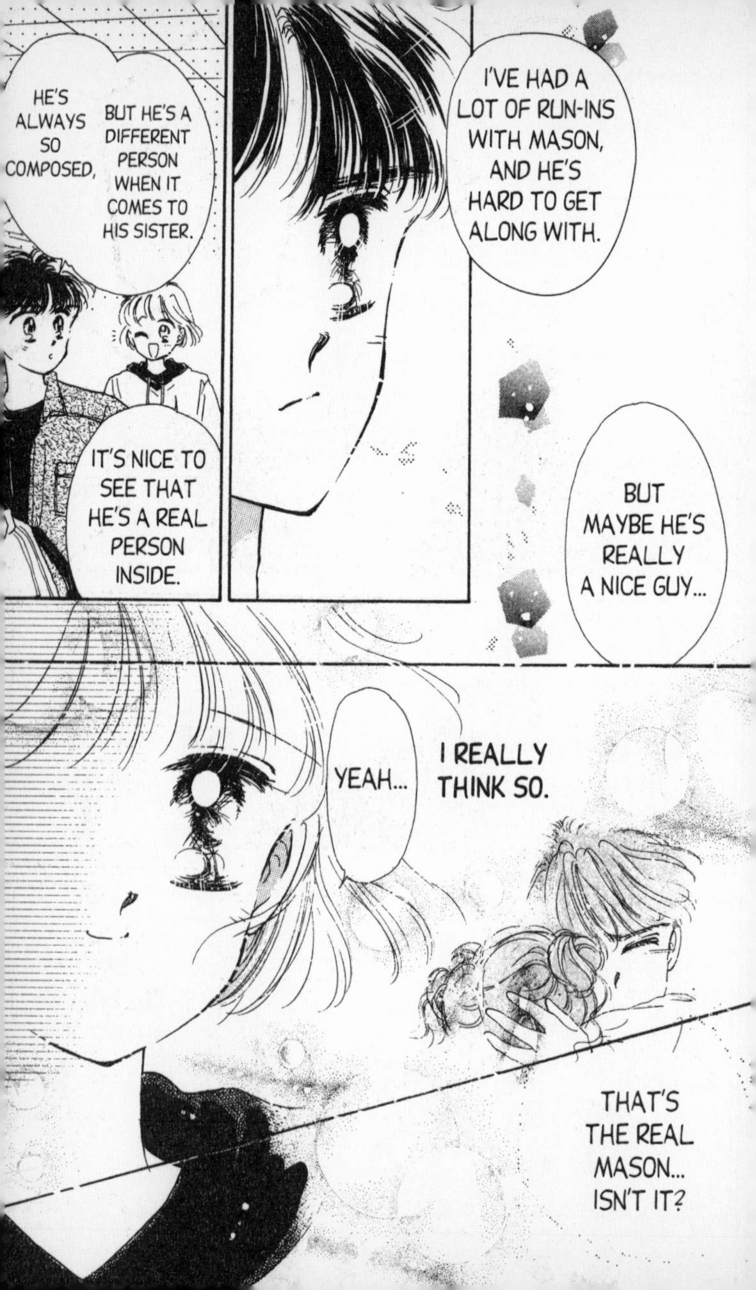
HE'S ALWAYS SO COMPOSED,
BUT HE'S A DIFFERENT PERSON WHEN IT COMES TO HIS SISTER.
IT'S NICE TO SEE THAT HE'S A REAL PERSON INSIDE.
I'VE HAD A LOT OF RUN-INS WITH MASON, AND HE'S HARD TO GET ALONG WITH.
BUT MAYBE HE'S REALLY A NICE GUY...
YEAH...
I REALLY THINK SO.
THAT'S THE REAL MASON... ISN'T IT?

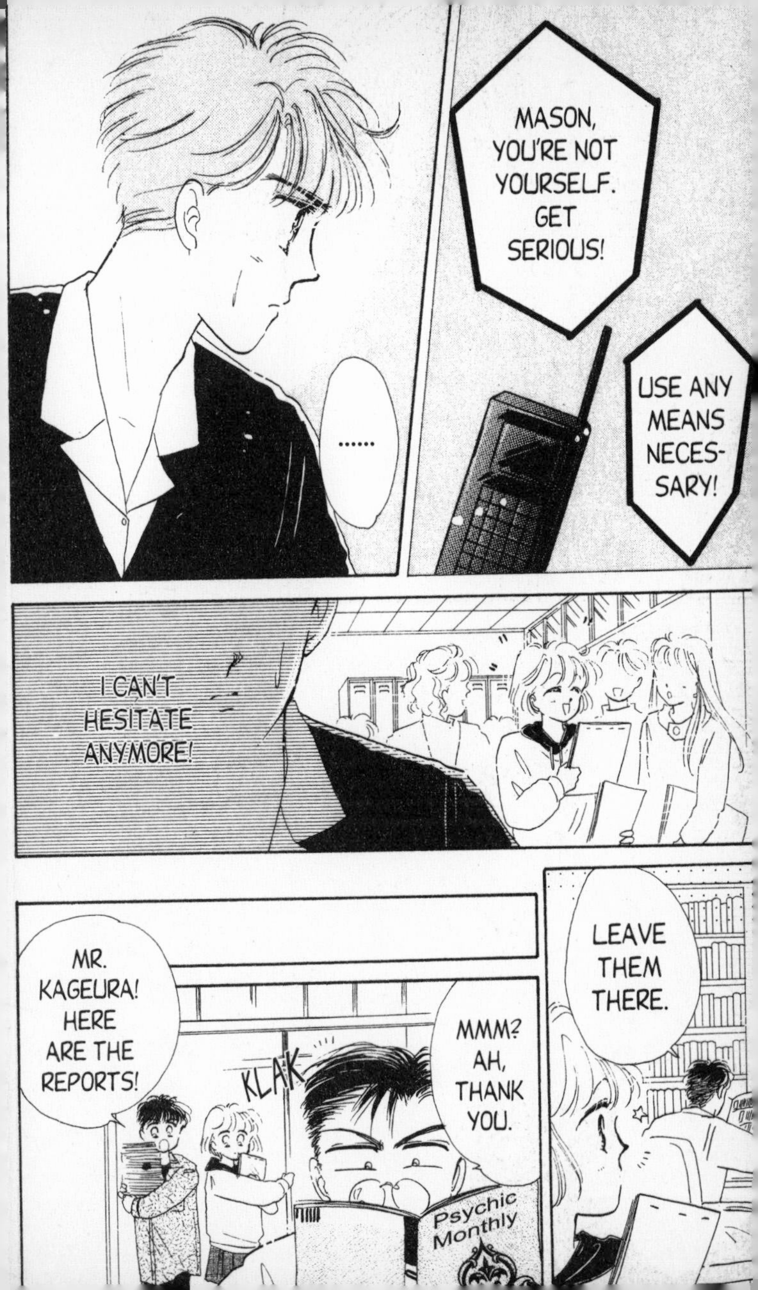
......
MASON, YOU'RE NOT YOURSELF. GET SERIOUS!
USE ANY MEANS NECES-SARY!
I CAN'T HESITATE ANYMORE!
MR. KAGEURA! HERE ARE THE REPORTS!
KLAK
MMM? AH, THANK YOU.
Psychic Monthly
LEAVE THEM THERE.

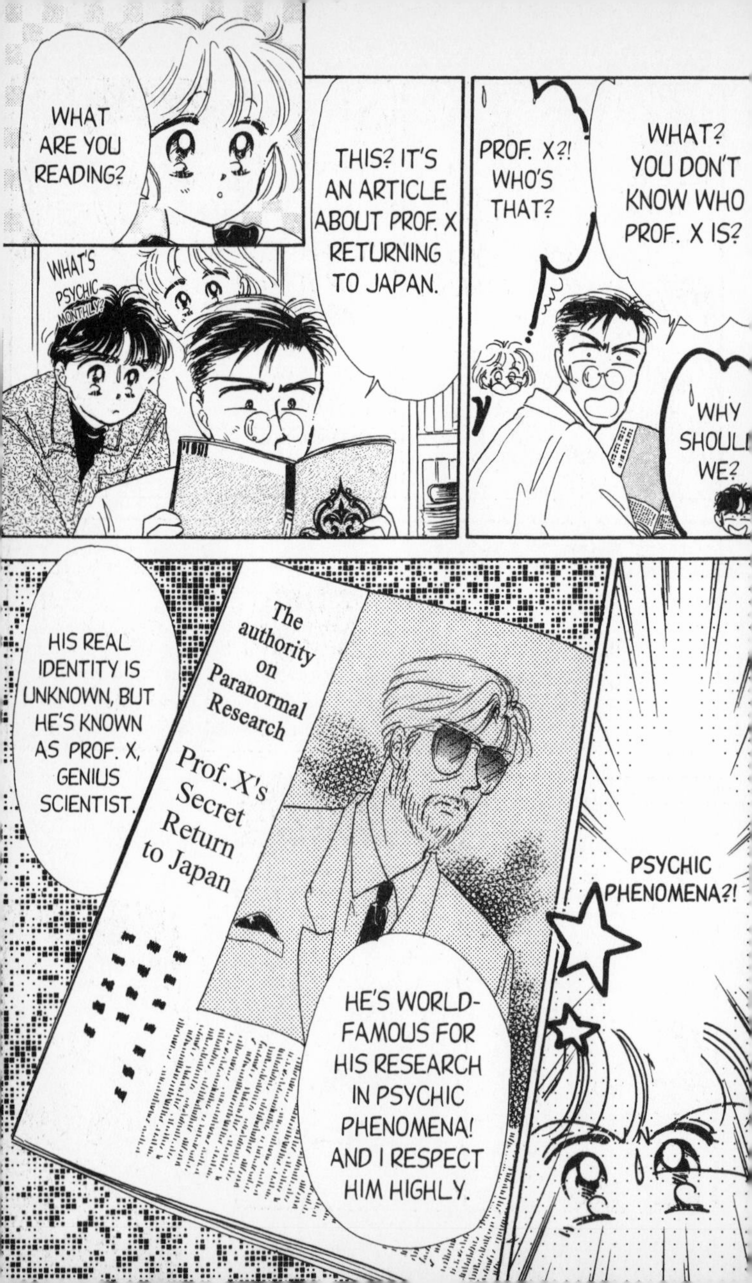
WHAT ARE YOU READING?
WHAT'S PSYCHIC MONTHLY?
THIS? IT'S AN ARTICLE ABOUT PROF. X RETURNING TO JAPAN.
PROF. X?! WHO'S THAT?
WHAT? YOU DON'T KNOW WHO PROF. X IS?
WHY SHOULD WE?
HIS REAL IDENTITY IS UNKNOWN, BUT HE'S KNOWN AS PROF. X, GENIUS SCIENTIST.
The authority on Paranormal Research
Prof. X's Secret Return to Japan
HE'S WORLD-FAMOUS FOR HIS RESEARCH IN PSYCHIC PHENOMENA! AND I RESPECT HIM HIGHLY.
PSYCHIC PHENOMENA?!

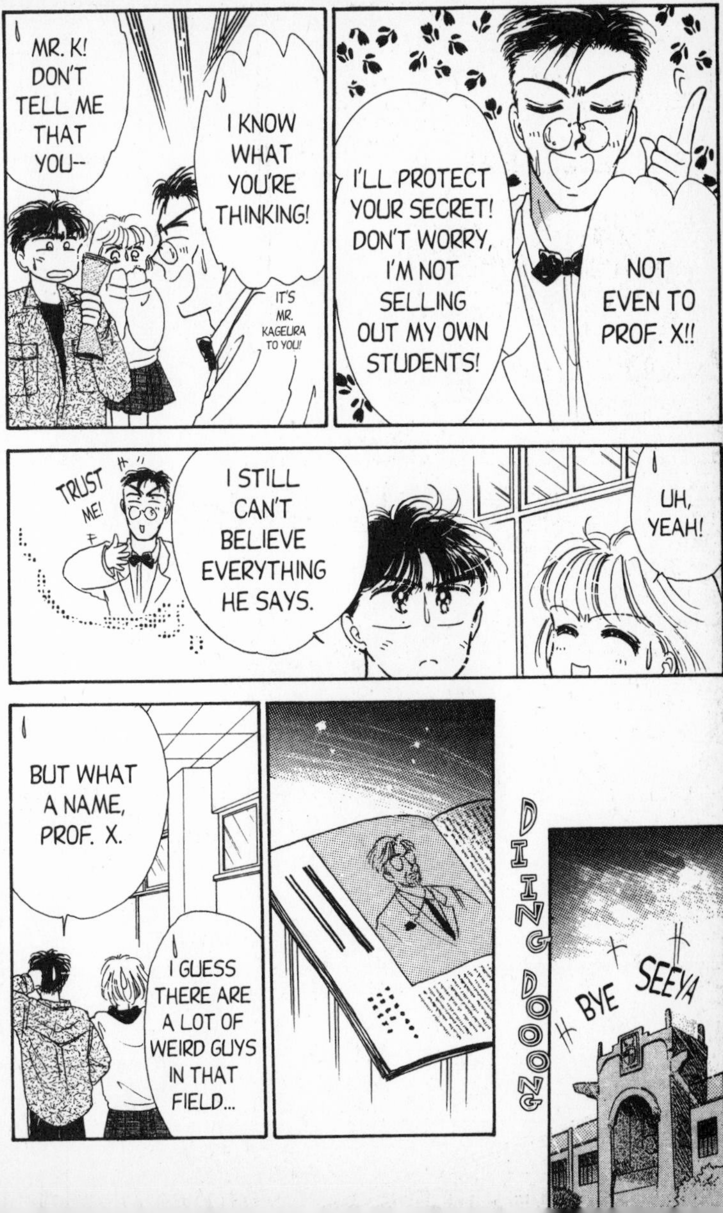
MR. K! DON'T TELL ME THAT YOU--
I KNOW WHAT YOU'RE THINKING!
IT'S MR. KAGEURA TO YOU!
I'LL PROTECT YOUR SECRET! DON'T WORRY, I'M NOT SELLING OUT MY OWN STUDENTS!
NOT EVEN TO PROF. X!!
TRUST ME!
I STILL CAN'T BELIEVE EVERYTHING HE SAYS.
UH, YEAH!
BUT WHAT A NAME, PROF. X.
I GUESS THERE ARE A LOT OF WEIRD GUYS IN THAT FIELD...
DIIING DOOONG
BYE
SEEYA

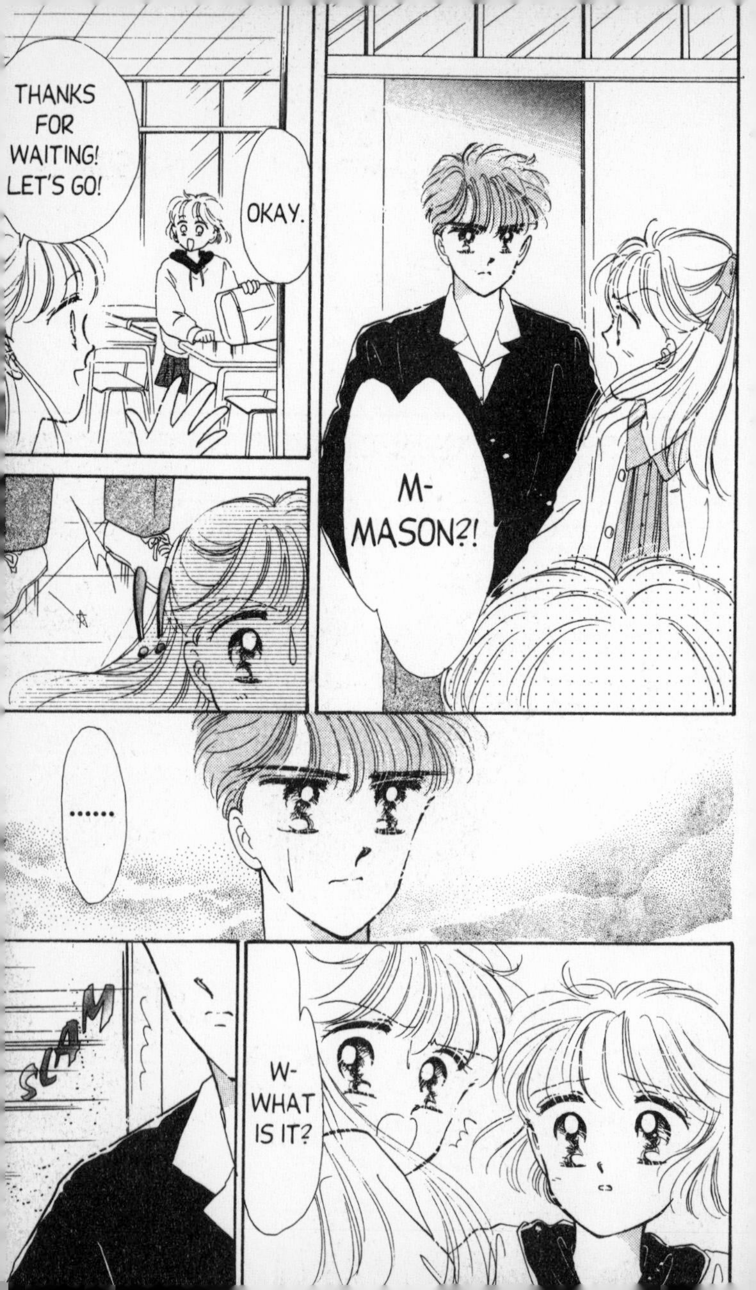
THANKS FOR WAITING! LET'S GO!
OKAY.
M-MASON?!
......
SLAM
W-WHAT IS IT?

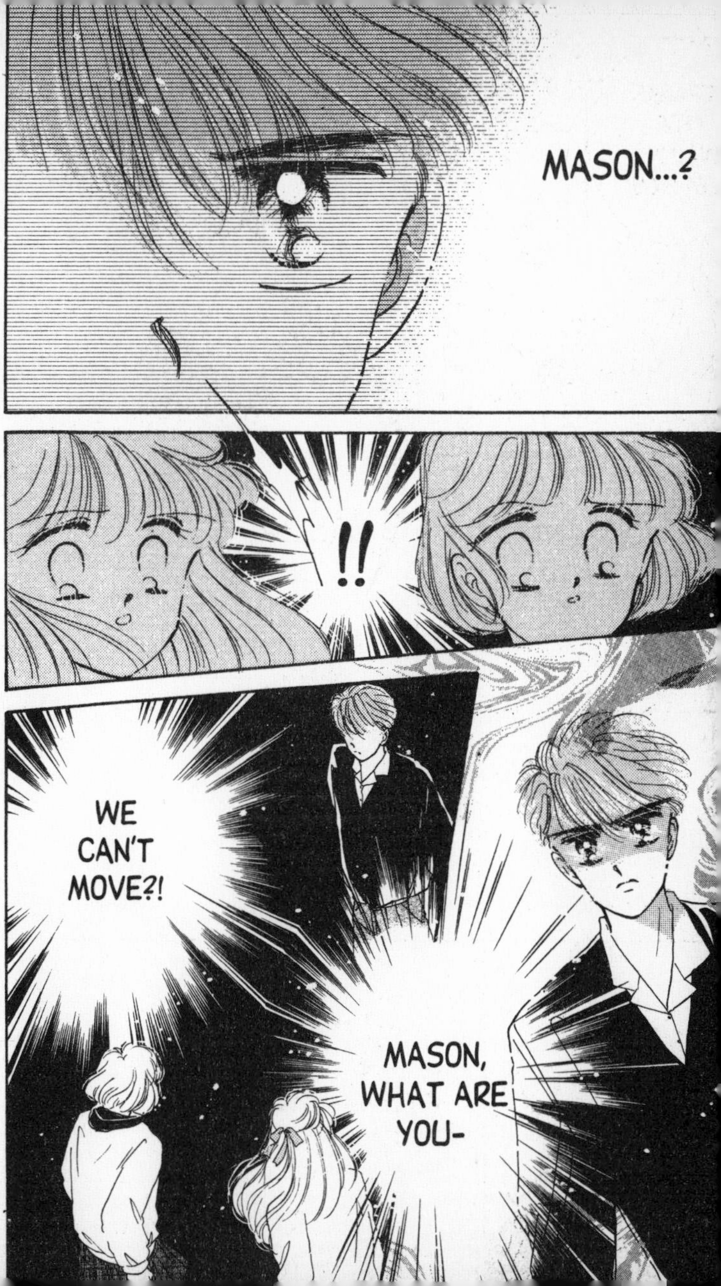
MASON...?
!!
WE CAN'T MOVE?!
MASON, WHAT ARE YOU-

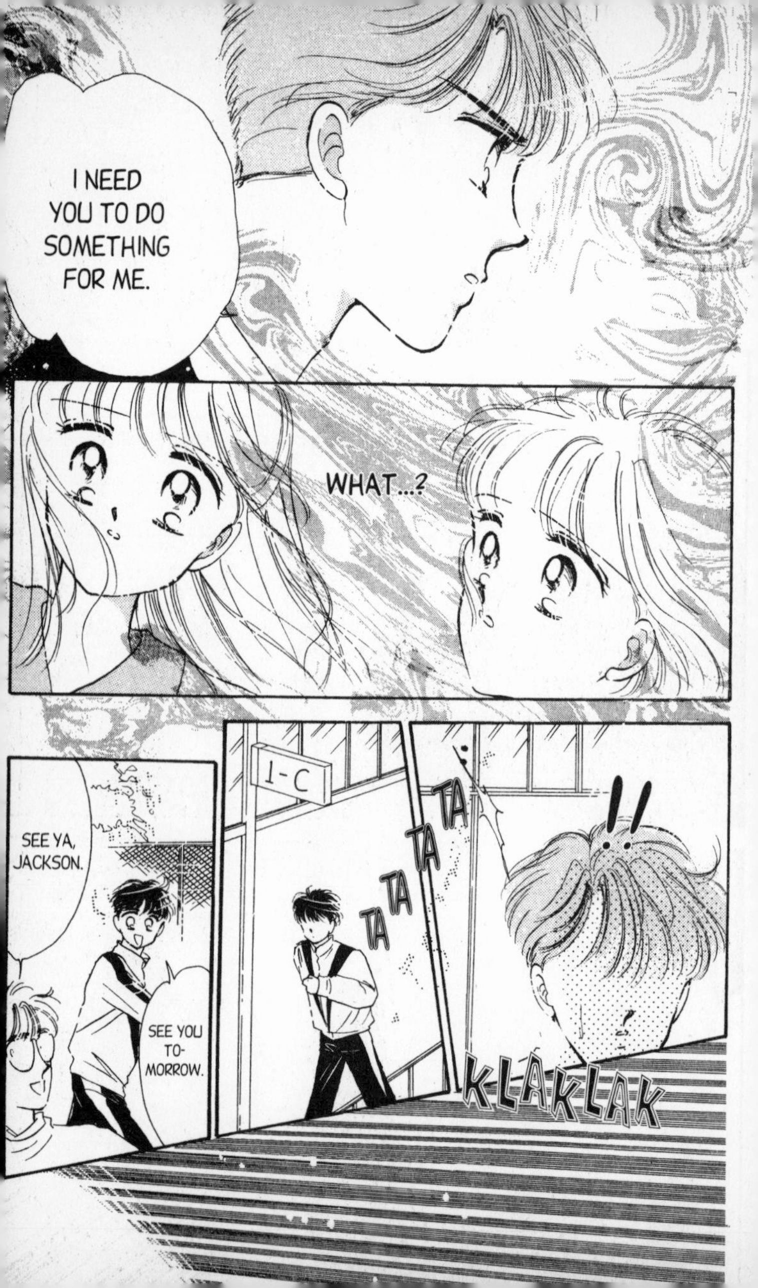
I NEED YOU TO DO SOMETHING FOR ME.
WHAT...?
SEE YA, JACKSON.
SEE YOU TO-MORROW.
1-C
TA TA TA TA TA
!!
KLAKLAK

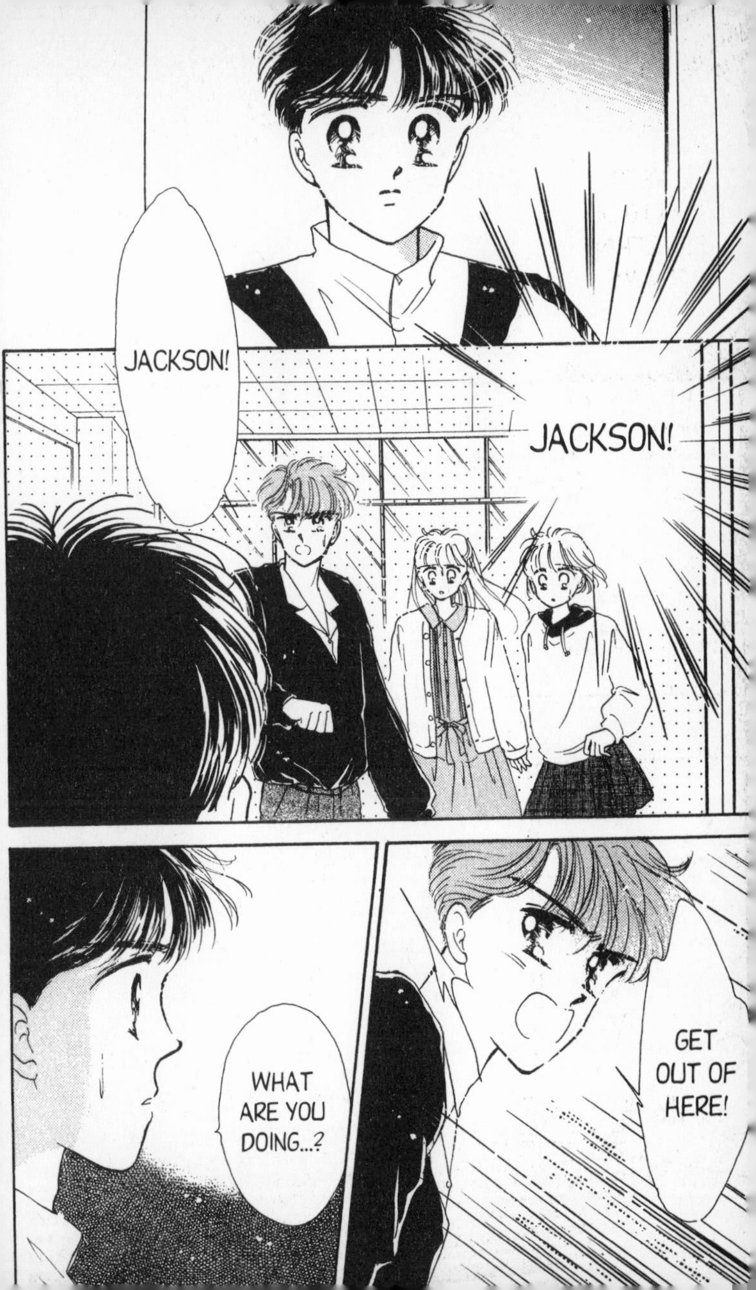
JACKSON!
JACKSON!
WHAT ARE YOU DOING...?
GET OUT OF HERE!

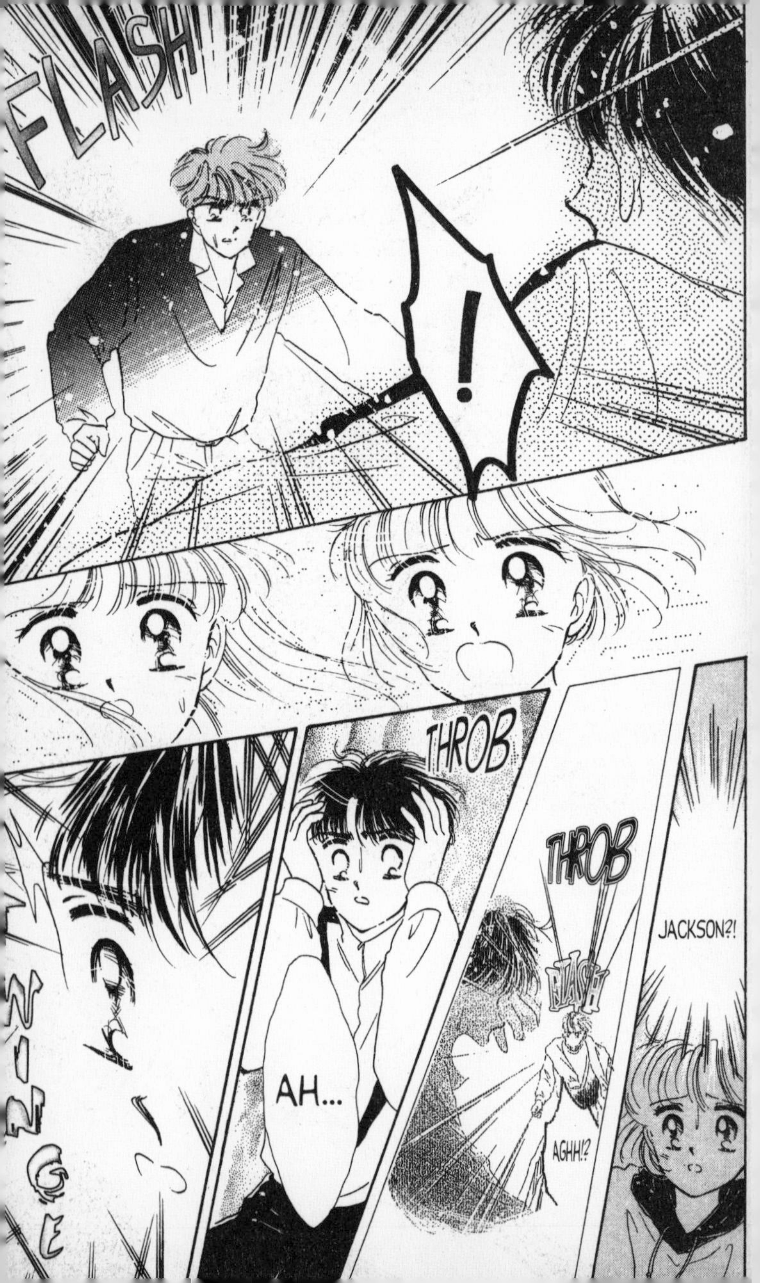
FLASH
!
WINGE
THROB
AH...
THROB
FLASH
AGHH!?
JACKSON?!

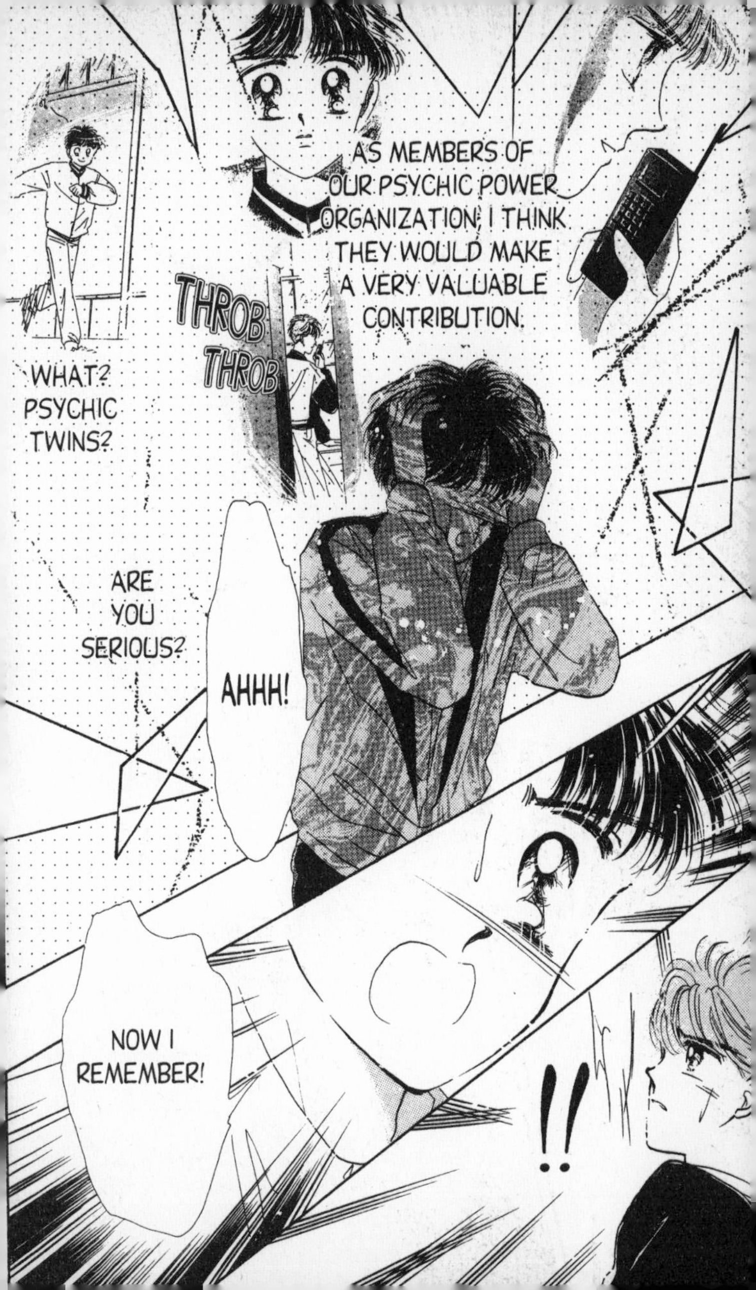

AS MEMBERS OF OUR PSYCHIC POWER ORGANIZATION, I THINK THEY WOULD MAKE A VERY VALUABLE CONTRIBUTION.
WHAT? PSYCHIC TWINS?
THROB THROB
ARE YOU SERIOUS?
AHHH!
NOW I REMEMBER!
!!

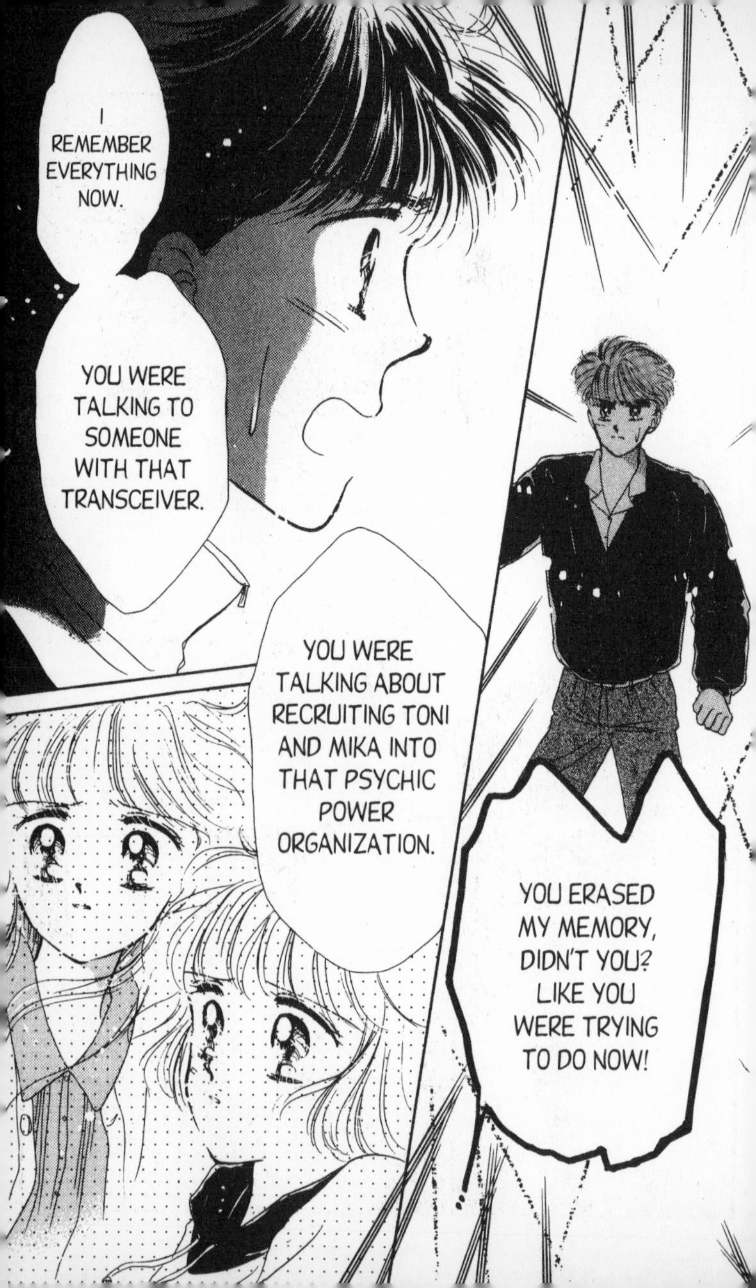
I REMEMBER EVERYTHING NOW.
YOU WERE TALKING TO SOMEONE WITH THAT TRANSCEIVER.
YOU WERE TALKING ABOUT RECRUITING TONI AND MIKA INTO THAT PSYCHIC POWER ORGANIZATION.
YOU ERASED MY MEMORY, DIDN'T YOU? LIKE YOU WERE TRYING TO DO NOW!

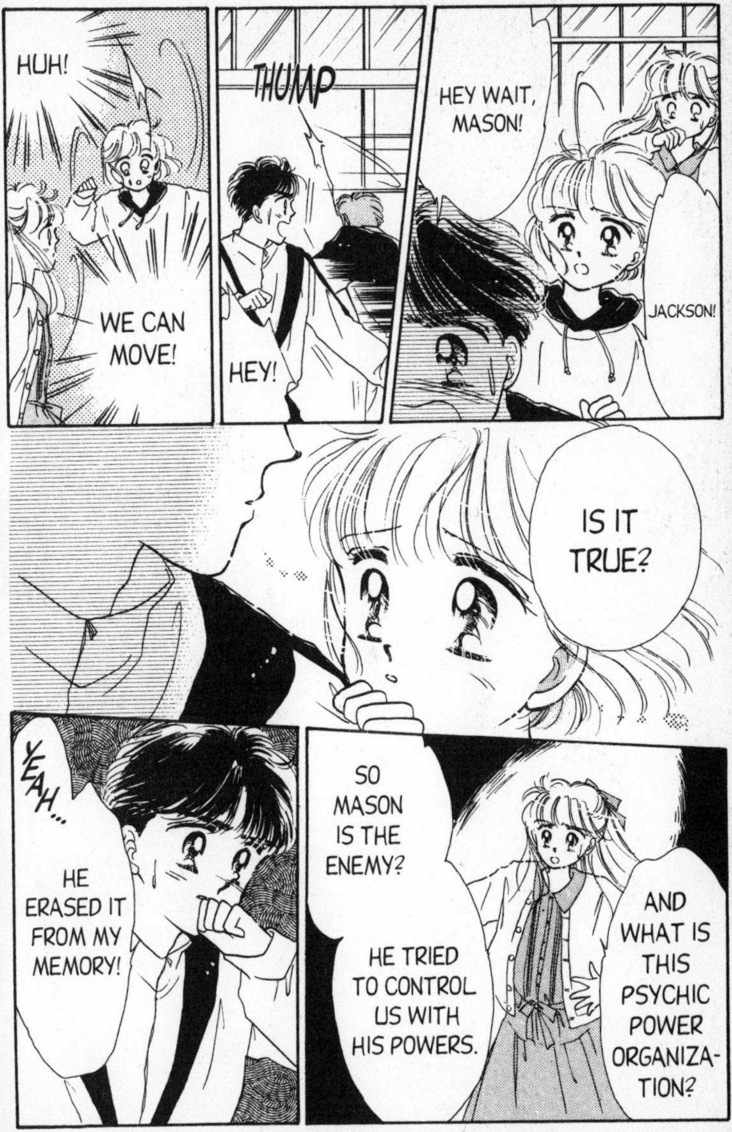
HUH!
WE CAN MOVE!
THUMP
HEY!
HEY WAIT, MASON!
JACKSON!
IS IT TRUE?
YEAH...
HE ERASED IT FROM MY MEMORY!
SO MASON IS THE ENEMY?
HE TRIED TO CONTROL US WITH HIS POWERS.
AND WHAT IS THIS PSYCHIC POWER ORGANIZA-TION?

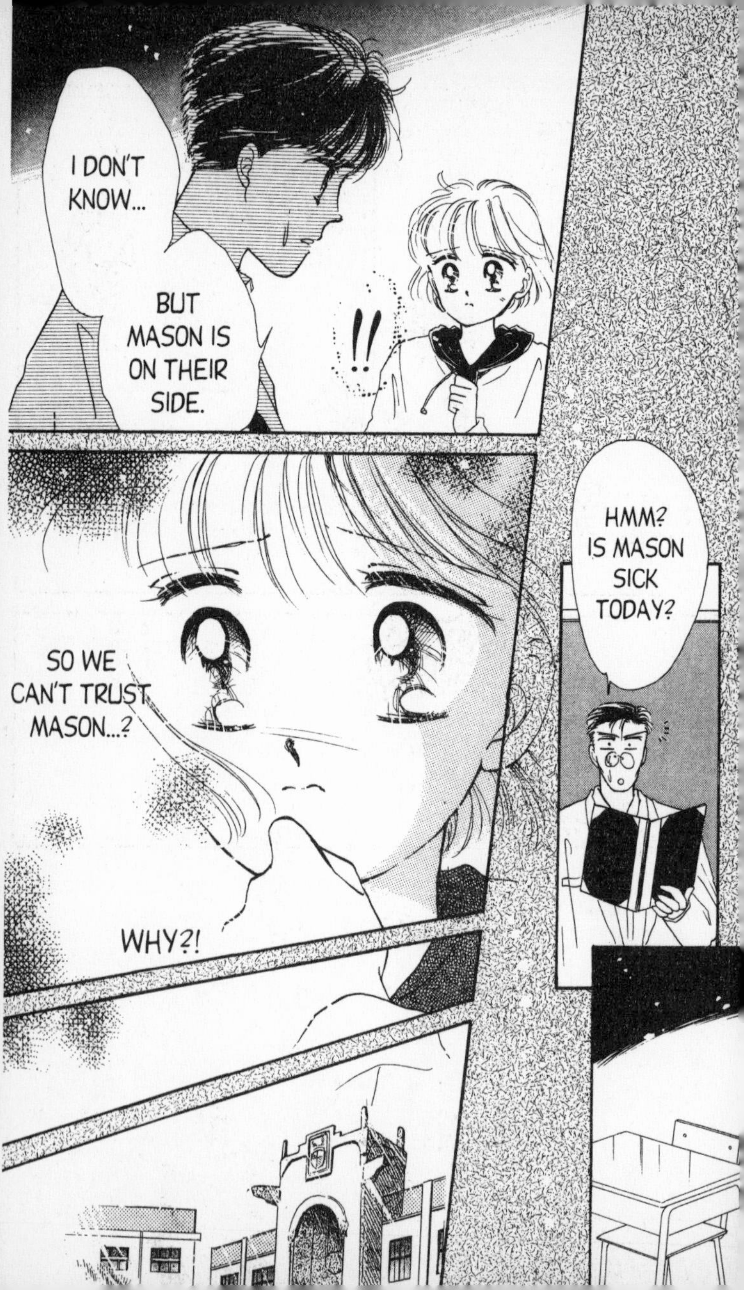
I DON'T KNOW...
BUT MASON IS ON THEIR SIDE.
!!
SO WE CAN'T TRUST MASON...?
WHY?!
HMM? IS MASON SICK TODAY?

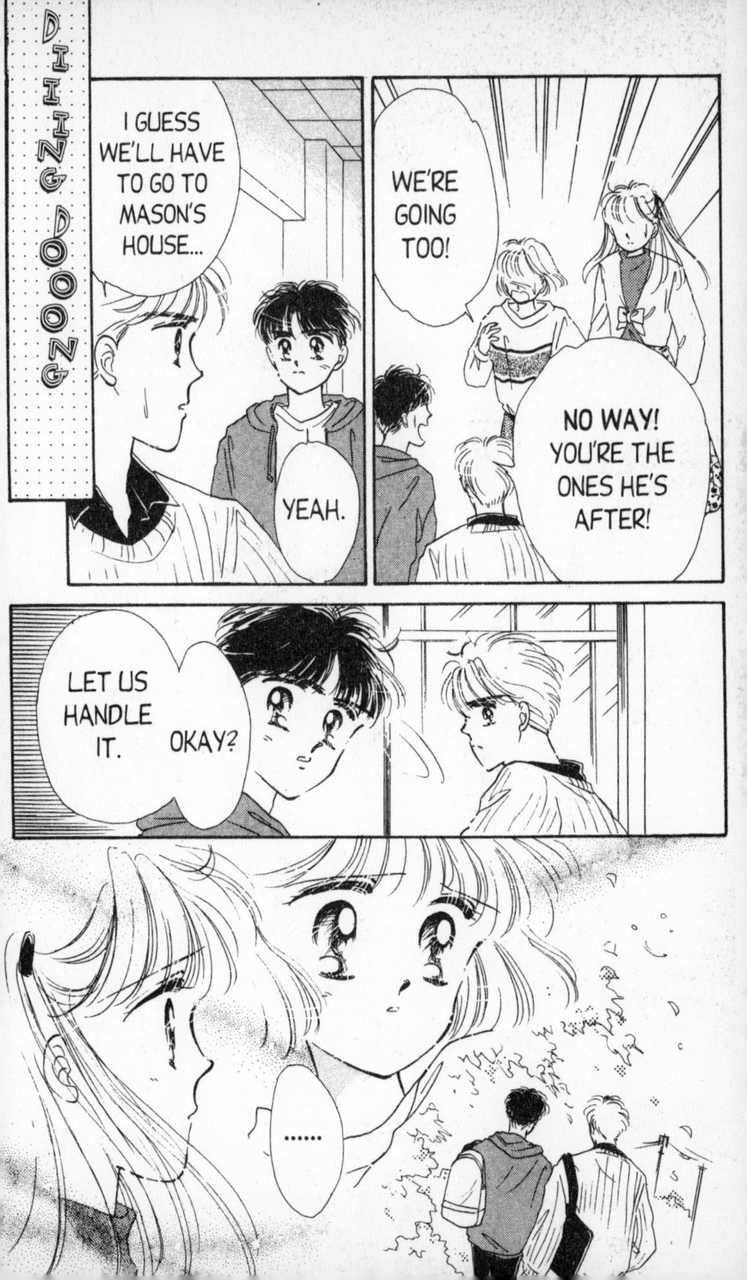
DIIING DOOONG
I GUESS WE'LL HAVE TO GO TO MASON'S HOUSE...
YEAH.
WE'RE GOING TOO!
NO WAY! YOU'RE THE ONES HE'S AFTER!
LET US HANDLE IT.
OKAY?
......

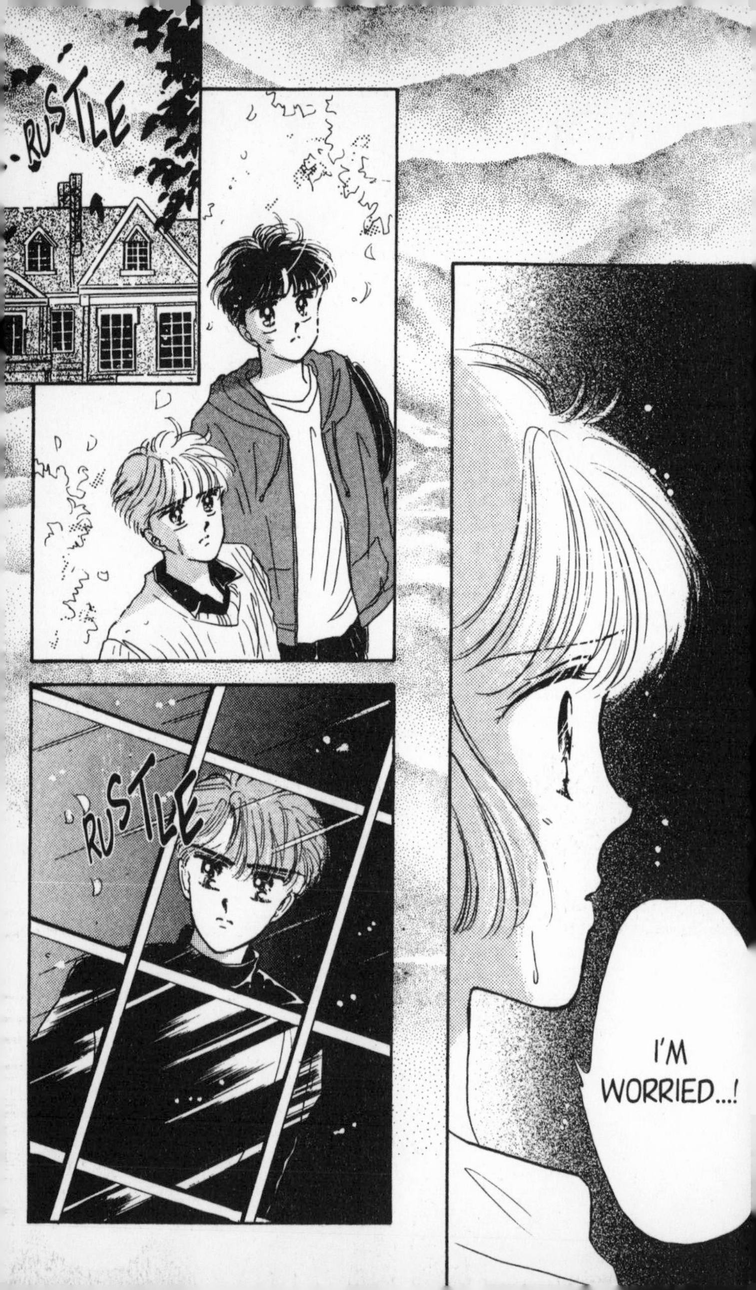
RUSTLE
RUSTLE
I'M WORRIED...!

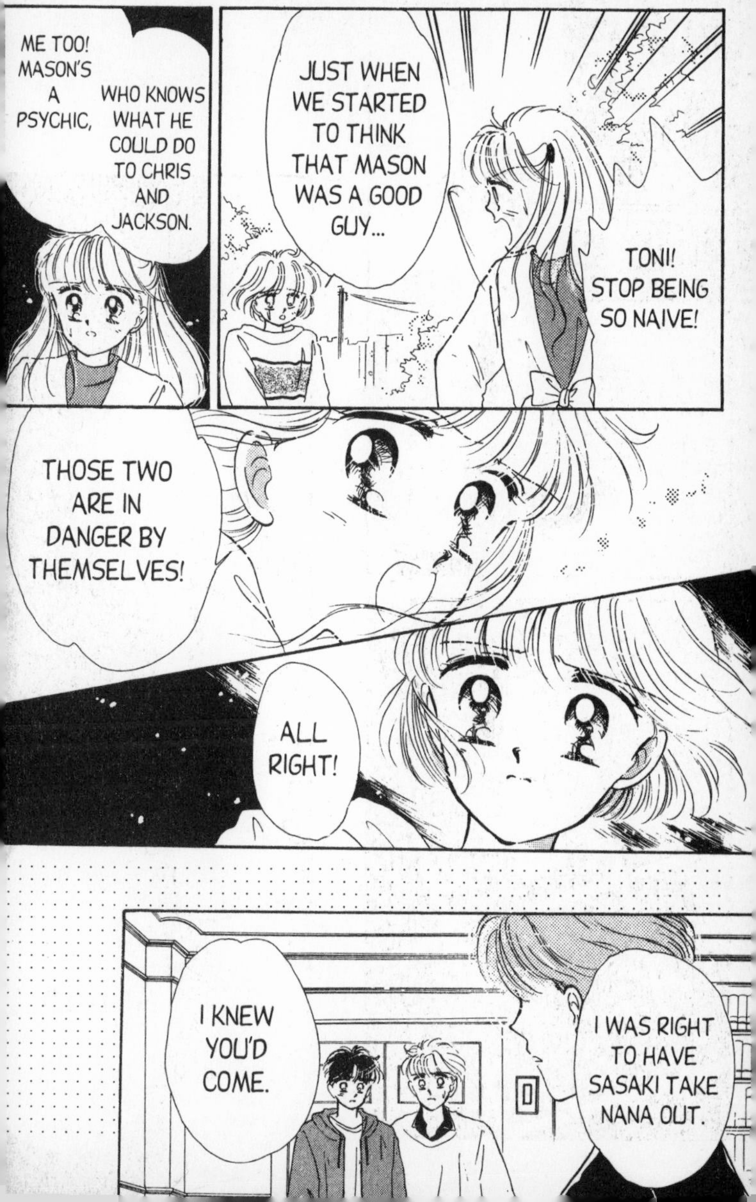
ME TOO! MASON'S A PSYCHIC,
WHO KNOWS WHAT HE COULD DO TO CHRIS AND JACKSON.
JUST WHEN WE STARTED TO THINK THAT MASON WAS A GOOD GUY...
TONI! STOP BEING SO NAIVE!
THOSE TWO ARE IN DANGER BY THEMSELVES!
ALL RIGHT!
I KNEW YOU'D COME.
I WAS RIGHT TO HAVE SASAKI TAKE NANA OUT.

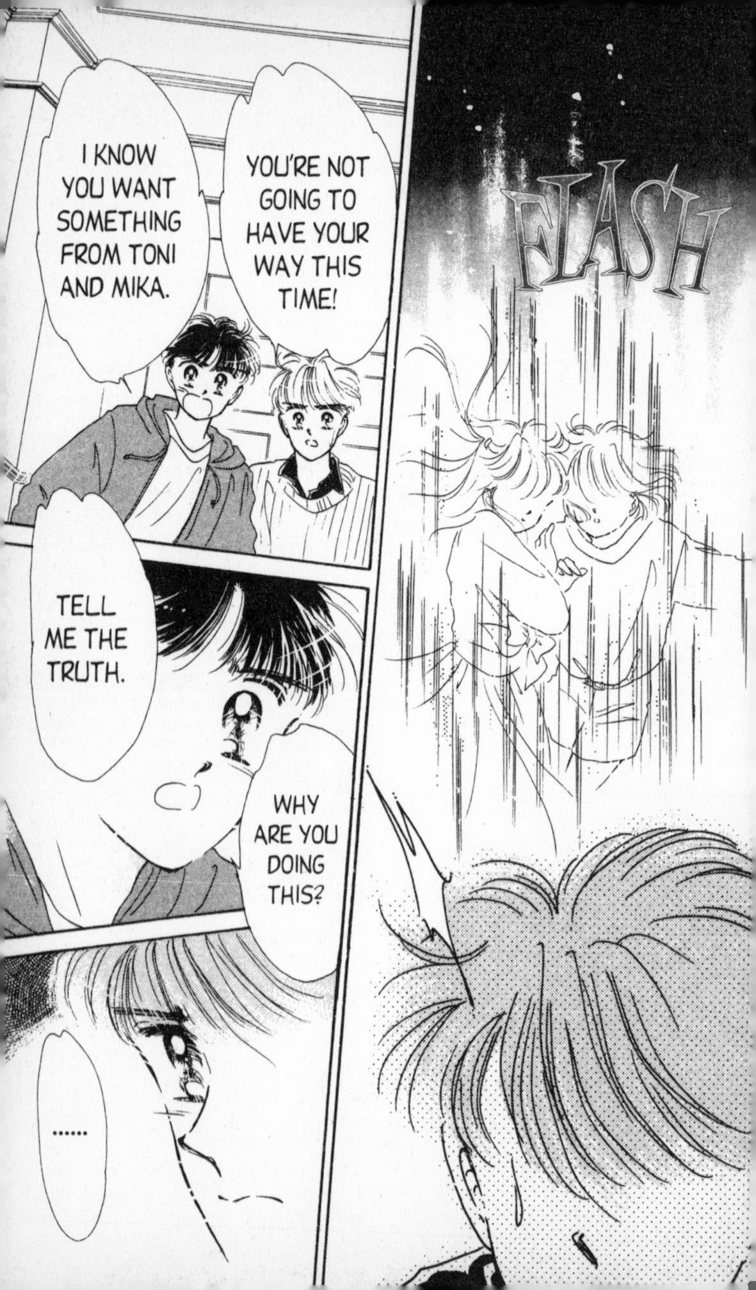
I KNOW YOU WANT SOMETHING FROM TONI AND MIKA.
YOU'RE NOT GOING TO HAVE YOUR WAY THIS TIME!
TELL ME THE TRUTH.
WHY ARE YOU DOING THIS?
......
FLASH

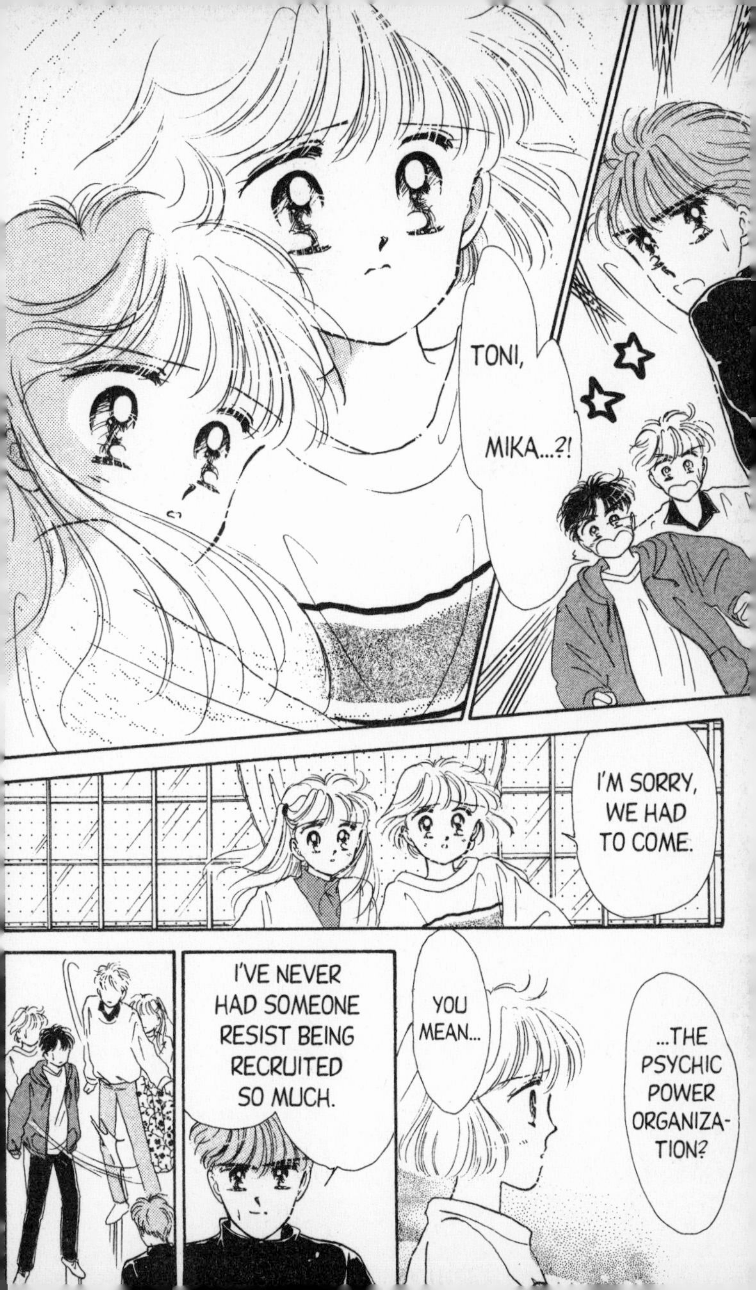
TONI, MIKA...?!
I'M SORRY, WE HAD TO COME.
I'VE NEVER HAD SOMEONE RESIST BEING RECRUITED SO MUCH.
YOU MEAN...
...THE PSYCHIC POWER ORGANIZA-TION?

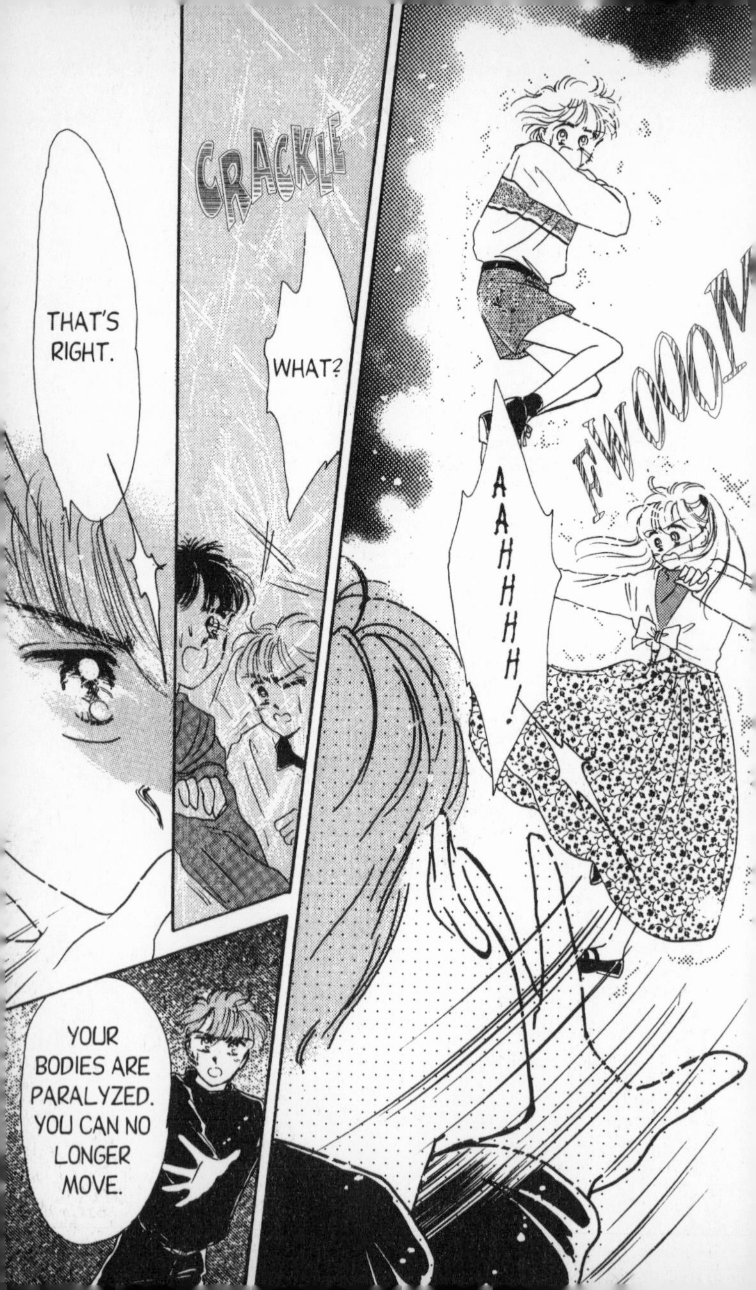
THAT'S RIGHT.
CRACKLE
WHAT?
YOUR BODIES ARE PARALYZED. YOU CAN NO LONGER MOVE.
FWOOOM
AAHHHHH!

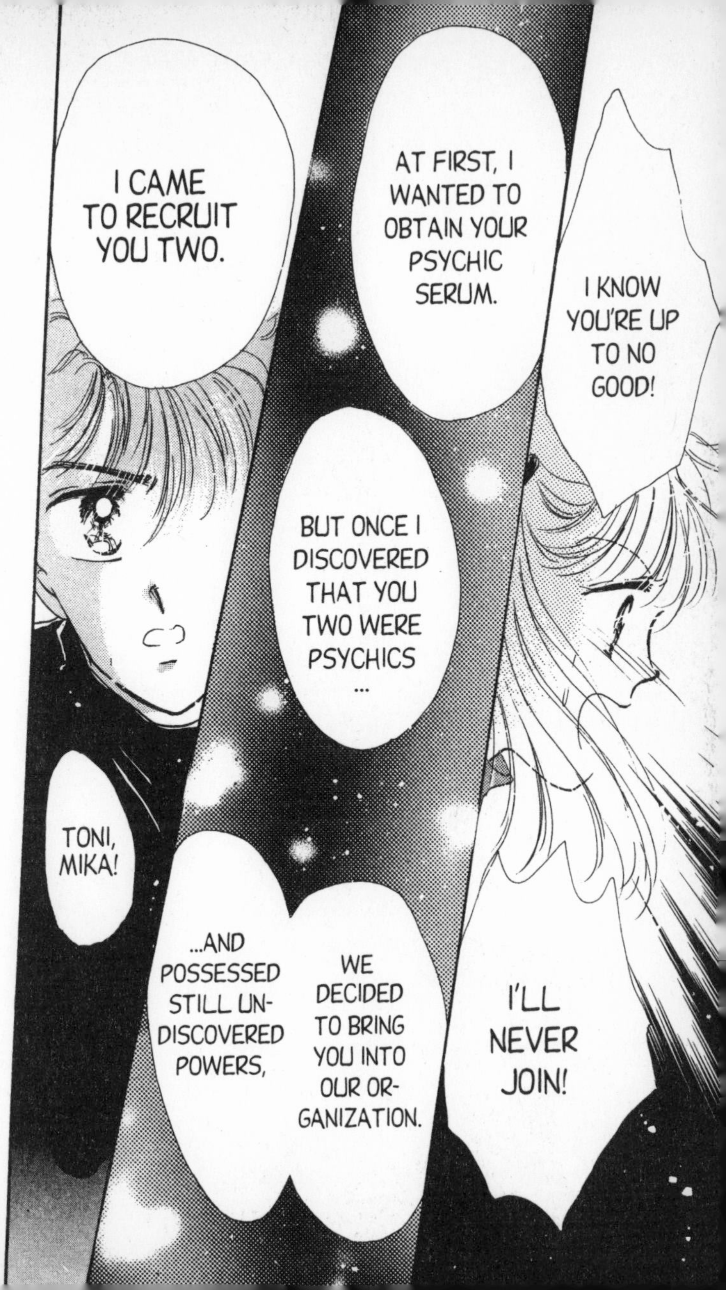
I CAME TO RECRUIT YOU TWO.
TONI, MIKA!
AT FIRST, I WANTED TO OBTAIN YOUR PSYCHIC SERUM.
BUT ONCE I DISCOVERED THAT YOU TWO WERE PSYCHICS ...
...AND POSSESSED STILL UN-DISCOVERED POWERS,
WE DECIDED TO BRING YOU INTO OUR OR-GANIZATION.
I KNOW YOU'RE UP TO NO GOOD!
I'LL NEVER JOIN!

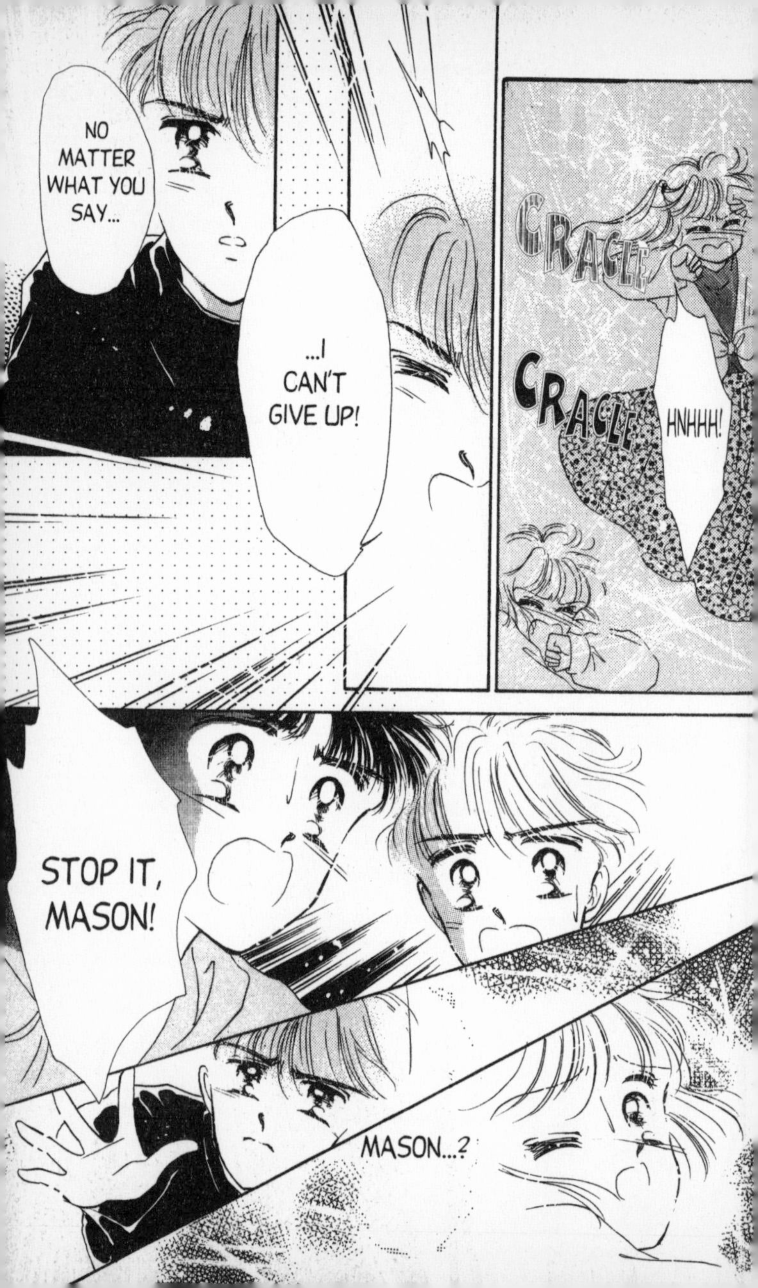
NO MATTER WHAT YOU SAY...
...I CAN'T GIVE UP!
CRACLE
CRACLE
HNHHH!
STOP IT, MASON!
MASON...?

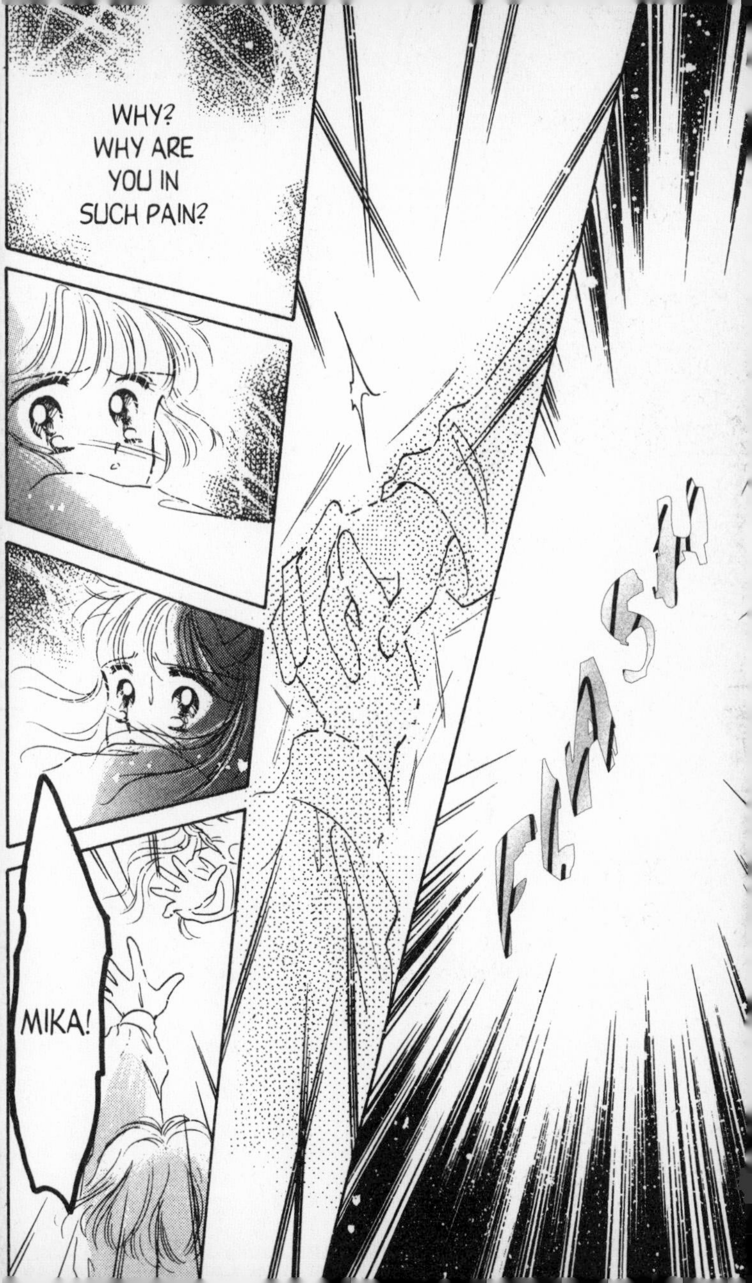
WHY?
WHY ARE YOU IN SUCH PAIN?
MIKA!
FLASH

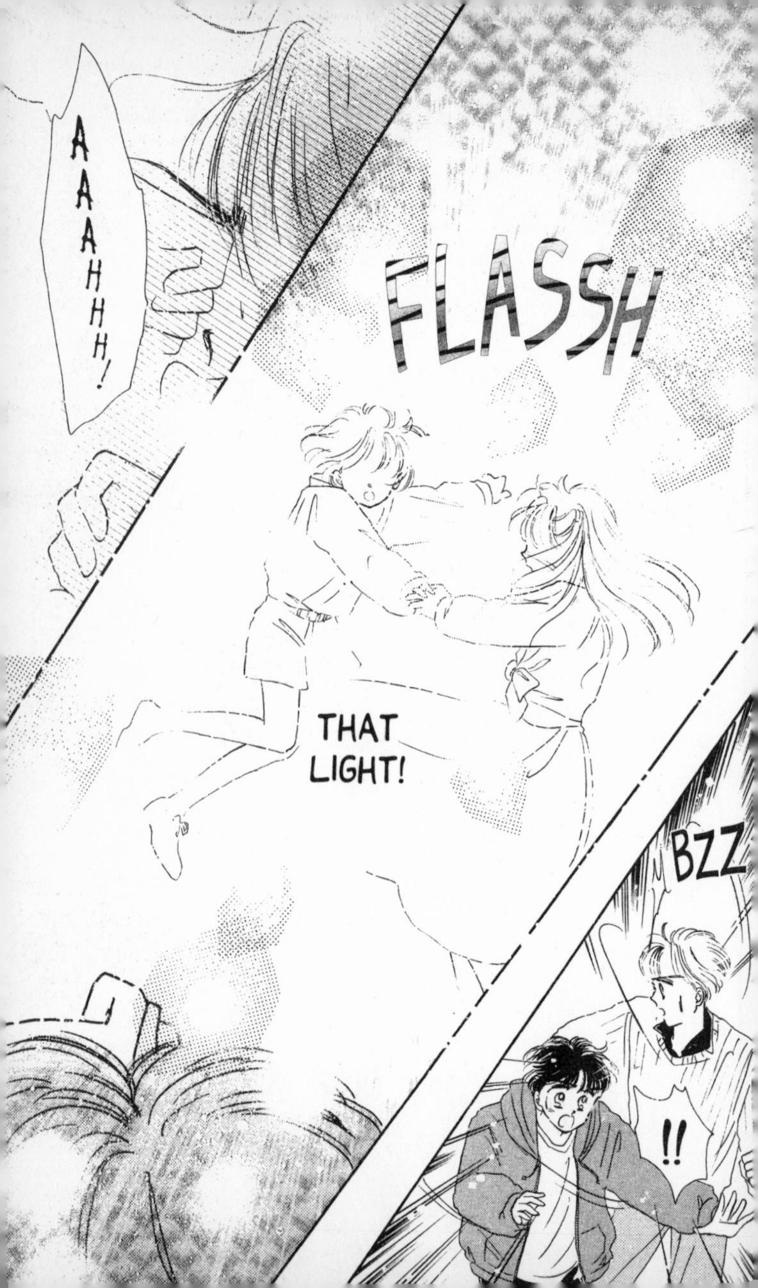
AAAAHHHH!
FLASSH
THAT LIGHT!
BZZ
!!

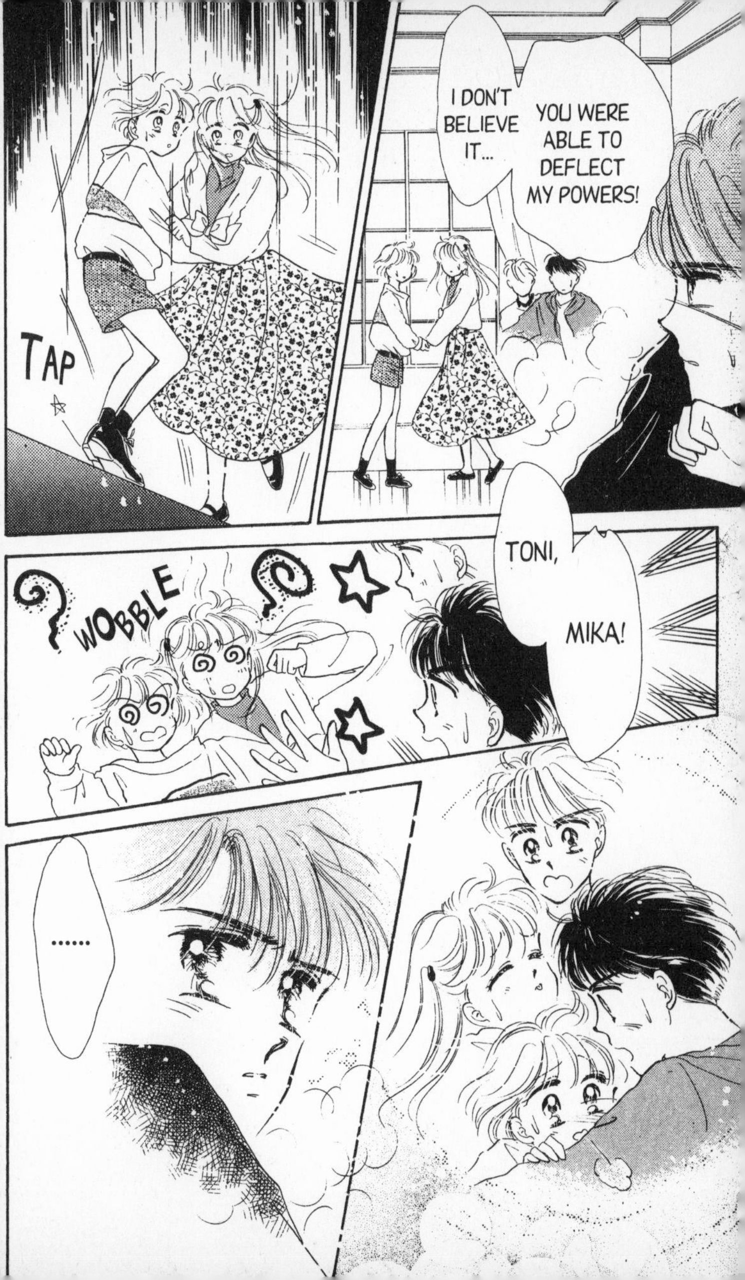
TAP
I DON'T BELIEVE IT...
YOU WERE ABLE TO DEFLECT MY POWERS!
WOBBLE
TONI,
MIKA!
......

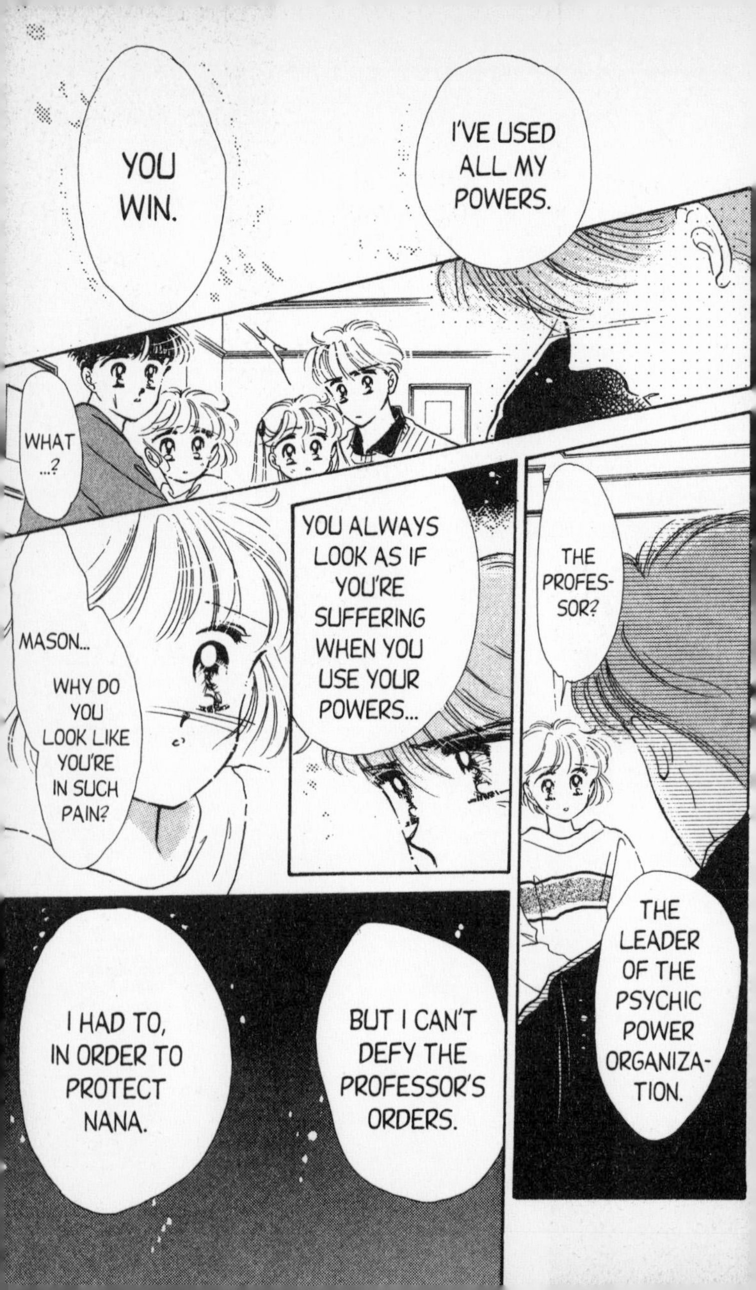
YOU WIN.
I'VE USED ALL MY POWERS.
WHAT ...?
MASON... WHY DO YOU LOOK LIKE YOU'RE IN SUCH PAIN?
YOU ALWAYS LOOK AS IF YOU'RE SUFFERING WHEN YOU USE YOUR POWERS...
I HAD TO, IN ORDER TO PROTECT NANA.
BUT I CAN'T DEFY THE PROFESSOR'S ORDERS.
THE PROFES-SOR?
THE LEADER OF THE PSYCHIC POWER ORGANIZA-TION.

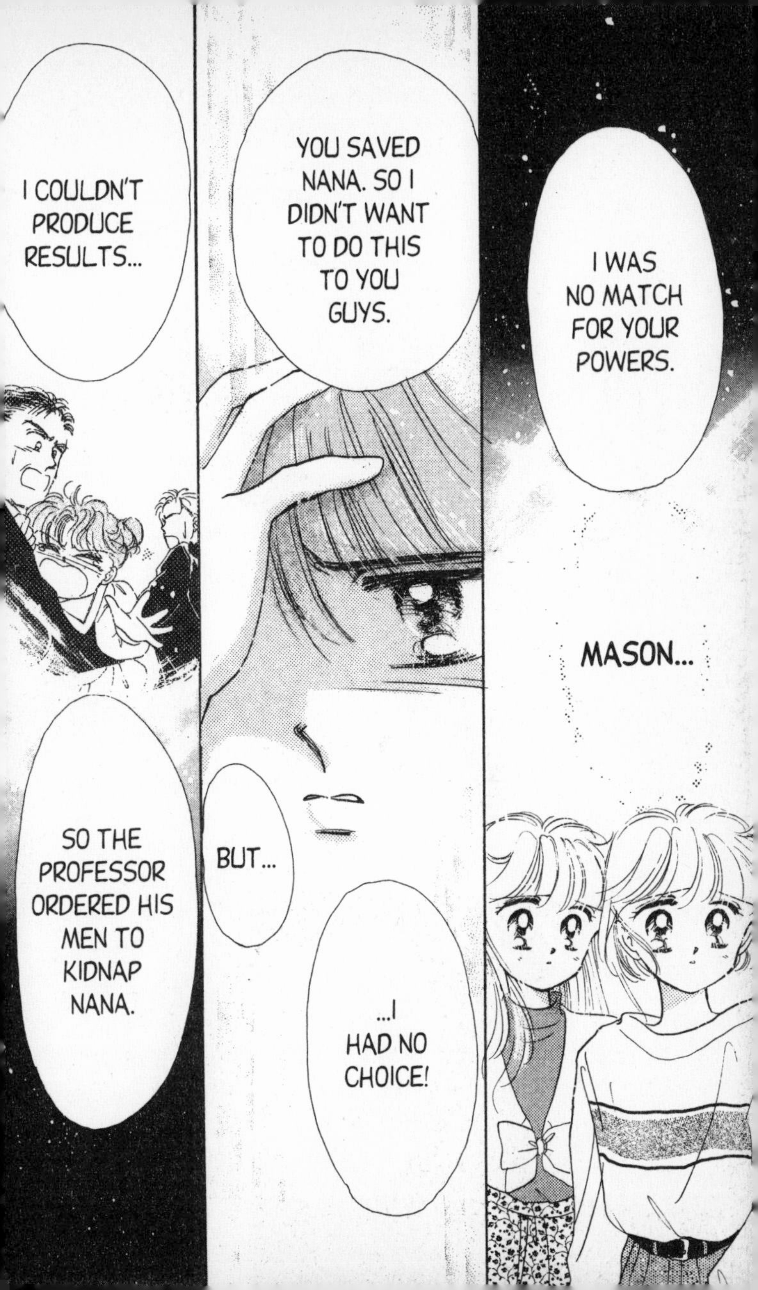
I WAS NO MATCH FOR YOUR POWERS.
MASON...
YOU SAVED NANA. SO I DIDN'T WANT TO DO THIS TO YOU GUYS.
BUT...
...I HAD NO CHOICE!
I COULDN'T PRODUCE RESULTS...
SO THE PROFESSOR ORDERED HIS MEN TO KIDNAP NANA.

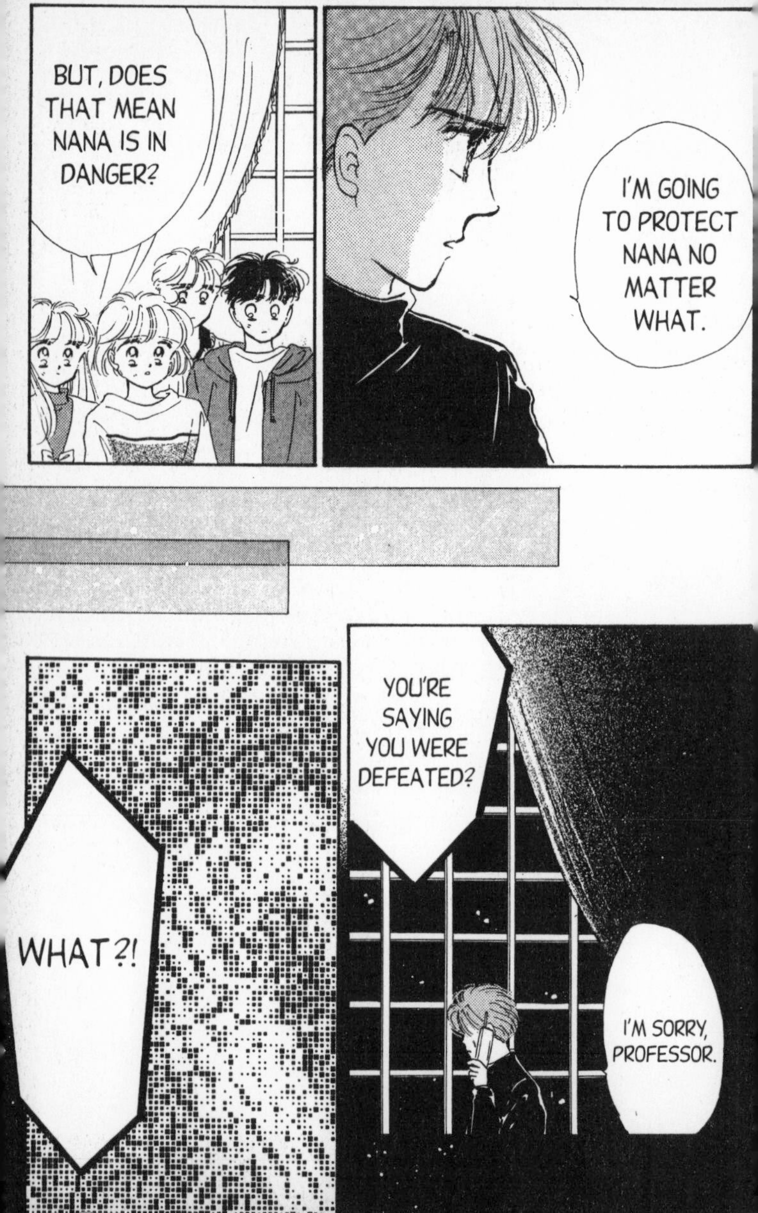
BUT, DOES THAT MEAN NANA IS IN DANGER?
I'M GOING TO PROTECT NANA NO MATTER WHAT.
WHAT?!
YOU'RE SAYING YOU WERE DEFEATED?
I'M SORRY, PROFESSOR.

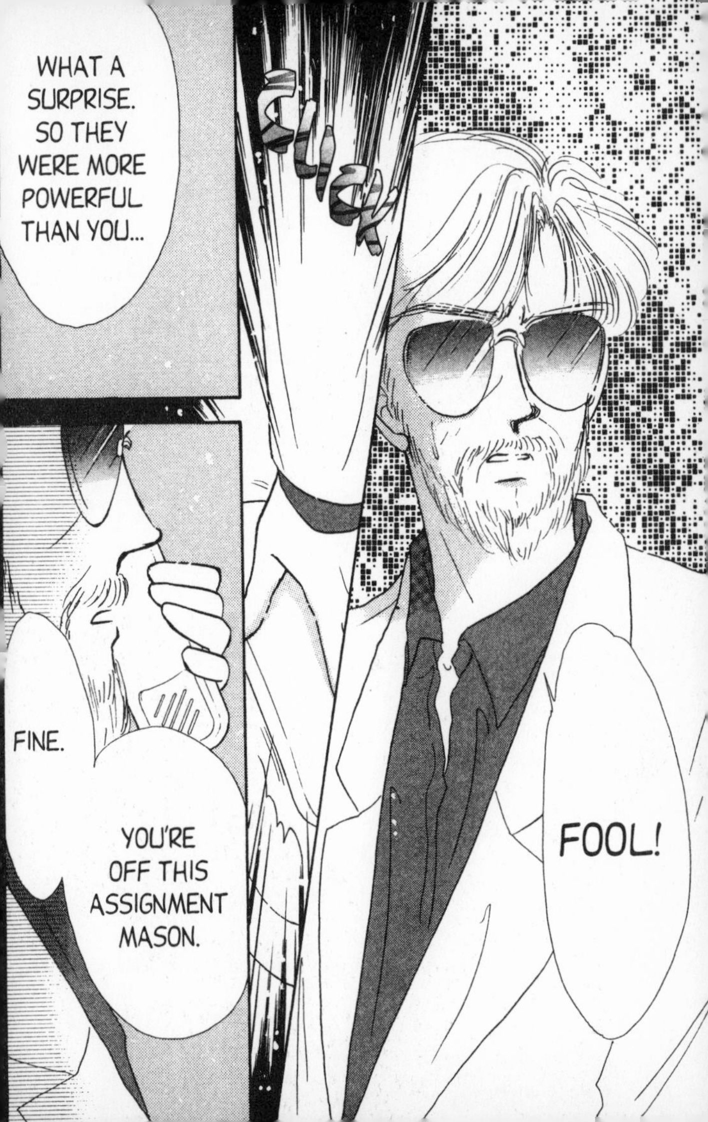
WHAT A SURPRISE. SO THEY WERE MORE POWERFUL THAN YOU...
FINE.
YOU'RE OFF THIS ASSIGNMENT MASON.
CLICK
FOOL!

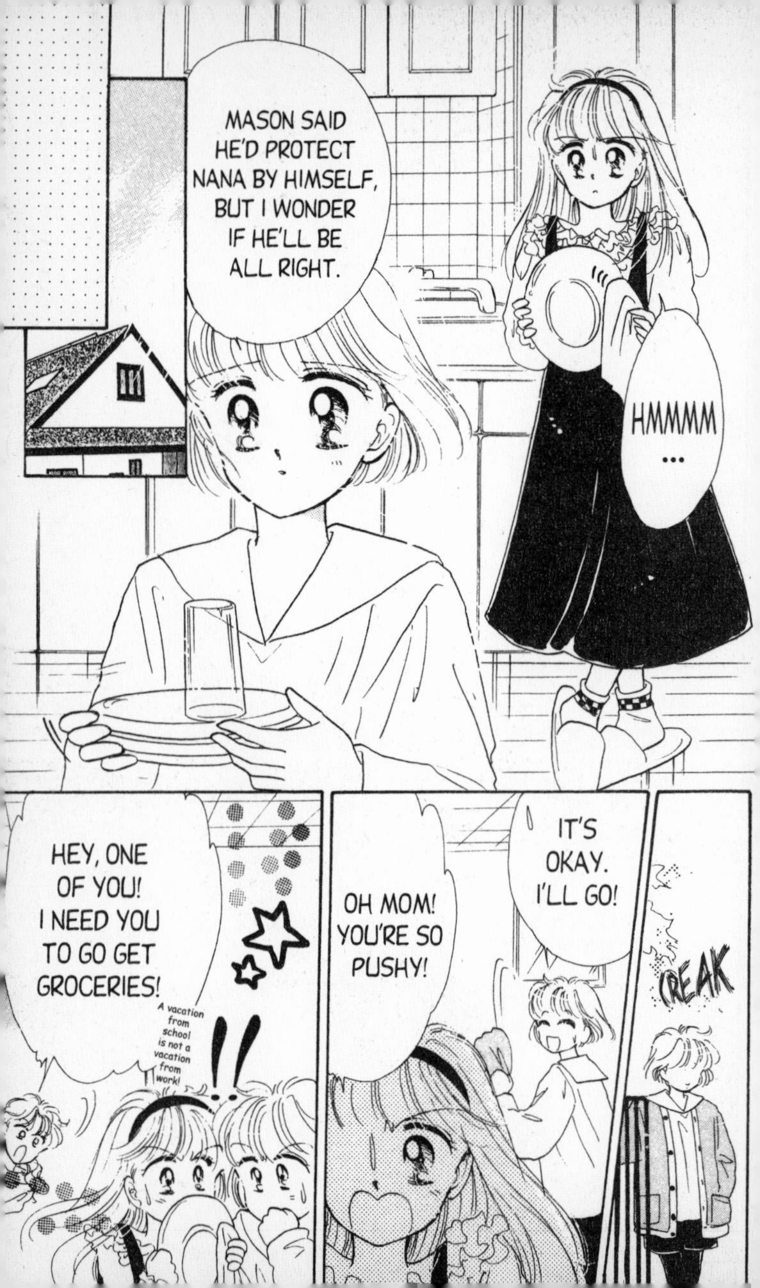
MASON SAID HE'D PROTECT NANA BY HIMSELF, BUT I WONDER IF HE'LL BE ALL RIGHT.
HMMMM ...
HEY, ONE OF YOU! I NEED YOU TO GO GET GROCERIES!
A vacation from school is not a vacation from work!
!!
OH MOM! YOU'RE SO PUSHY!
IT'S OKAY. I'LL GO!
CREAK

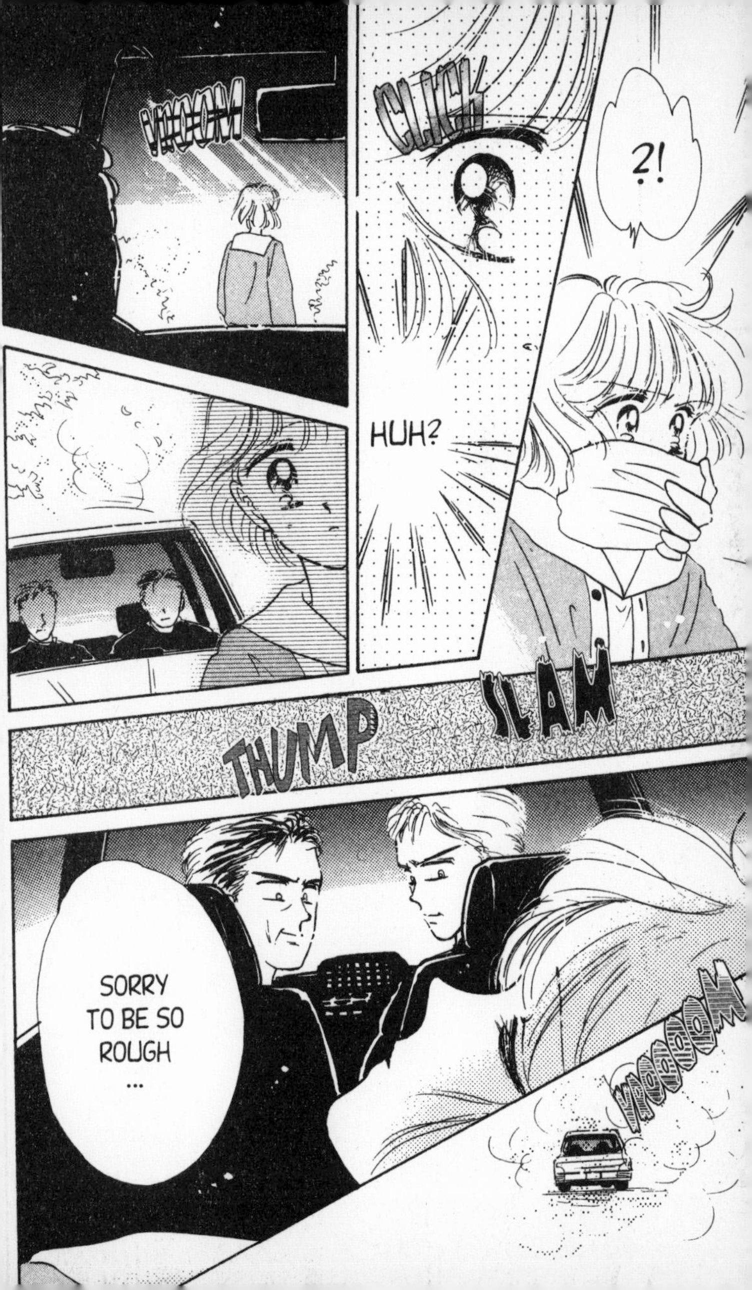
VROOM
CLICK
?!
HUH?
THUMP
SLAM
SORRY TO BE SO ROUGH ...
VROOOOM

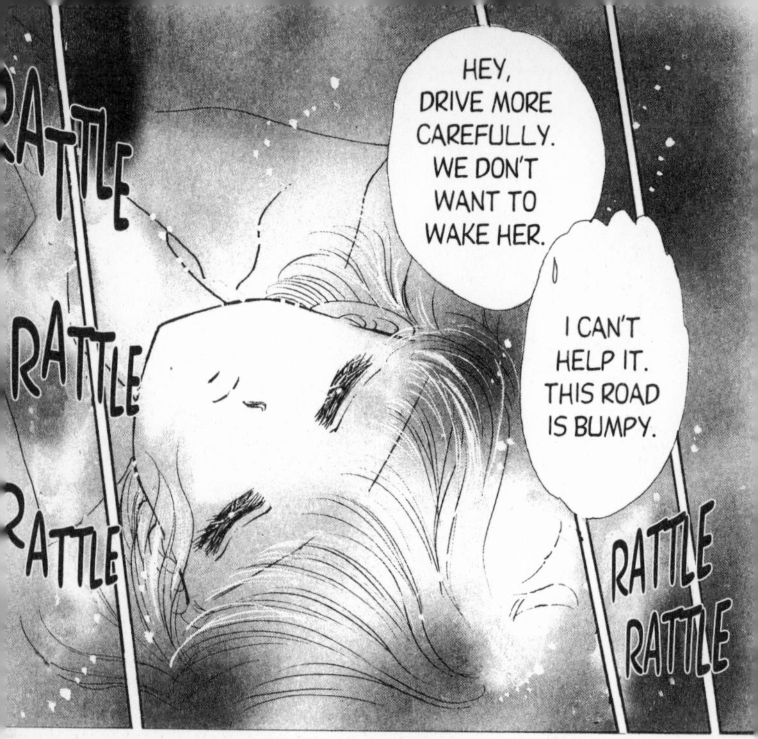
RATTLE
HEY, DRIVE MORE CAREFULLY. WE DON'T WANT TO WAKE HER.
RATTLE
I CAN'T HELP IT. THIS ROAD IS BUMPY.
RATTLE
RATTLE RATTLE

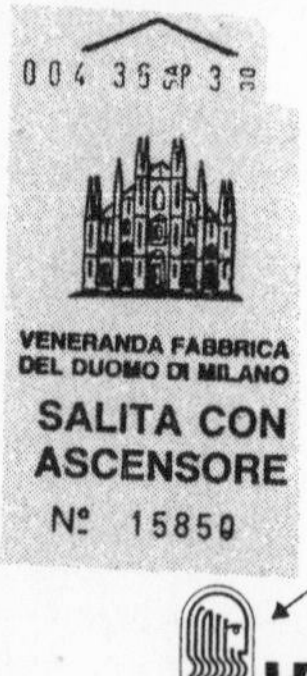
004 35 SP 3 30
VENERANDA FABBRICA DEL DUOMO DI MILANO
SALITA CON ASCENSORE
Nº 15850

◀A TICKET FROM WHEN I WENT TO THE ROOFTOP OF THE DUOMO.

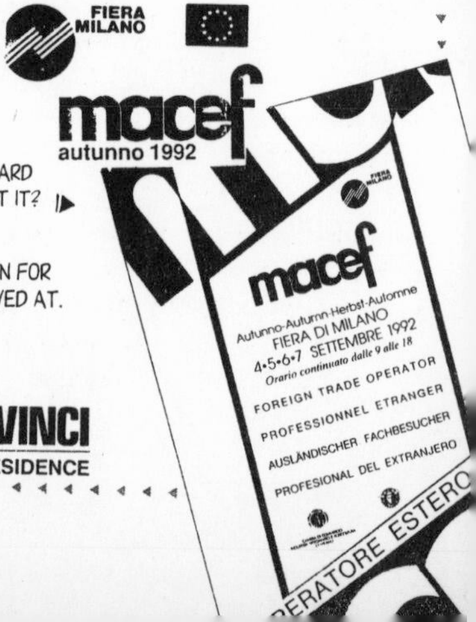
FIERA MILANO
macef
autunno 1992
macef
Autunno-Autumn-Herbst-Automne
FIERA DI MILANO
4•5•6•7 SETTEMBRE 1992
Orario continuato dalle 9 alle 18
FOREIGN TRADE OPERATOR
PROFESSIONNEL ETRANGER
AUSLÄNDISCHER FACHBESUCHER
PROFESIONAL DEL EXTRANJERO
OPERATORE ESTERO

A FOREIGNER ENTRY CARD FOR MACEF. CUTE, ISN'T IT? ▶

▼ I LIKE THE DESIGN FOR THE HOTEL I STAYED AT.

LEONARDO DA VINCI
HOTEL CENTRO CONGRESSI RESIDENCE

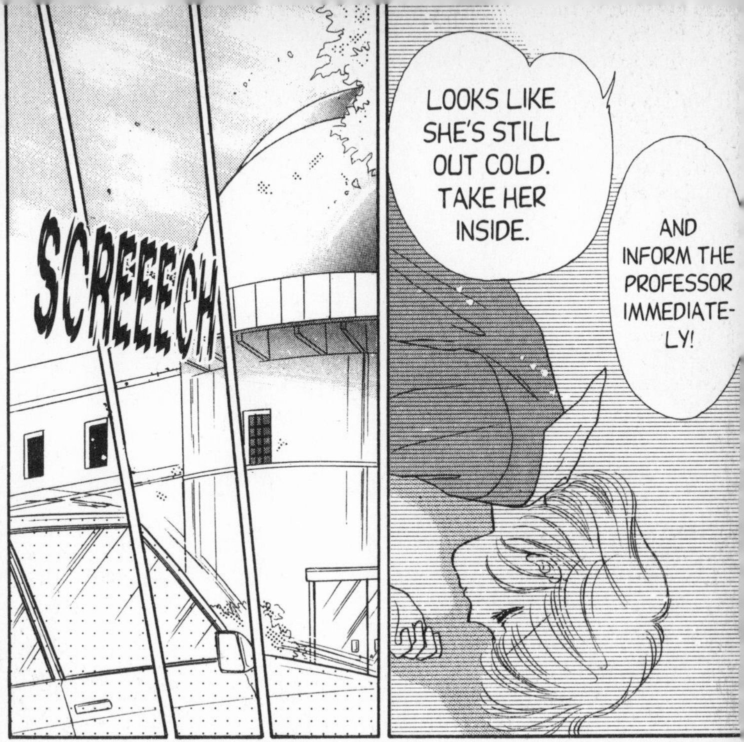
SCREEECH
LOOKS LIKE SHE'S STILL OUT COLD. TAKE HER INSIDE.
AND INFORM THE PROFESSOR IMMEDIATE-LY!

BONUS

Milan Part 1: Via London, I finally arrived in Milan at 9:00PM. Time difference, 8 hours. (Although there is no time difference for a manga artist!) The following morning my day began! First, I visited the international open market at Macef. I had fun looking at all the items for sale, but the place was so huge I was exhausted. There were some strange novelty items, like the Piccolo Bonsai (mini-bonsai). The next day was a tour of the city. I went to the Duomo cathedral, Galilea Emmanuel II arcade, Santa Maria Cathedral (where Da Vinci's Last Supper is displayed), and many other places. The view from the rooftop of the Duomo cathedral was spectacular! You either climb the stairs or take the elevator- you climbers out there, you've got guts!

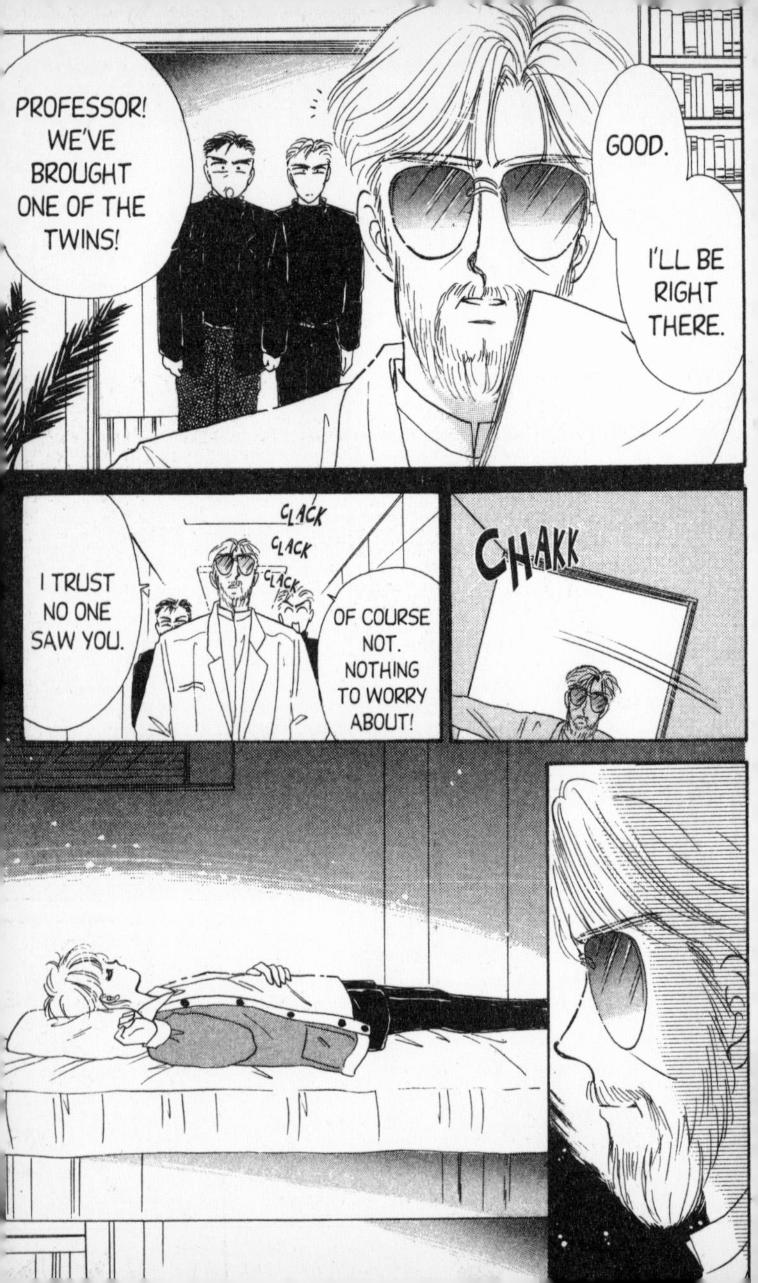
PROFESSOR! WE'VE BROUGHT ONE OF THE TWINS!
GOOD.
I'LL BE RIGHT THERE.
I TRUST NO ONE SAW YOU.
CLACK
CLACK
CLACK
OF COURSE NOT. NOTHING TO WORRY ABOUT!
CHAKK

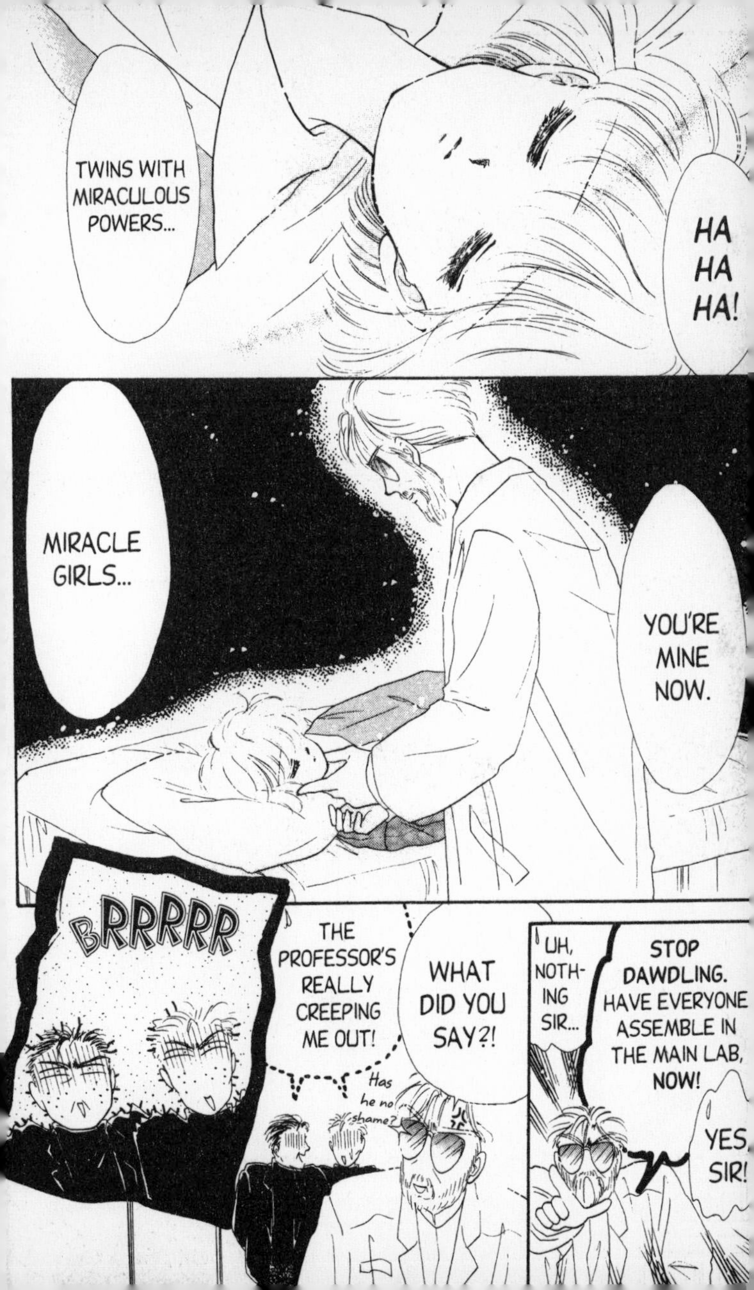
TWINS WITH MIRACULOUS POWERS...
HA HA HA!
MIRACLE GIRLS...
YOU'RE MINE NOW.
BRRRRR
THE PROFESSOR'S REALLY CREEPING ME OUT!
WHAT DID YOU SAY?!
Has he no shame?
UH, NOTH-ING SIR...
STOP DAWDLING. HAVE EVERYONE ASSEMBLE IN THE MAIN LAB, NOW!
YES SIR!

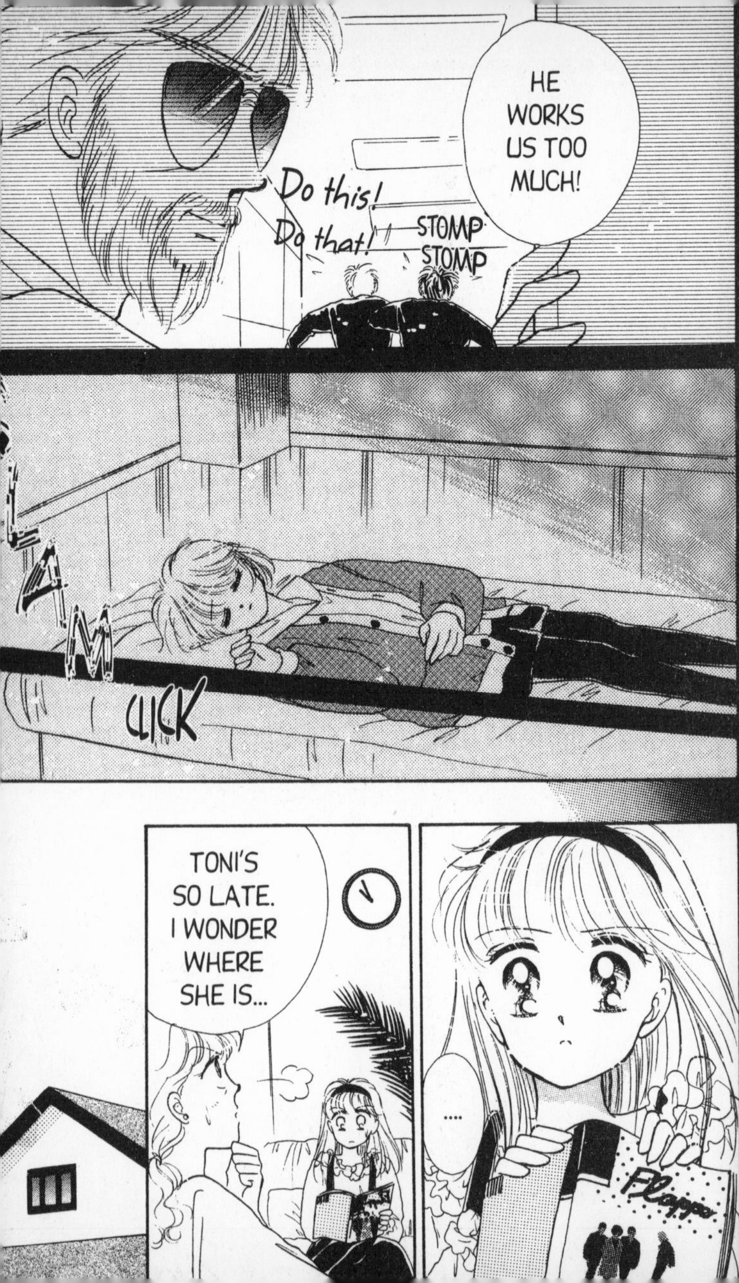
Do this!
Do that!
STOMP STOMP
HE WORKS US TOO MUCH!
CLICK
TONI'S SO LATE. I WONDER WHERE SHE IS...
....
Flappo

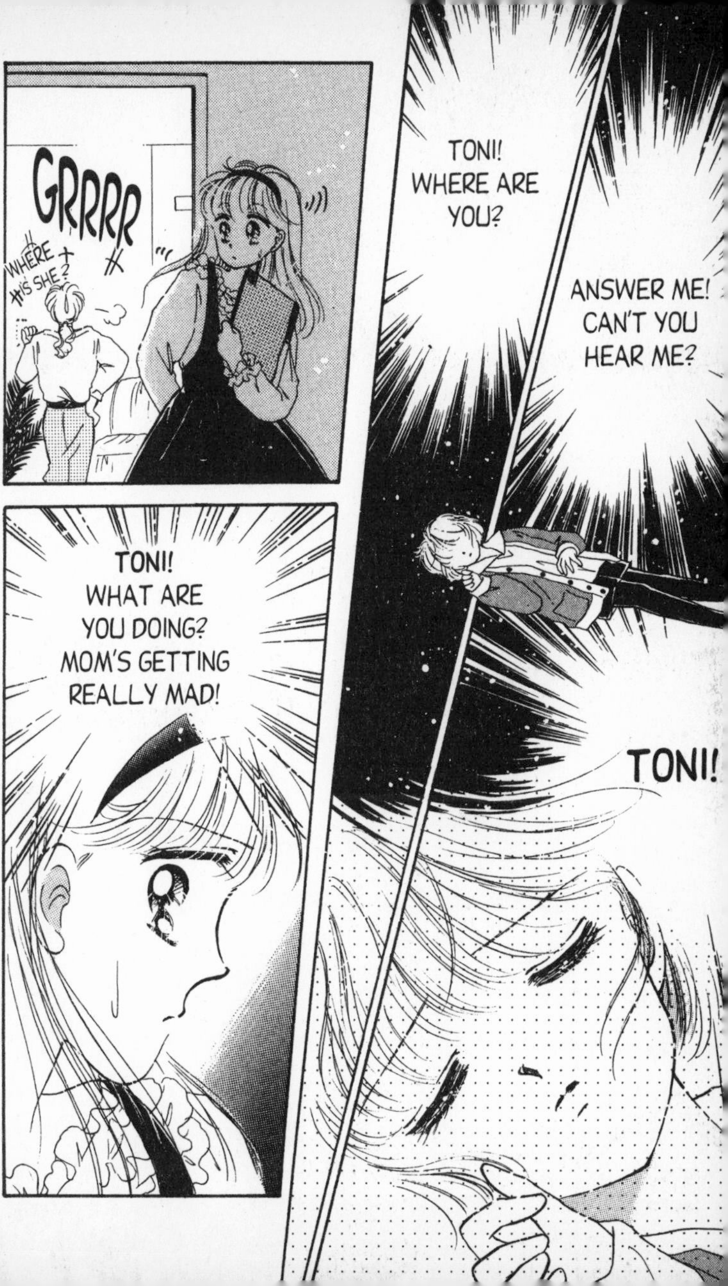
GRRRR
WHERE IS SHE?
TONI! WHAT ARE YOU DOING? MOM'S GETTING REALLY MAD!
TONI! WHERE ARE YOU?
ANSWER ME! CAN'T YOU HEAR ME?
TONI!

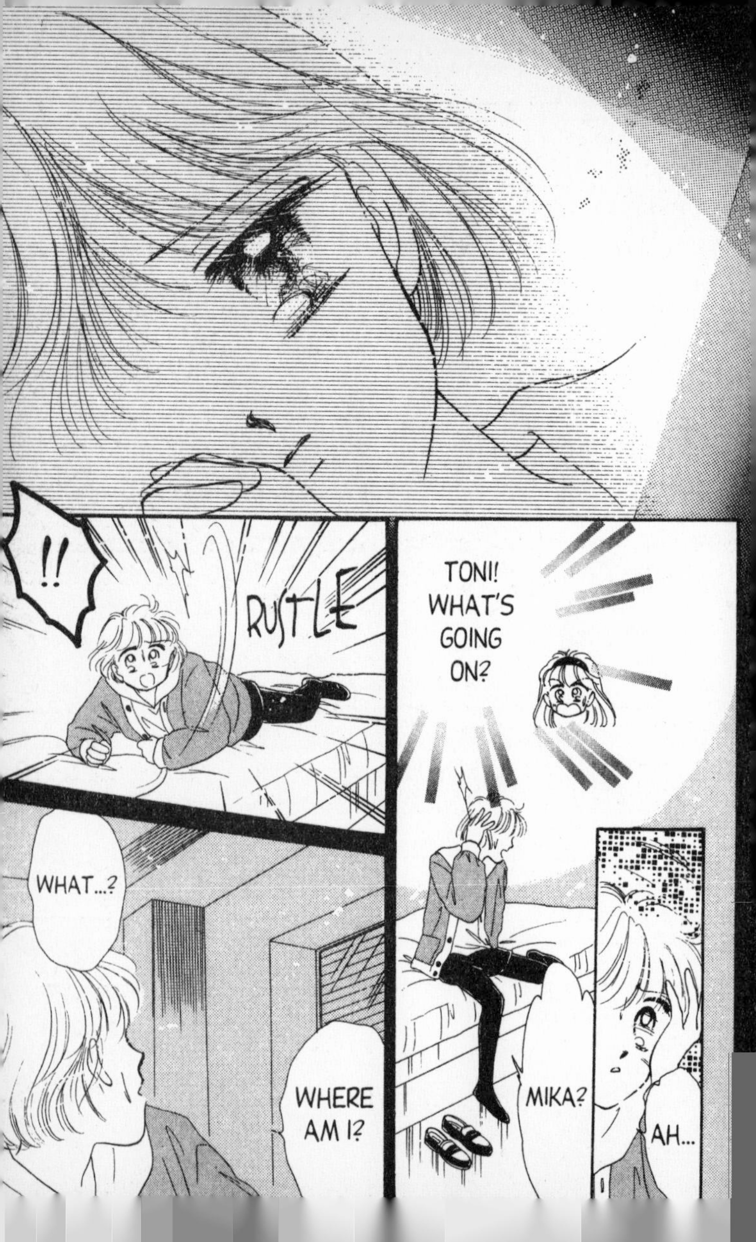
!!
RUSTLE
WHAT...?
WHERE AM I?
TONI! WHAT'S GOING ON?
MIKA?
AH...

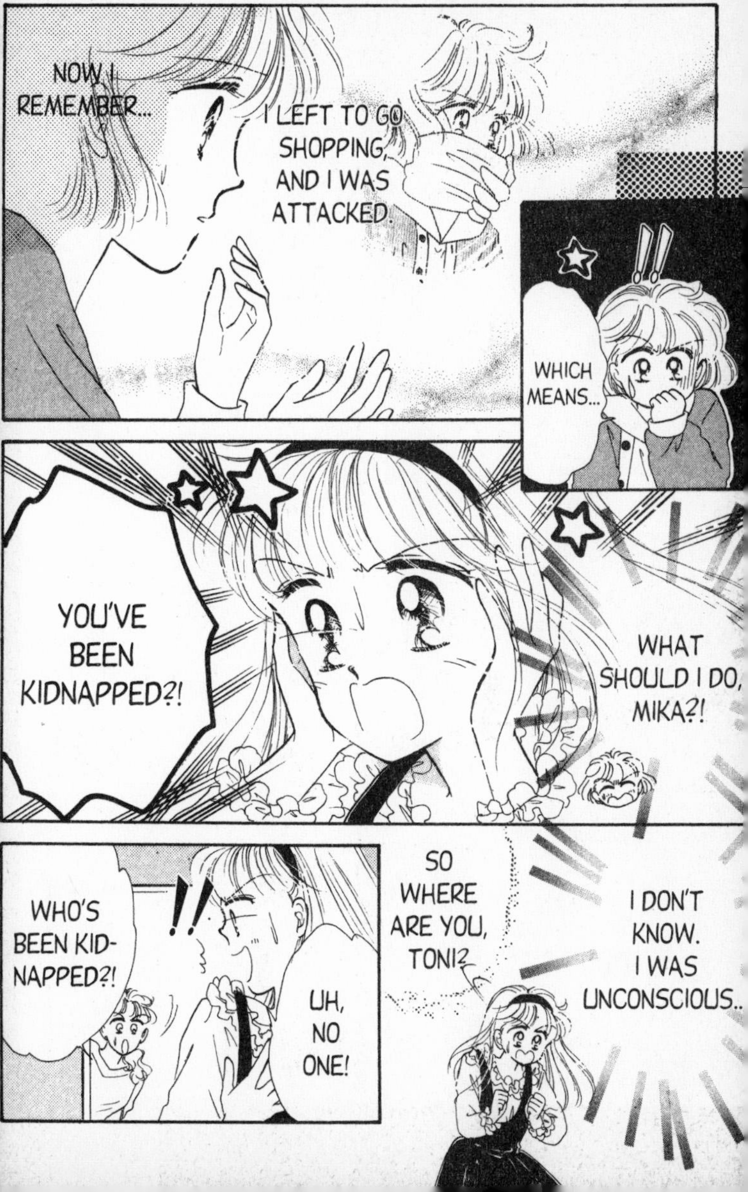
NOW I REMEMBER...
I LEFT TO GO SHOPPING, AND I WAS ATTACKED.
WHICH MEANS...
YOU'VE BEEN KIDNAPPED?!
WHAT SHOULD I DO, MIKA?!
WHO'S BEEN KID-NAPPED?!
UH, NO ONE!
SO WHERE ARE YOU, TONI?
I DON'T KNOW. I WAS UNCONSCIOUS...

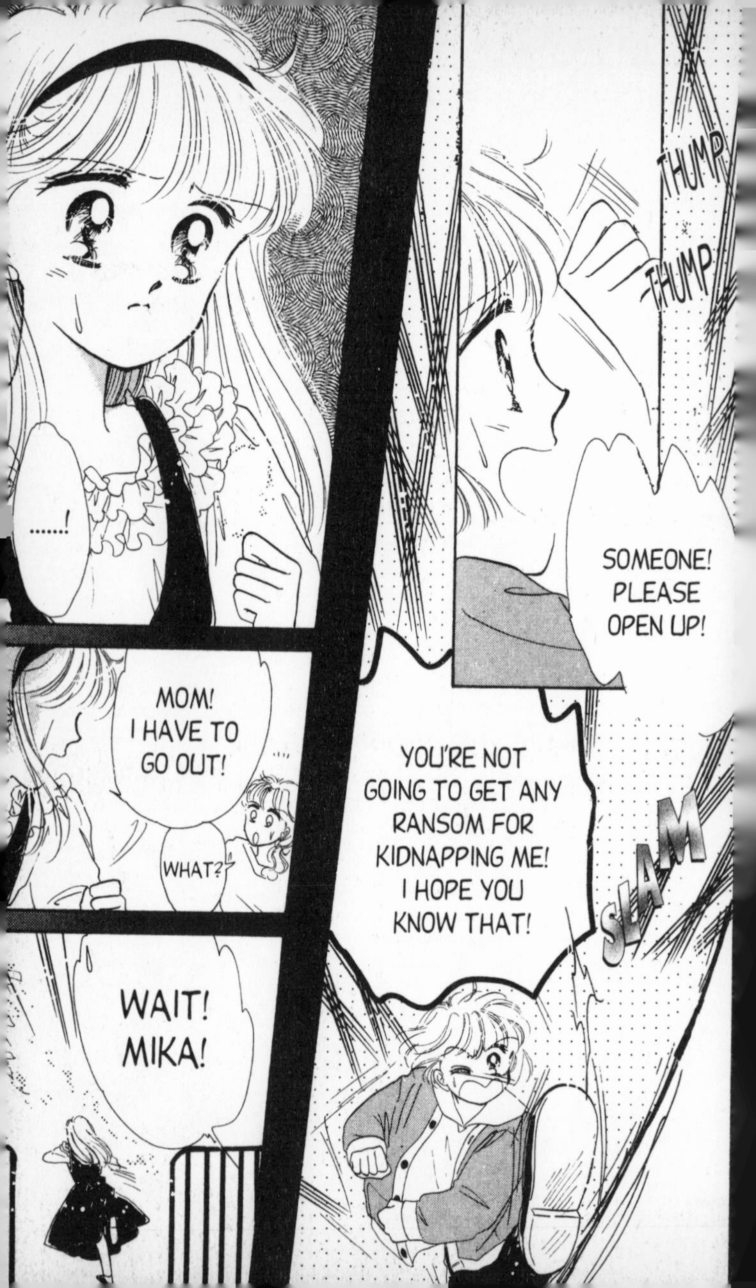
.......!
MOM! I HAVE TO GO OUT!
WHAT?
WAIT! MIKA!
THUMP
THUMP
SOMEONE! PLEASE OPEN UP!
YOU'RE NOT GOING TO GET ANY RANSOM FOR KIDNAPPING ME! I HOPE YOU KNOW THAT!
SLAM

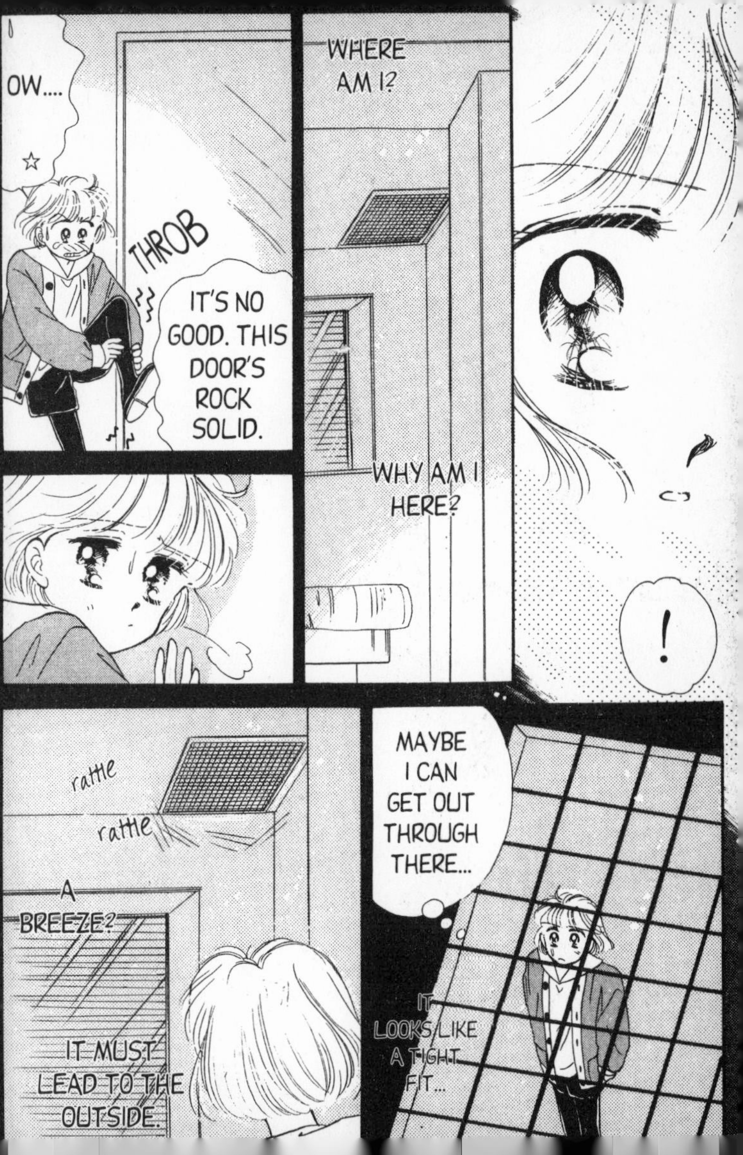
OW....
THROB
IT'S NO GOOD. THIS DOOR'S ROCK SOLID.
WHERE AM I?
WHY AM I HERE?
!
rattle
rattle
A BREEZE?
IT MUST LEAD TO THE OUTSIDE.
MAYBE I CAN GET OUT THROUGH THERE...
IT LOOKS LIKE A TIGHT FIT...

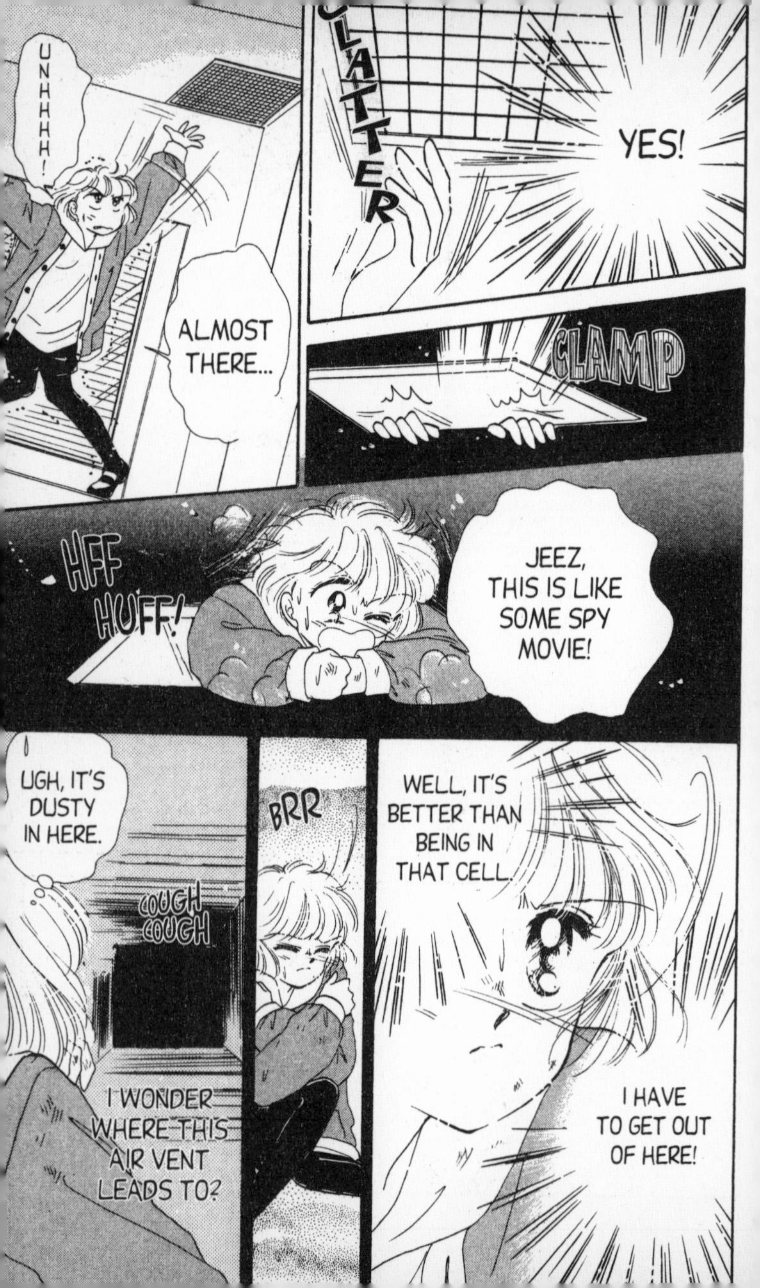
UNHHHH!
ALMOST THERE...
CLATTER
YES!
CLAMP
HFF HUFF!
JEEZ, THIS IS LIKE SOME SPY MOVIE!
UGH, IT'S DUSTY IN HERE.
COUGH COUGH
I WONDER WHERE THIS AIR VENT LEADS TO?
BRR
WELL, IT'S BETTER THAN BEING IN THAT CELL.
I HAVE TO GET OUT OF HERE!

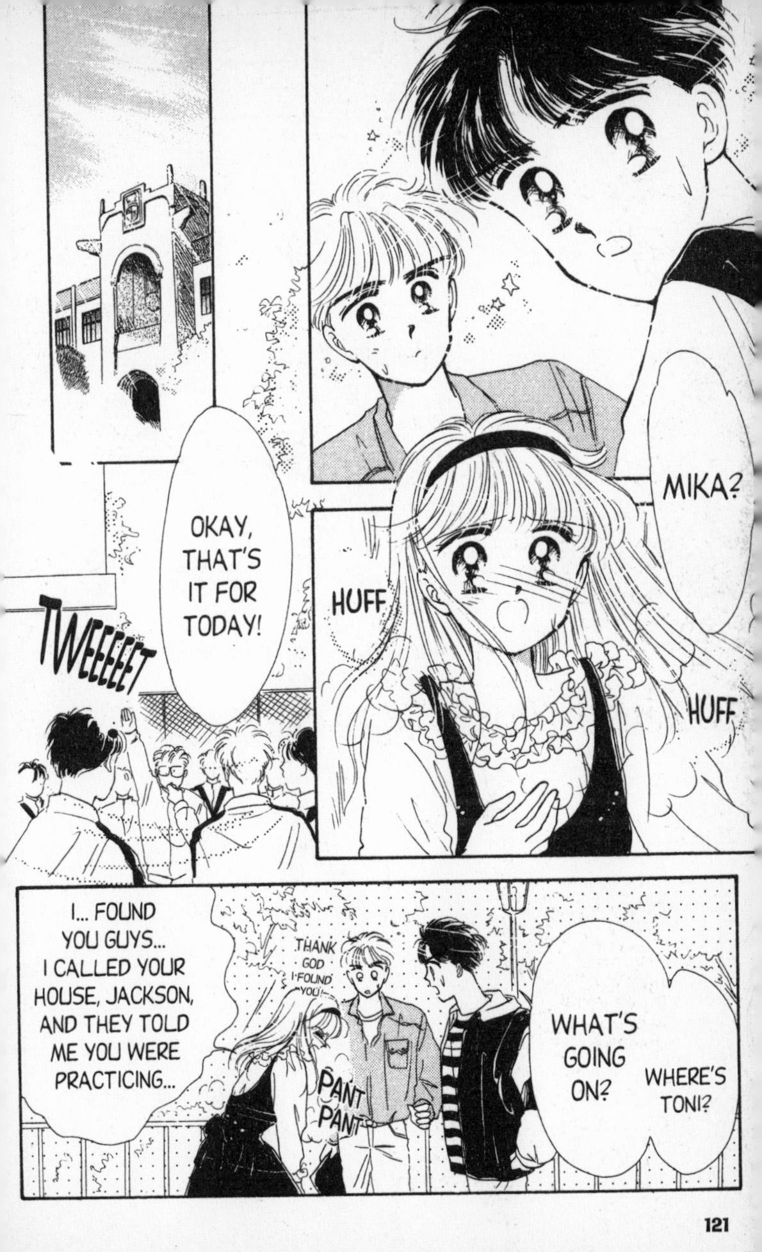
OKAY, THAT'S IT FOR TODAY!
TWEEEEEET
MIKA?
HUFF
HUFF
I... FOUND YOU GUYS... I CALLED YOUR HOUSE, JACKSON, AND THEY TOLD ME YOU WERE PRACTICING...
THANK GOD I FOUND YOU!
PANT PANT
WHAT'S GOING ON?
WHERE'S TONI?

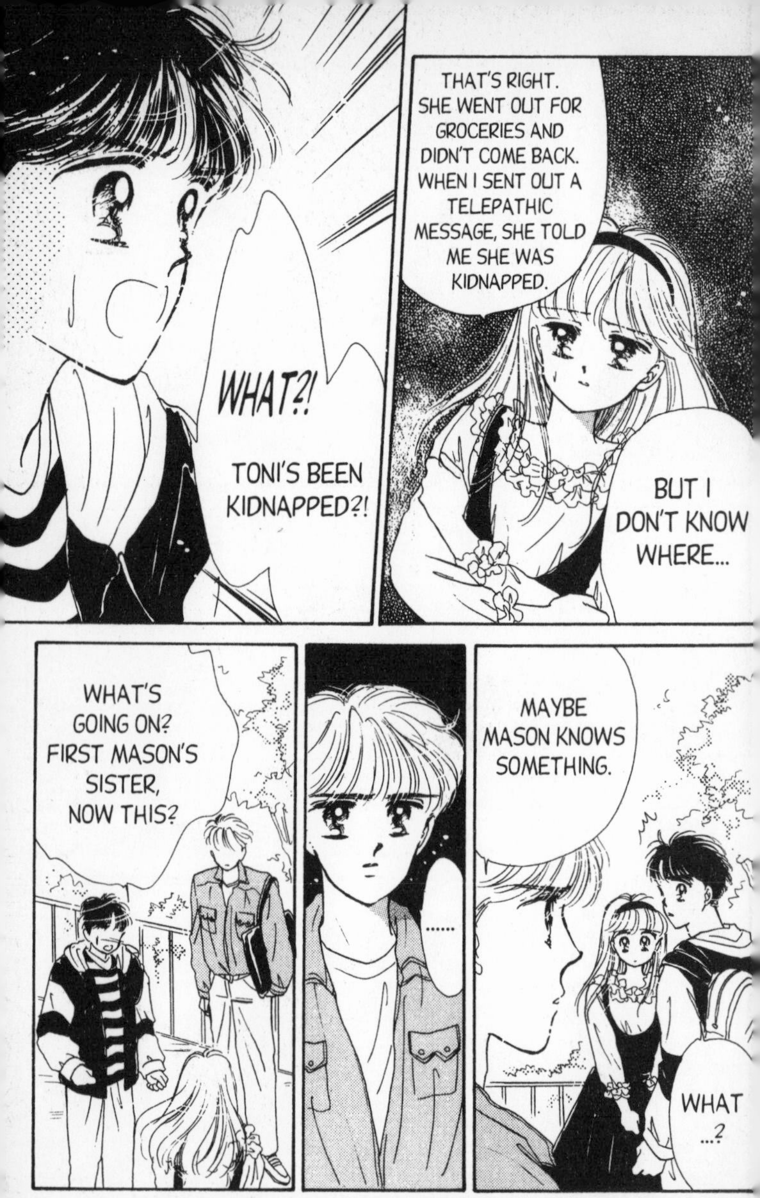
WHAT?!
TONI'S BEEN KIDNAPPED?!
THAT'S RIGHT. SHE WENT OUT FOR GROCERIES AND DIDN'T COME BACK. WHEN I SENT OUT A TELEPATHIC MESSAGE, SHE TOLD ME SHE WAS KIDNAPPED.
BUT I DON'T KNOW WHERE...
WHAT'S GOING ON? FIRST MASON'S SISTER, NOW THIS?
......
MAYBE MASON KNOWS SOMETHING.
WHAT ...?

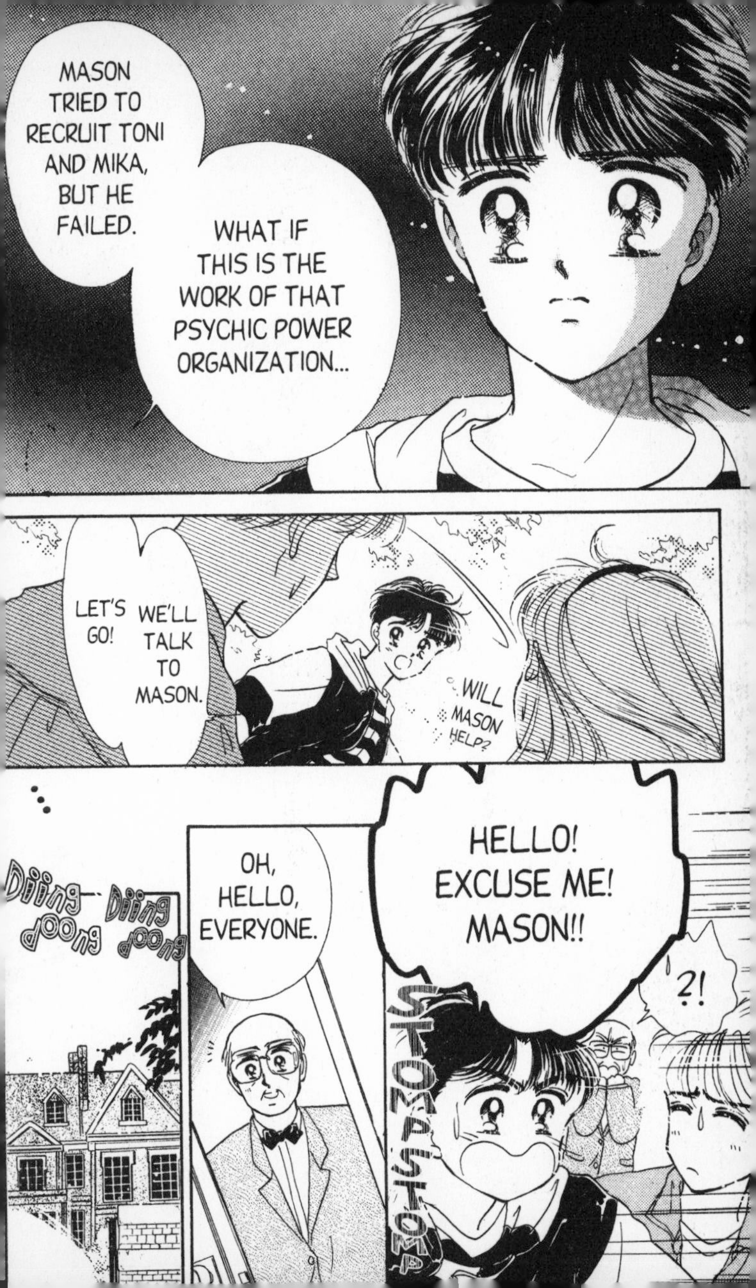
MASON TRIED TO RECRUIT TONI AND MIKA, BUT HE FAILED.
WHAT IF THIS IS THE WORK OF THAT PSYCHIC POWER ORGANIZATION...
LET'S GO!
WE'LL TALK TO MASON.
WILL MASON HELP?
...
Diiing-- doong Diiing doong
OH, HELLO, EVERYONE.
HELLO! EXCUSE ME! MASON!!
STOMP STOMP
?!

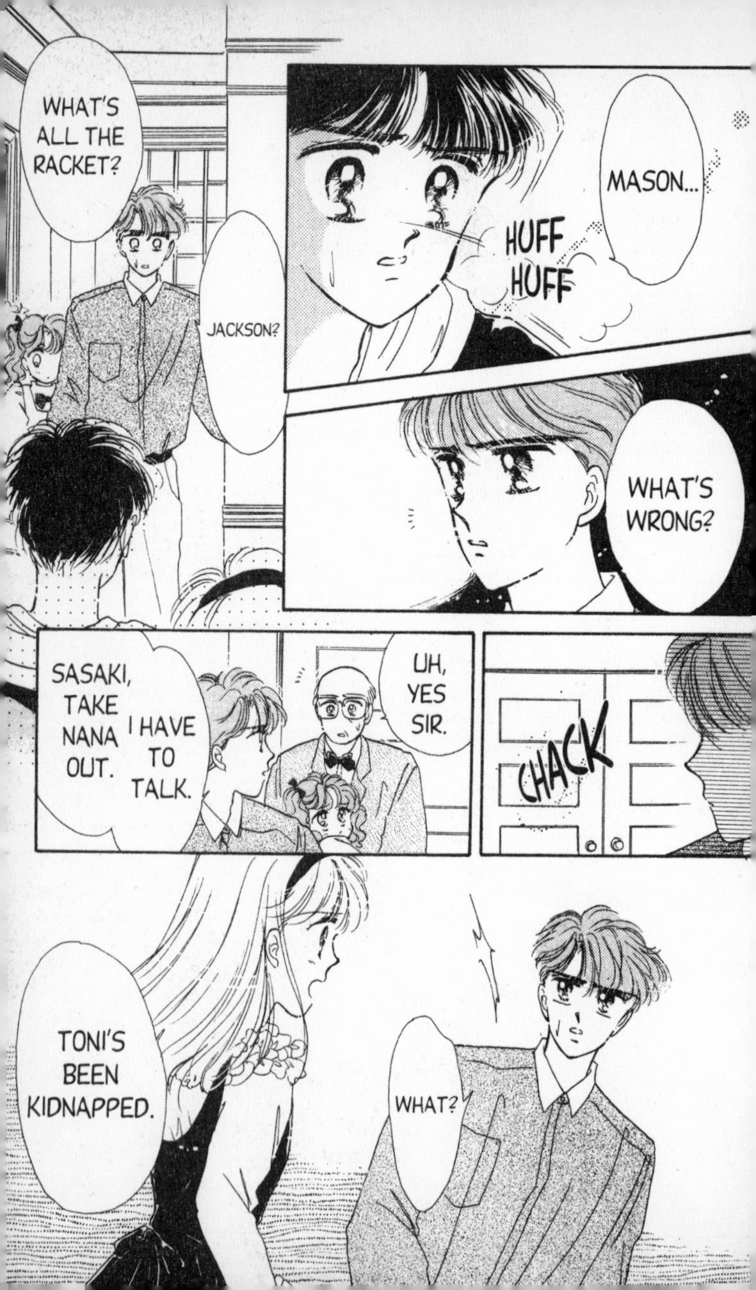
WHAT'S ALL THE RACKET?
JACKSON?
MASON...
HUFF HUFF
WHAT'S WRONG?
SASAKI, TAKE NANA OUT.
I HAVE TO TALK.
UH, YES SIR.
CHACK
TONI'S BEEN KIDNAPPED.
WHAT?

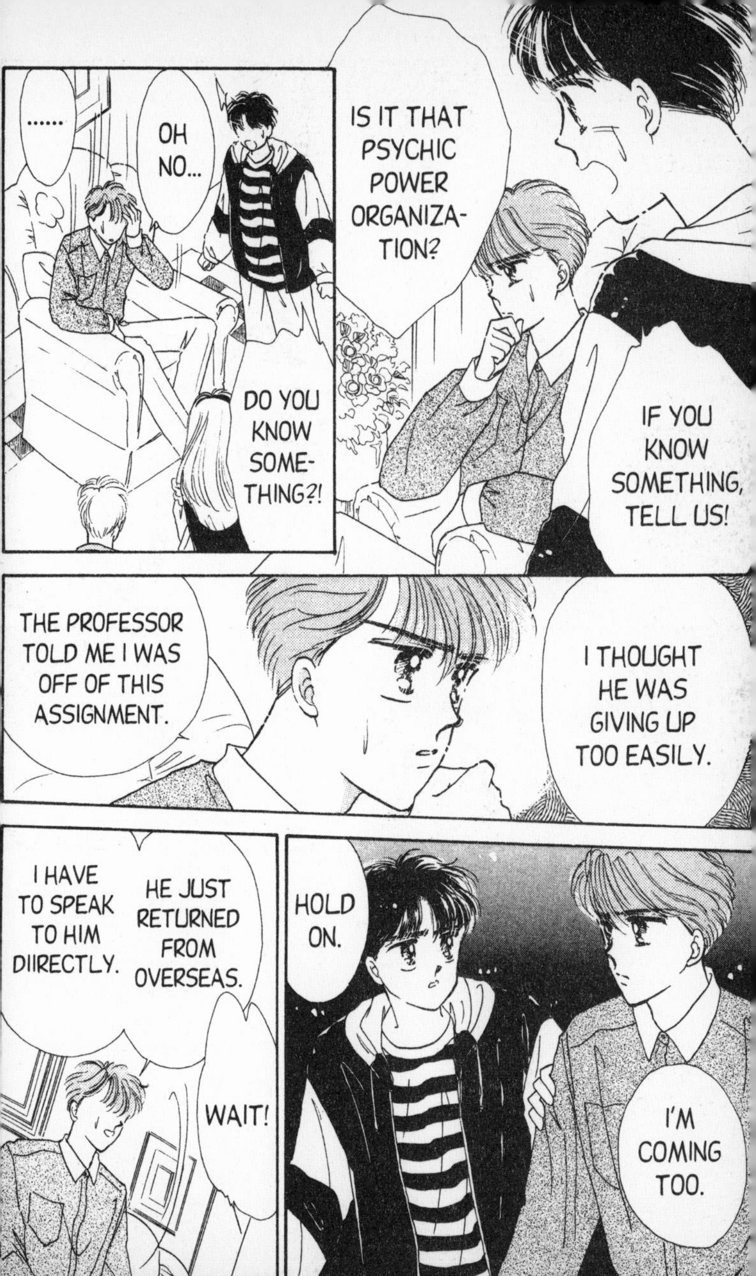
......
OH NO...
DO YOU KNOW SOMETHING?!
IS IT THAT PSYCHIC POWER ORGANIZATION?
IF YOU KNOW SOMETHING, TELL US!
THE PROFESSOR TOLD ME I WAS OFF OF THIS ASSIGNMENT.
I THOUGHT HE WAS GIVING UP TOO EASILY.
I HAVE TO SPEAK TO HIM DIIRECTLY.
HE JUST RETURNED FROM OVERSEAS.
WAIT!
HOLD ON.
I'M COMING TOO.

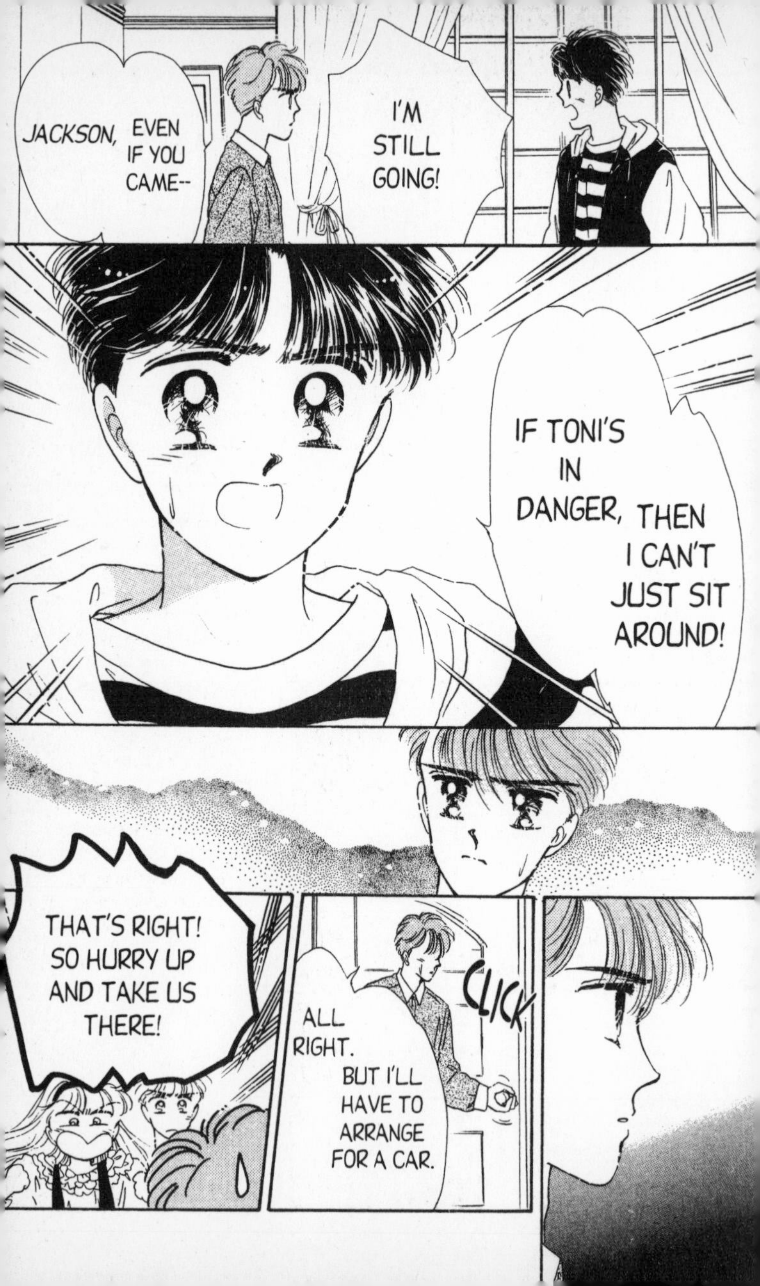

JACKSON, EVEN IF YOU CAME--
I'M STILL GOING!
IF TONI'S IN DANGER, THEN I CAN'T JUST SIT AROUND!
THAT'S RIGHT! SO HURRY UP AND TAKE US THERE!
ALL RIGHT. BUT I'LL HAVE TO ARRANGE FOR A CAR.
CLICK

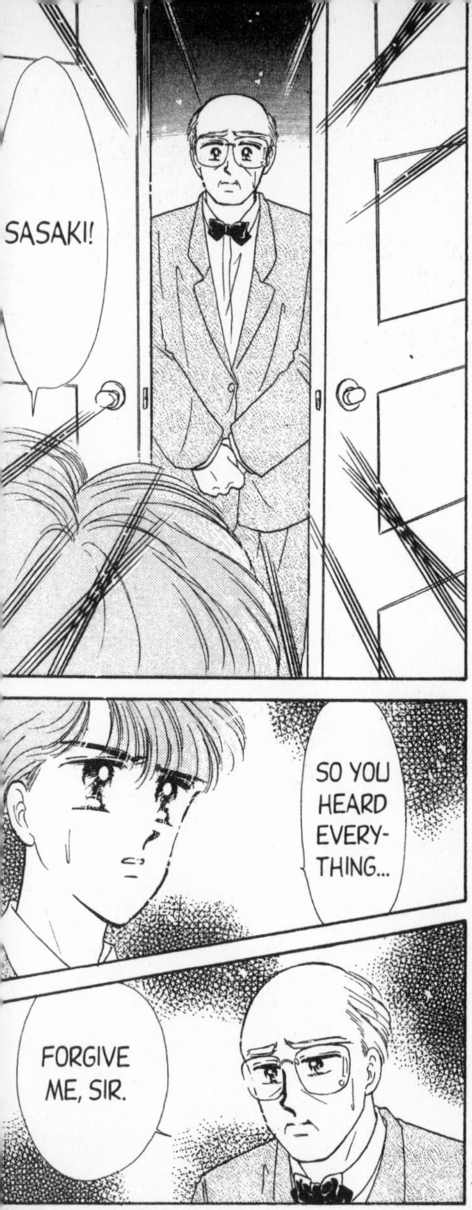
SASAKI!
SO YOU HEARD EVERYTHING...
FORGIVE ME, SIR.

BONUS

Milan, Part 2:
In Milan, all the taxis are yellow, but there are different models. I rode in sportscars and even a Mercedes Benz!
I'm sorry, but a Mercedes doesn't look good in yellow...
Most shops in Italy close in the afternoon (from around noon until 3 or 4), so I usually found something to eat (the restaurants stay open).
The restaurants here are amazing! They bring you pizza as soon as you sit at your table.
There were five of us for that one pizza, but at another table two people downed a whole pizza and more. Wow.
And for dessert, the sherbert I ordered came in a huge bowl.
Maybe it was because it was all girls at our table, but they gave us lots of candy too!

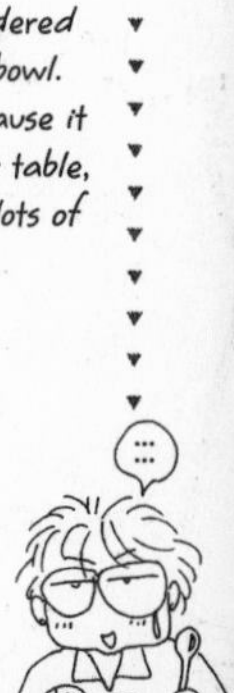

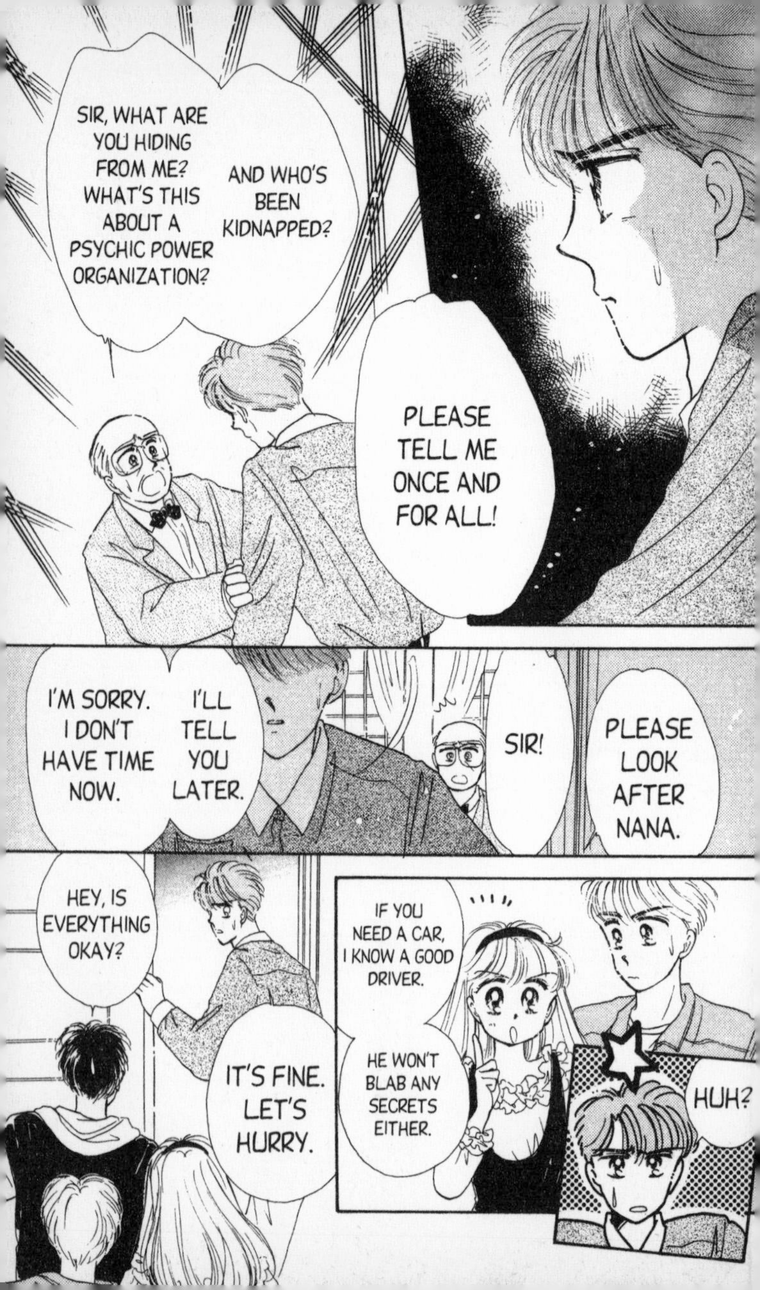
SIR, WHAT ARE YOU HIDING FROM ME? WHAT'S THIS ABOUT A PSYCHIC POWER ORGANIZATION?
AND WHO'S BEEN KIDNAPPED?
PLEASE TELL ME ONCE AND FOR ALL!
I'M SORRY. I DON'T HAVE TIME NOW.
I'LL TELL YOU LATER.
SIR!
PLEASE LOOK AFTER NANA.
HEY, IS EVERYTHING OKAY?
IT'S FINE. LET'S HURRY.
IF YOU NEED A CAR, I KNOW A GOOD DRIVER.
HE WON'T BLAB ANY SECRETS EITHER.
HUH?

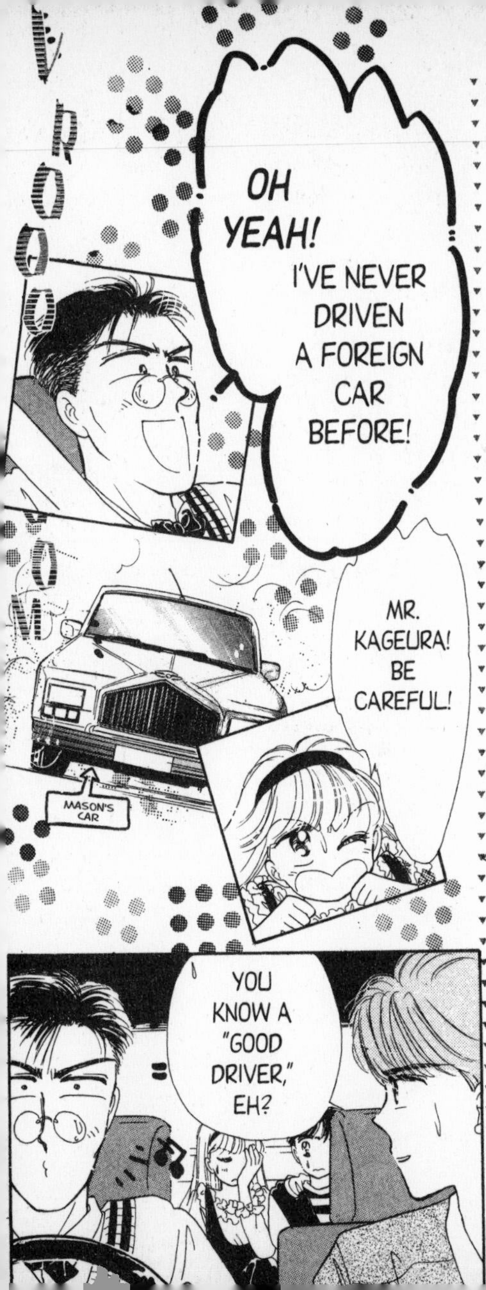
OH YEAH! I'VE NEVER DRIVEN A FOREIGN CAR BEFORE!
MR. KAGEURA! BE CAREFUL!
MASON'S CAR
YOU KNOW A "GOOD DRIVER," EH?

BONUS

Paris, Part 1.
After Milan, I arrived in Paris. Actually I don't remember what time it was. The airport is very futuristic, with its intersecting tubular escalators it looks like a space station! It's the kind of place that might show up in a science fiction movie or comic. And to top it all off, the boarding gates are called "satellites." During the flight I saw Mt. Monbraun (it looks like sugarcoated candy), so I was as happy as could be! Was it really Monbraun? I don't really know!

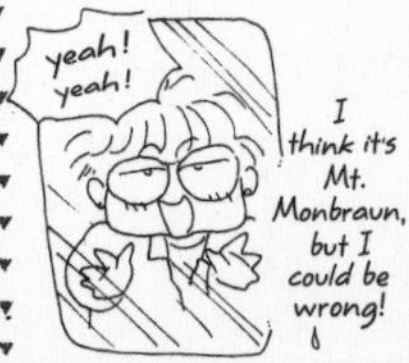
yeah! yeah!
I think it's Mt. Monbraun, but I could be wrong!

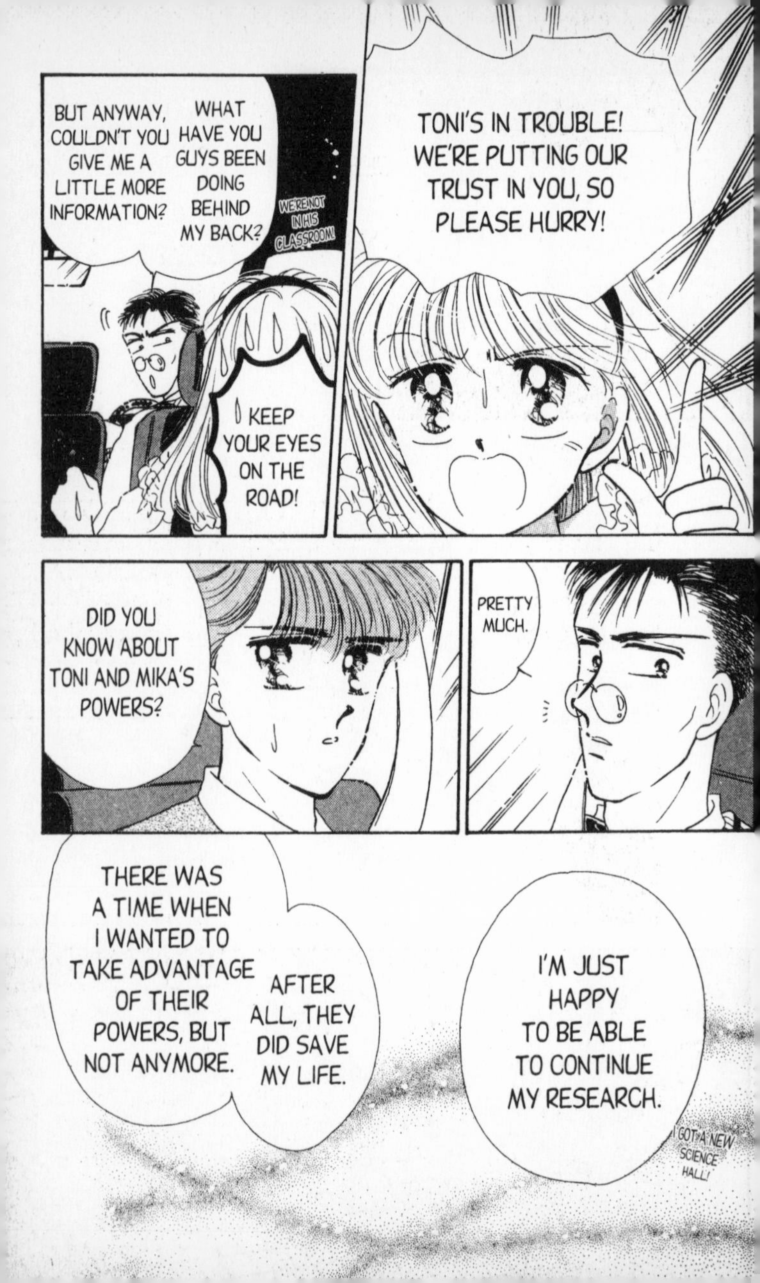
BUT ANYWAY, COULDN'T YOU GIVE ME A LITTLE MORE INFORMATION?
WHAT HAVE YOU GUYS BEEN DOING BEHIND MY BACK?
WE'RE NOT IN HIS CLASSROOM!
KEEP YOUR EYES ON THE ROAD!
TONI'S IN TROUBLE! WE'RE PUTTING OUR TRUST IN YOU, SO PLEASE HURRY!
DID YOU KNOW ABOUT TONI AND MIKA'S POWERS?
PRETTY MUCH.
THERE WAS A TIME WHEN I WANTED TO TAKE ADVANTAGE OF THEIR POWERS, BUT NOT ANYMORE.
AFTER ALL, THEY DID SAVE MY LIFE.
I'M JUST HAPPY TO BE ABLE TO CONTINUE MY RESEARCH.
I GOT A NEW SCIENCE HALL!

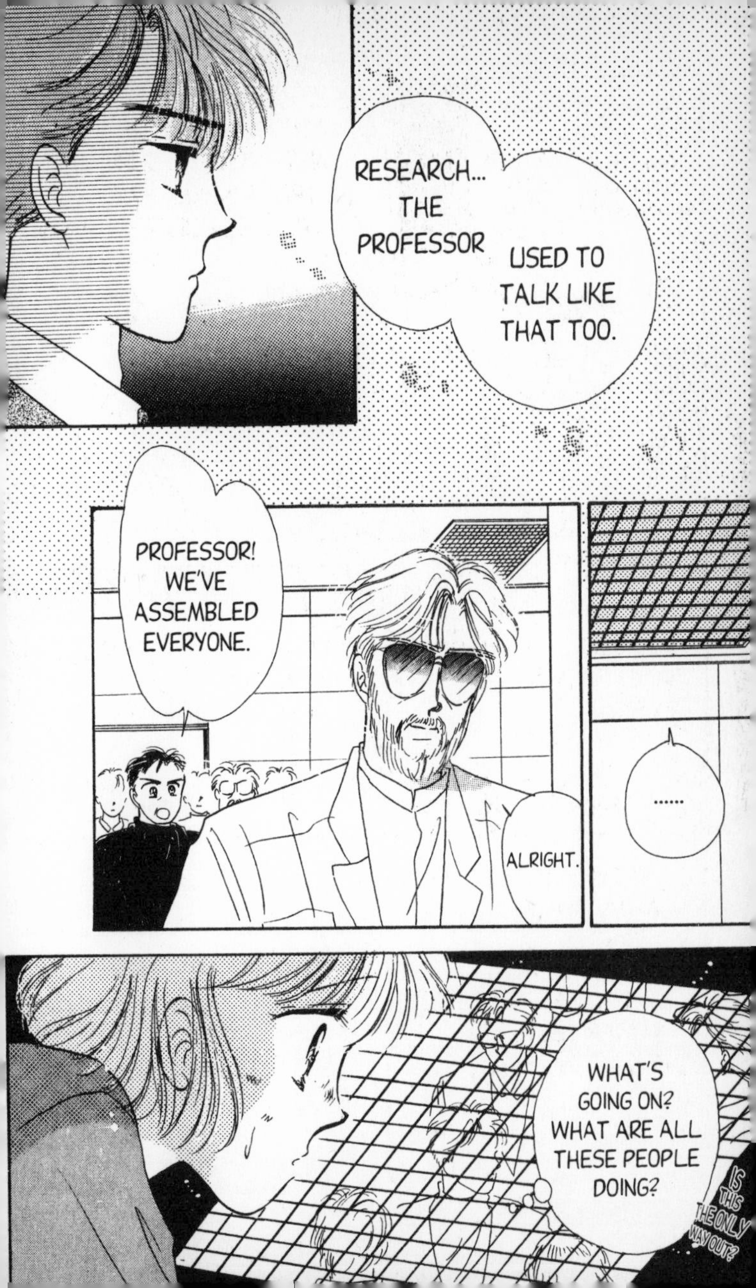
RESEARCH... THE PROFESSOR USED TO TALK LIKE THAT TOO.
PROFESSOR! WE'VE ASSEMBLED EVERYONE.
ALRIGHT.
......
WHAT'S GOING ON? WHAT ARE ALL THESE PEOPLE DOING?
IS THIS THE ONLY WAY OUT?

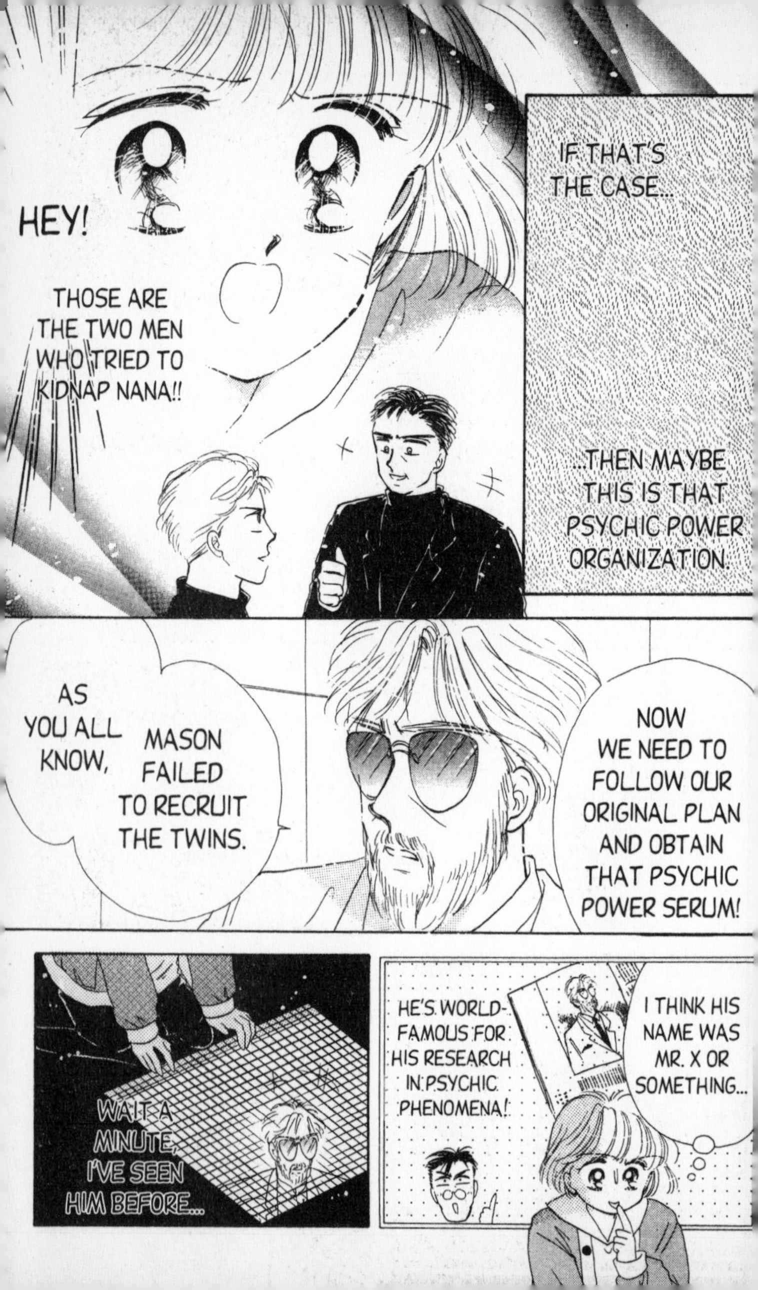
HEY!
THOSE ARE THE TWO MEN WHO TRIED TO KIDNAP NANA!!
IF THAT'S THE CASE...
...THEN MAYBE THIS IS THAT PSYCHIC POWER ORGANIZATION.
AS YOU ALL KNOW,
MASON FAILED TO RECRUIT THE TWINS.
NOW WE NEED TO FOLLOW OUR ORIGINAL PLAN AND OBTAIN THAT PSYCHIC POWER SERUM!
WAIT A MINUTE, I'VE SEEN HIM BEFORE...
HE'S WORLD-FAMOUS FOR HIS RESEARCH IN PSYCHIC PHENOMENA!
I THINK HIS NAME WAS MR. X OR SOMETHING...

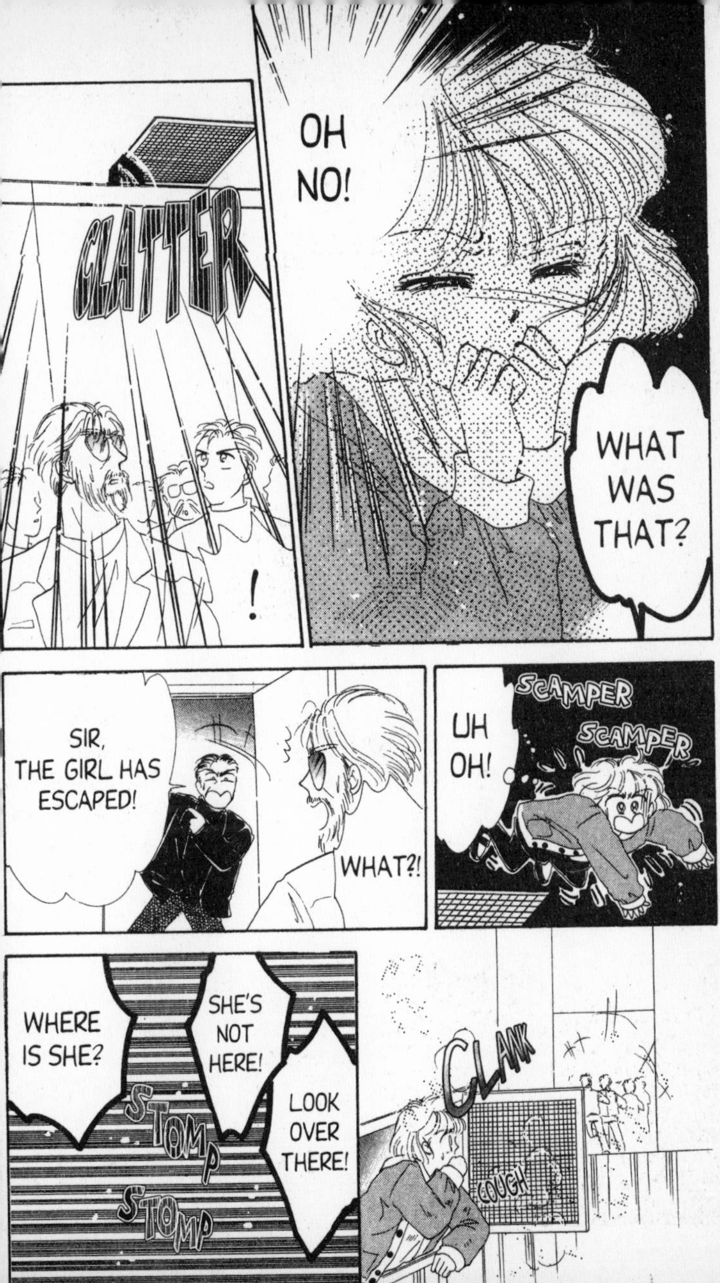
CLATTER
!
OH NO!
WHAT WAS THAT?
SIR, THE GIRL HAS ESCAPED!
WHAT?!
UH OH!
SCAMPER
SCAMPER
WHERE IS SHE?
SHE'S NOT HERE!
LOOK OVER THERE!
STOMP
STOMP
CLANK
COUGH

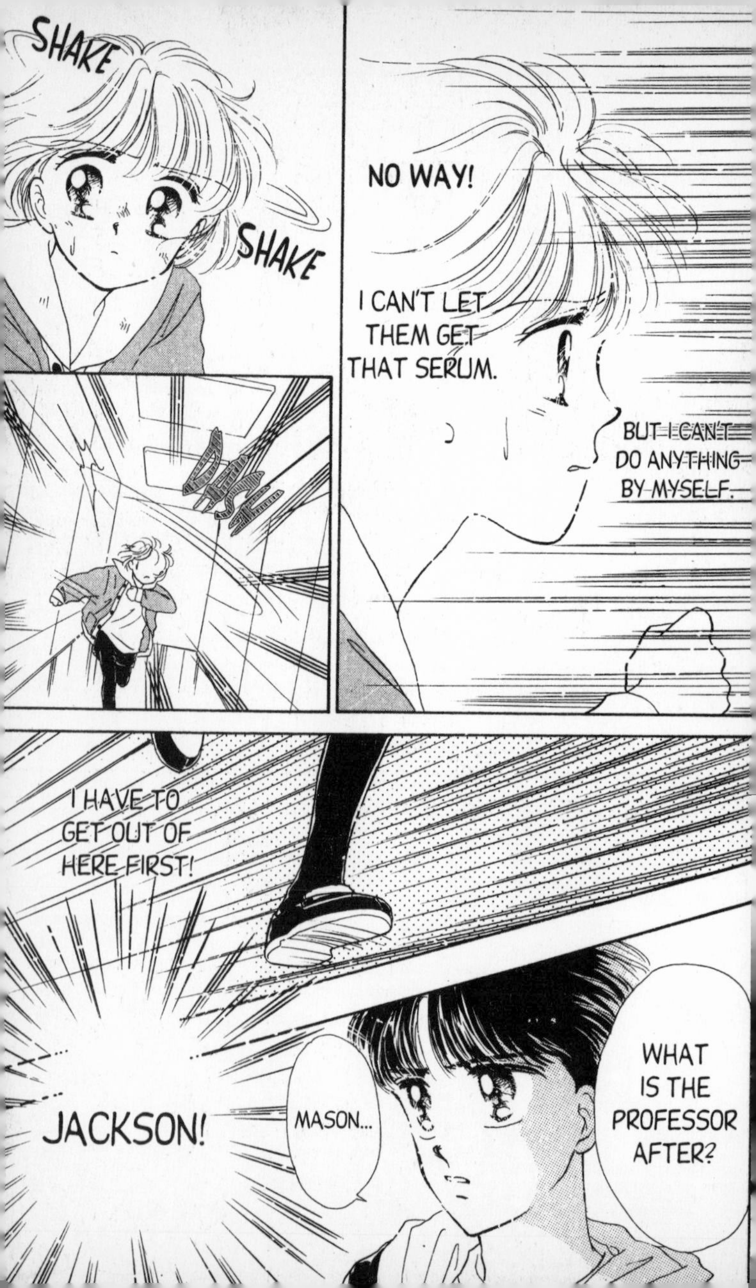
SHAKE
SHAKE
DASH
NO WAY!
I CAN'T LET THEM GET THAT SERUM.
BUT I CAN'T DO ANYTHING BY MYSELF.
I HAVE TO GET OUT OF HERE FIRST!
JACKSON!
MASON...
WHAT IS THE PROFESSOR AFTER?

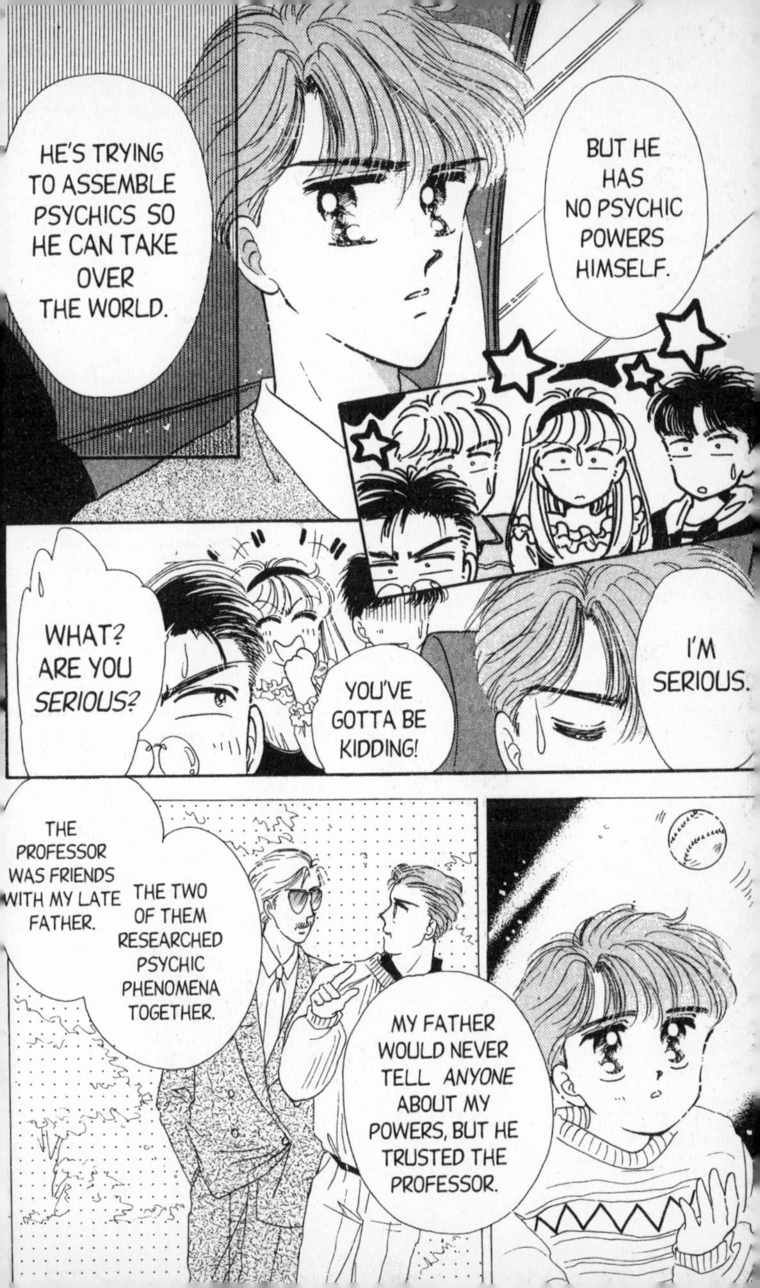
HE'S TRYING TO ASSEMBLE PSYCHICS SO HE CAN TAKE OVER THE WORLD.
BUT HE HAS NO PSYCHIC POWERS HIMSELF.
WHAT? ARE YOU *SERIOUS?*
YOU'VE GOTTA BE KIDDING!
I'M SERIOUS.
THE PROFESSOR WAS FRIENDS WITH MY LATE FATHER.
THE TWO OF THEM RESEARCHED PSYCHIC PHENOMENA TOGETHER.
MY FATHER WOULD NEVER TELL *ANYONE* ABOUT MY POWERS, BUT HE TRUSTED THE PROFESSOR.

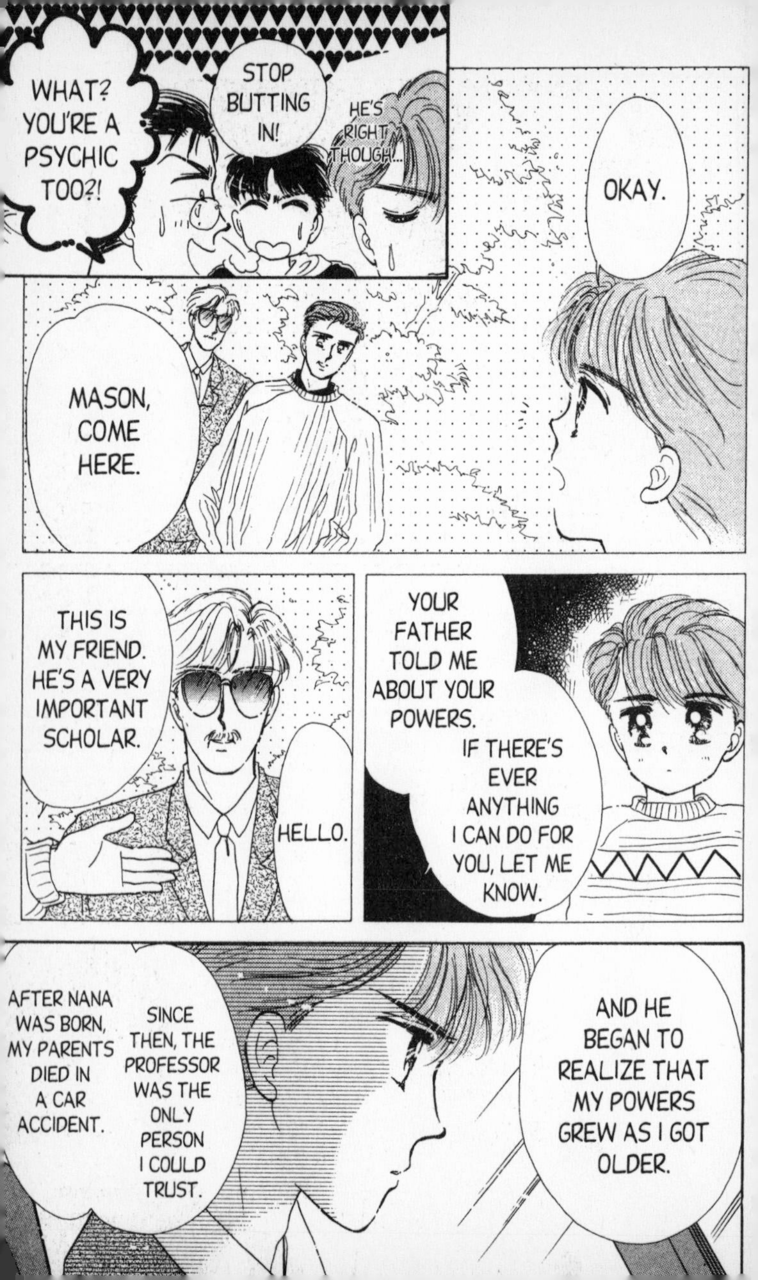
WHAT? YOU'RE A PSYCHIC TOO?!
STOP BUTTING IN!
HE'S RIGHT THOUGH...
MASON, COME HERE.
OKAY.
THIS IS MY FRIEND. HE'S A VERY IMPORTANT SCHOLAR.
HELLO.
YOUR FATHER TOLD ME ABOUT YOUR POWERS.
IF THERE'S EVER ANYTHING I CAN DO FOR YOU, LET ME KNOW.
AFTER NANA WAS BORN, MY PARENTS DIED IN A CAR ACCIDENT.
SINCE THEN, THE PROFESSOR WAS THE ONLY PERSON I COULD TRUST.
AND HE BEGAN TO REALIZE THAT MY POWERS GREW AS I GOT OLDER.

MASON, YOUR POWERS ARE TRULY UNIQUE.

I NEED YOUR HELP.

WE *NEED* TO ASSEMBLE OTHER PSYCHICS LIKE YOU.

WHILE THE PROFESSOR TRAVELED AROUND THE WORLD DOING HIS RESEARCH,

I TRANSFERRED FROM SCHOOL TO SCHOOL, SEARCHING FOR PSYCHICS.

BUT I NEVER MET ANYONE AS POWERFUL AS MYSELF.

I GUESS I BECAME ARROGANT.

I THOUGHT NO ONE COULD BEAT ME.

AND I *NEVER* THOUGHT YOU AND TONI COULD OVERPOWER ME.

SINCE I FAILED TO GET THE TWINS, I THINK HE'LL COME AFTER THE PSYCHIC SERUM.

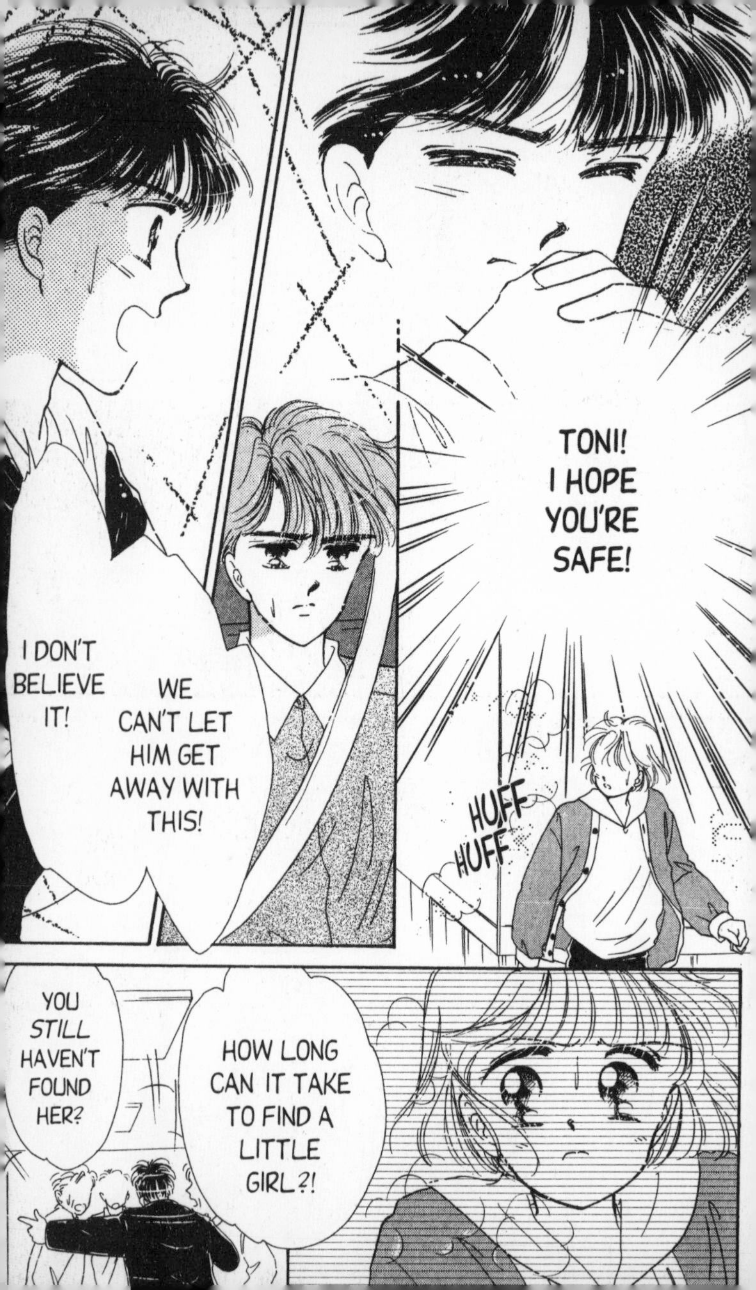
I DON'T BELIEVE IT!
WE CAN'T LET HIM GET AWAY WITH THIS!
TONI! I HOPE YOU'RE SAFE!
HUFF HUFF
YOU STILL HAVEN'T FOUND HER?
HOW LONG CAN IT TAKE TO FIND A LITTLE GIRL?!

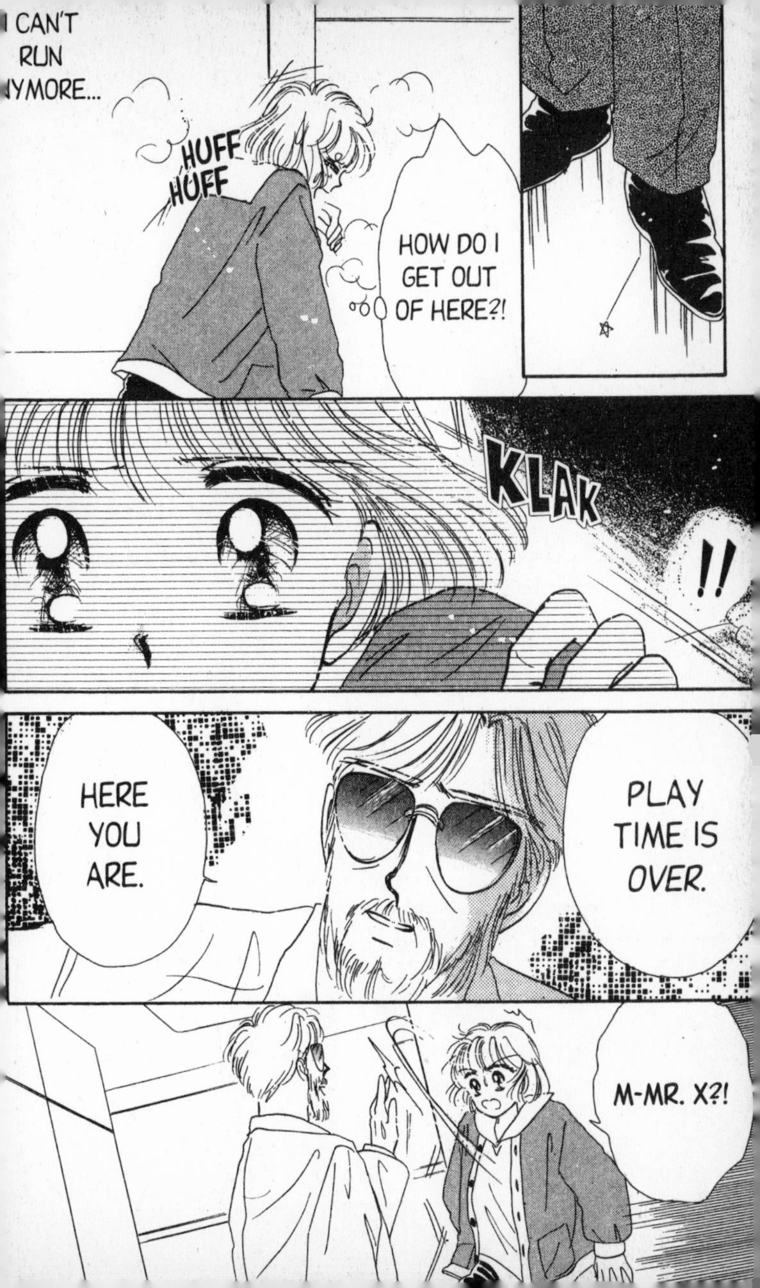
I CAN'T
RUN
NYMORE...
HUFF
HUFF
HOW DO I GET OUT OF HERE?!
KLAK
!!
HERE YOU ARE.
PLAY TIME IS OVER.
M-MR. X?!

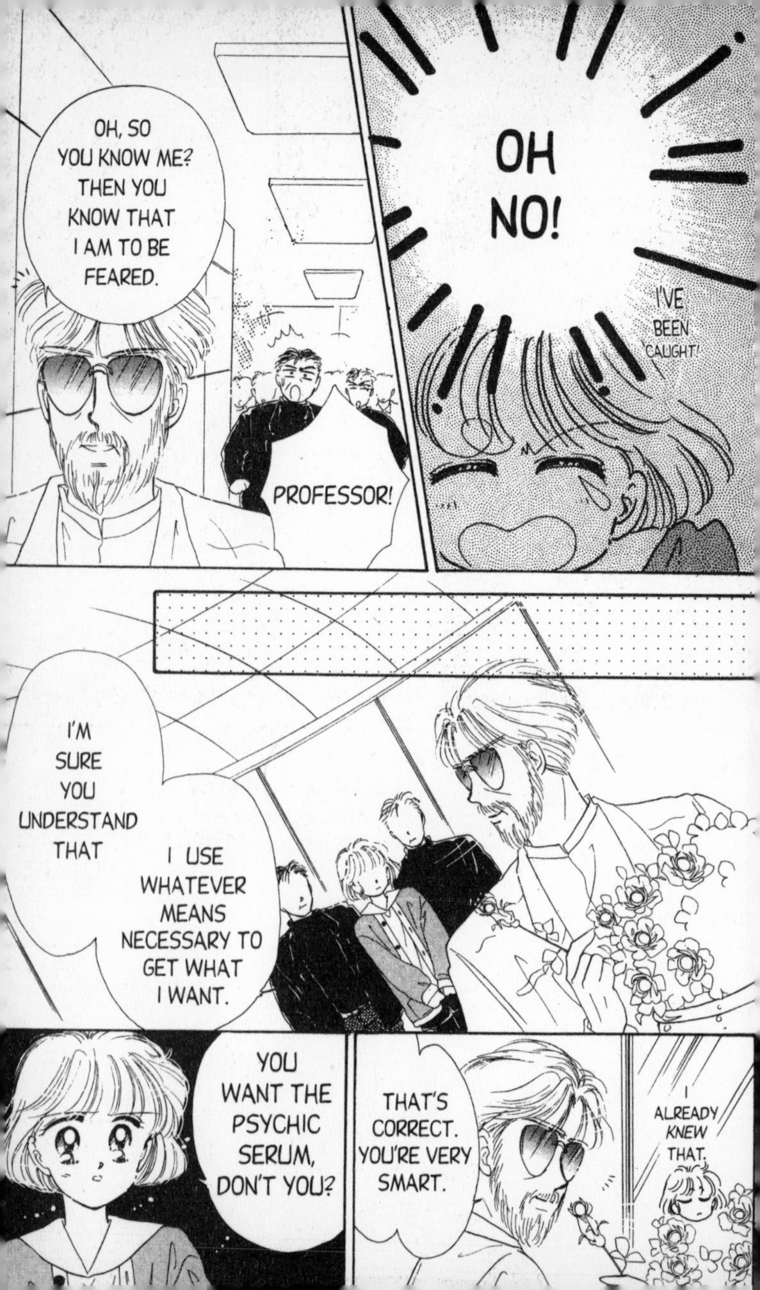
OH, SO YOU KNOW ME? THEN YOU KNOW THAT I AM TO BE FEARED.
PROFESSOR!
OH NO!
I'VE BEEN CAUGHT!
I'M SURE YOU UNDERSTAND THAT
I USE WHATEVER MEANS NECESSARY TO GET WHAT I WANT.
YOU WANT THE PSYCHIC SERUM, DON'T YOU?
THAT'S CORRECT. YOU'RE VERY SMART.
I ALREADY KNEW THAT.

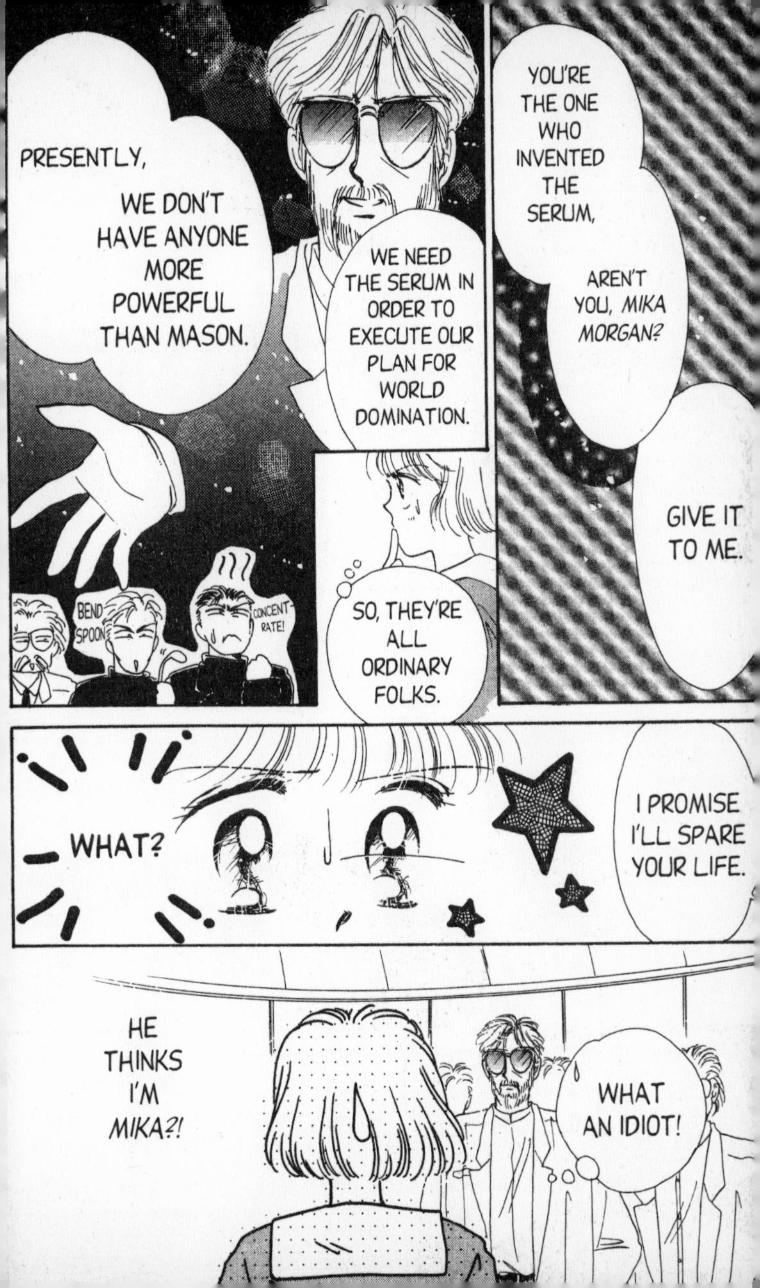
PRESENTLY,
WE DON'T HAVE ANYONE MORE POWERFUL THAN MASON.
WE NEED THE SERUM IN ORDER TO EXECUTE OUR PLAN FOR WORLD DOMINATION.
BEND SPOON
CONCENT-RATE!
SO, THEY'RE ALL ORDINARY FOLKS.
YOU'RE THE ONE WHO INVENTED THE SERUM,
AREN'T YOU, MIKA MORGAN?
GIVE IT TO ME.
WHAT?
I PROMISE I'LL SPARE YOUR LIFE.
HE THINKS I'M MIKA?!
WHAT AN IDIOT!

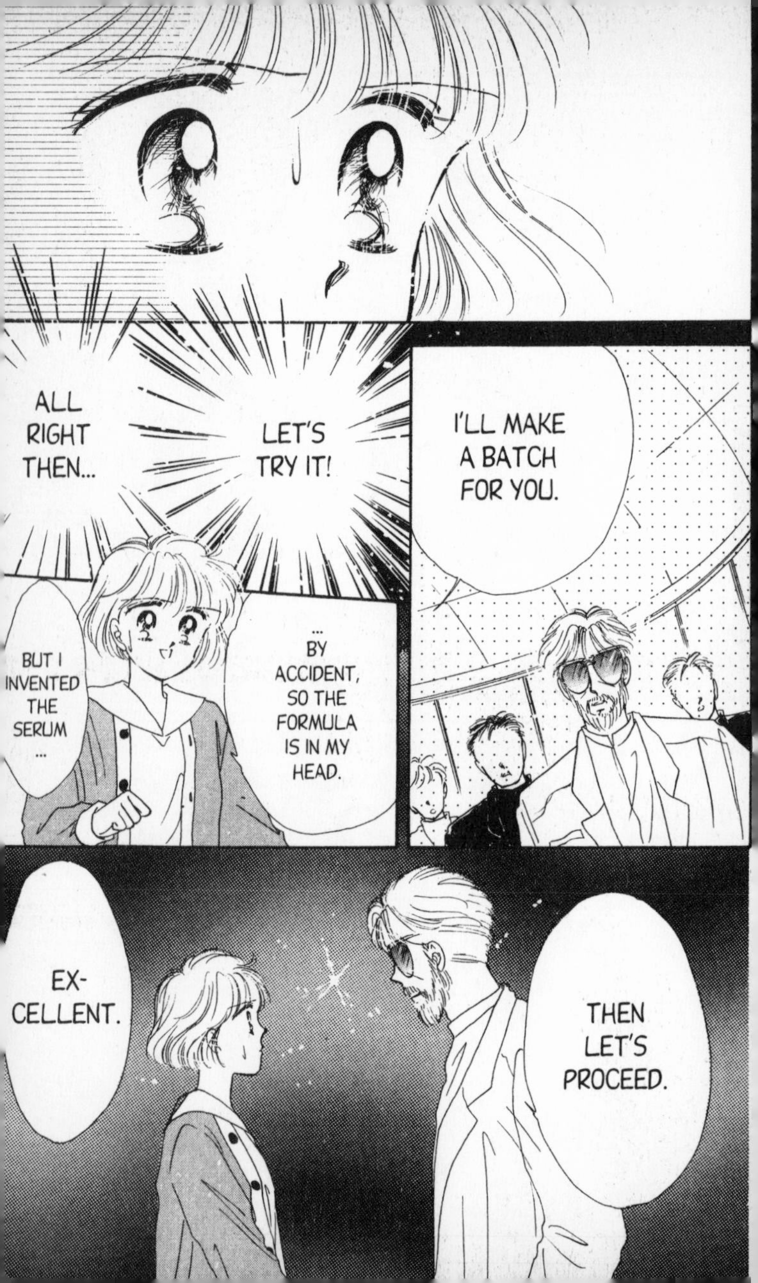
ALL RIGHT THEN...
LET'S TRY IT!
BUT I INVENTED THE SERUM ...
... BY ACCIDENT, SO THE FORMULA IS IN MY HEAD.
I'LL MAKE A BATCH FOR YOU.
EX-CELLENT.
THEN LET'S PROCEED.

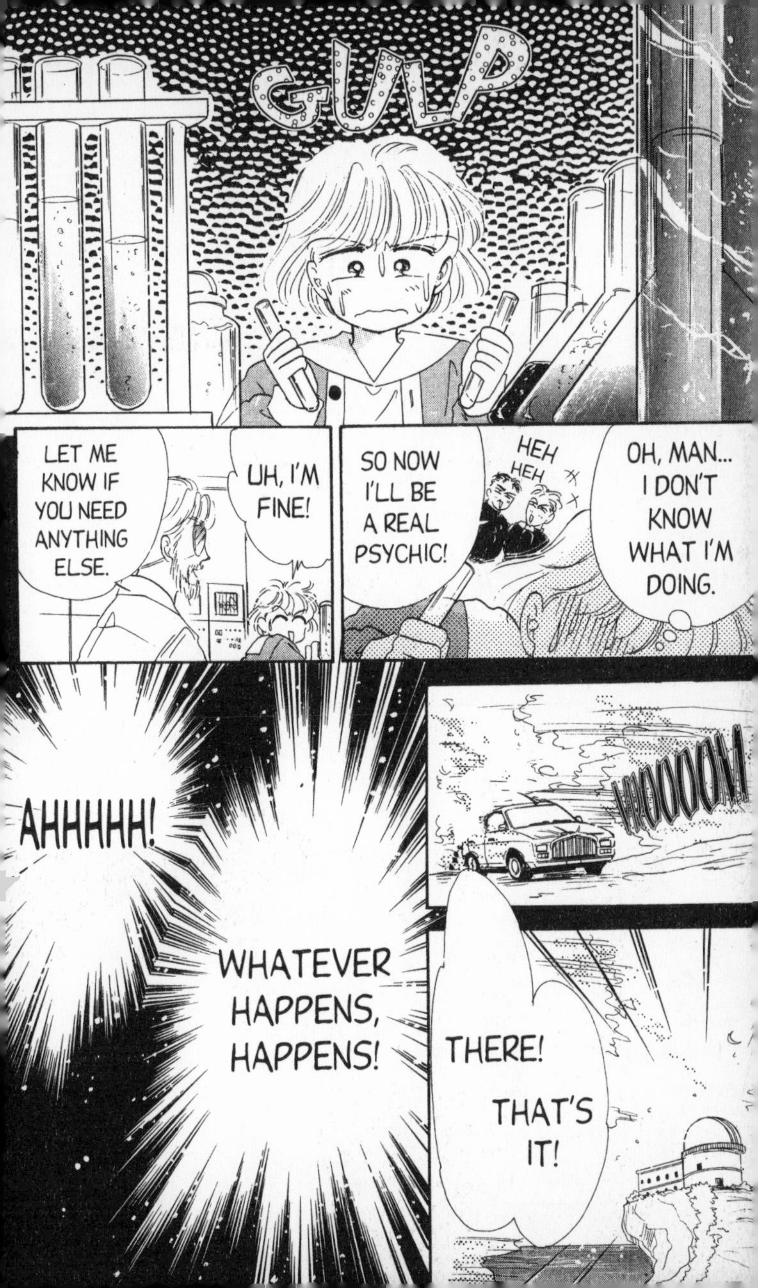
GULP
LET ME KNOW IF YOU NEED ANYTHING ELSE.
UH, I'M FINE!
SO NOW I'LL BE A REAL PSYCHIC!
HEH HEH
OH, MAN... I DON'T KNOW WHAT I'M DOING.
AHHHHH!
WHATEVER HAPPENS, HAPPENS!
VROOOOM
THERE!
THAT'S IT!

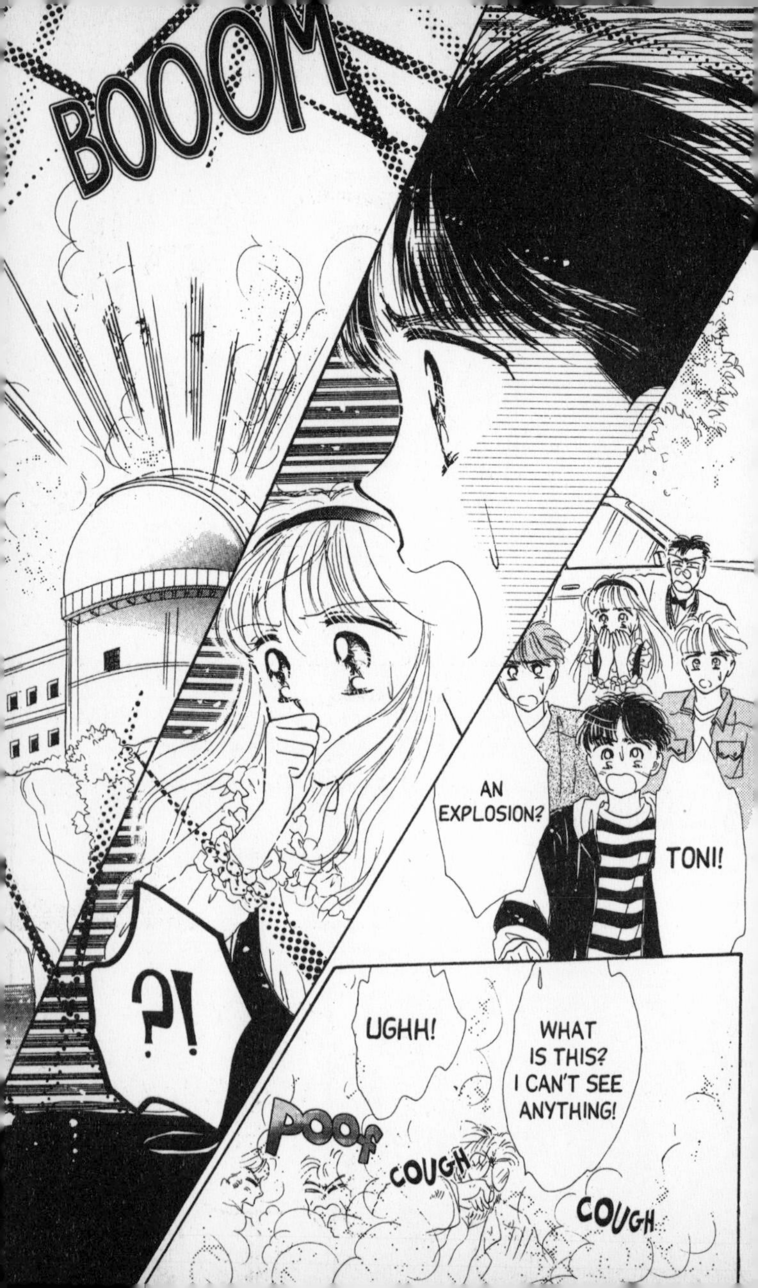
BOOOM
TONI!
AN EXPLOSION?
?!
WHAT IS THIS? I CAN'T SEE ANYTHING!
UGHH!
POOF
COUGH
COUGH

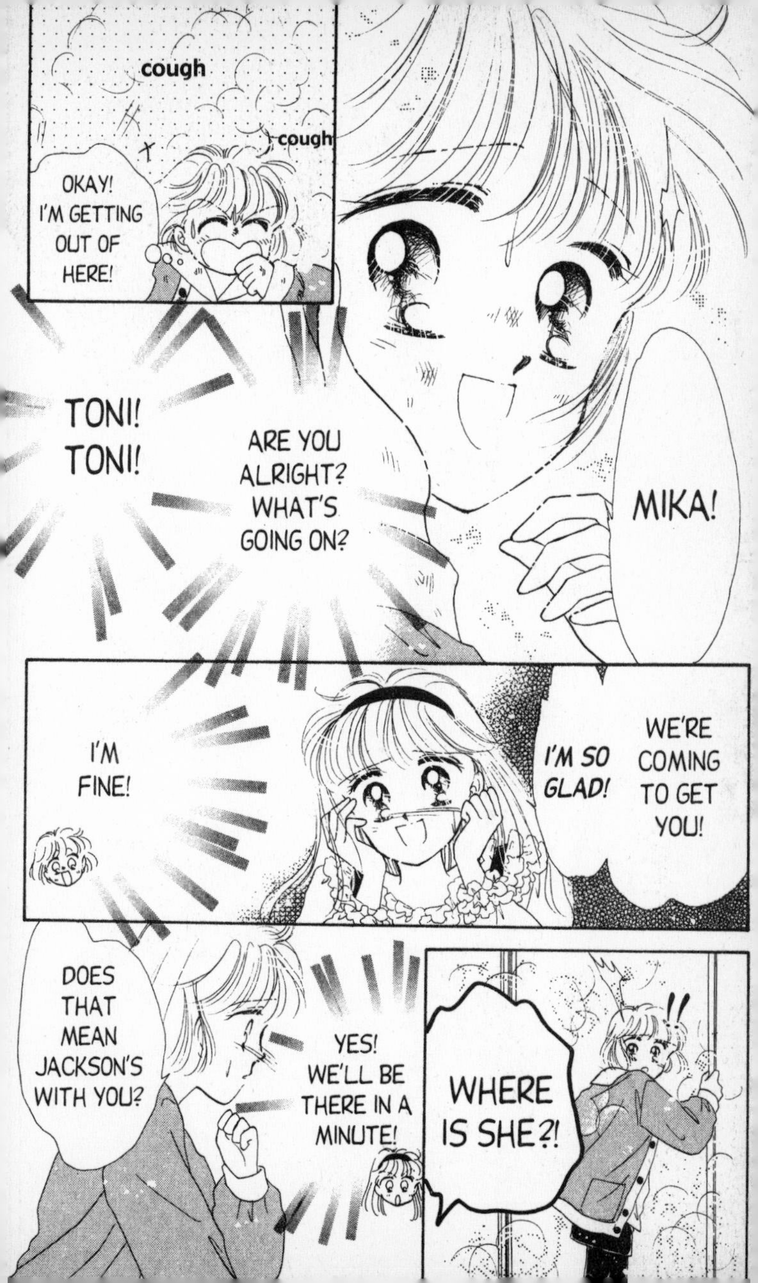
cough
cough
OKAY! I'M GETTING OUT OF HERE!
TONI! TONI!
ARE YOU ALRIGHT? WHAT'S GOING ON?
MIKA!
I'M FINE!
I'M SO GLAD!
WE'RE COMING TO GET YOU!
DOES THAT MEAN JACKSON'S WITH YOU?
YES! WE'LL BE THERE IN A MINUTE!
WHERE IS SHE?!
!!

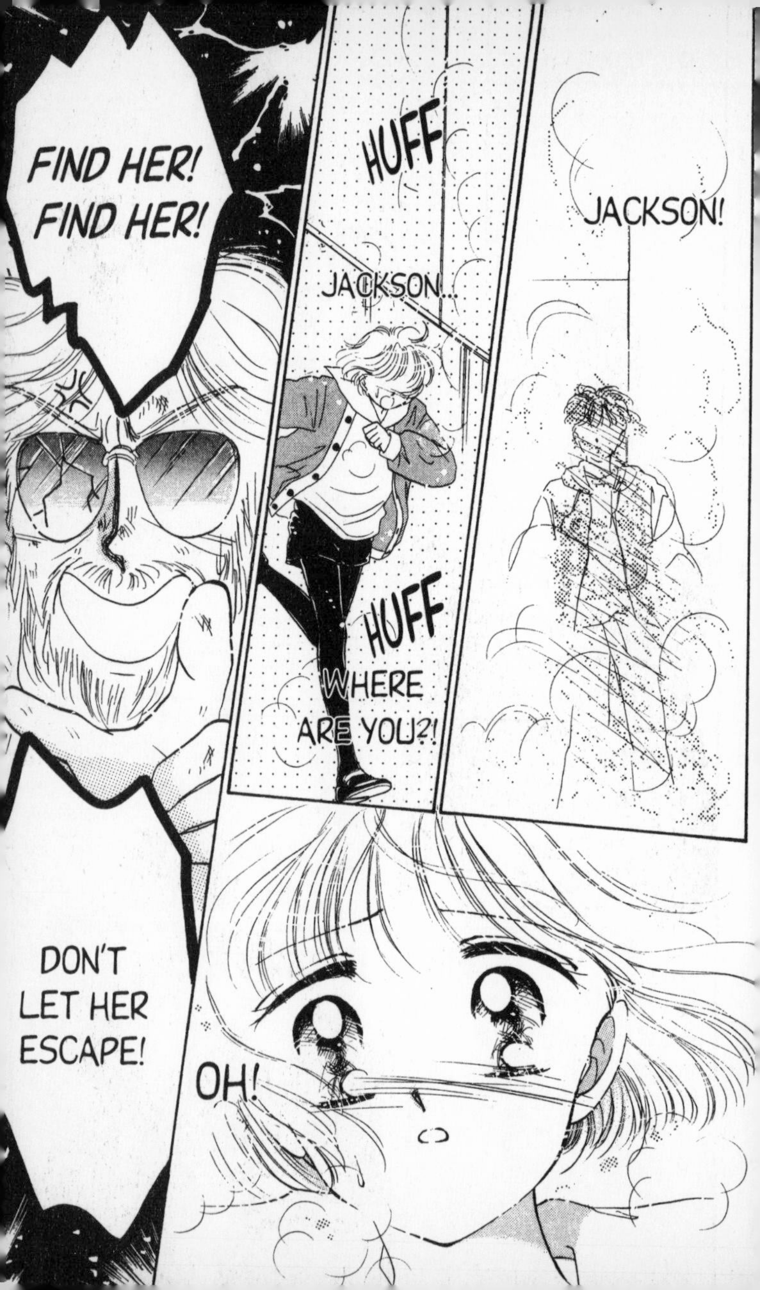
FIND HER! FIND HER!
DON'T LET HER ESCAPE!
HUFF
JACKSON...
HUFF
WHERE ARE YOU?!
JACKSON!
OH!

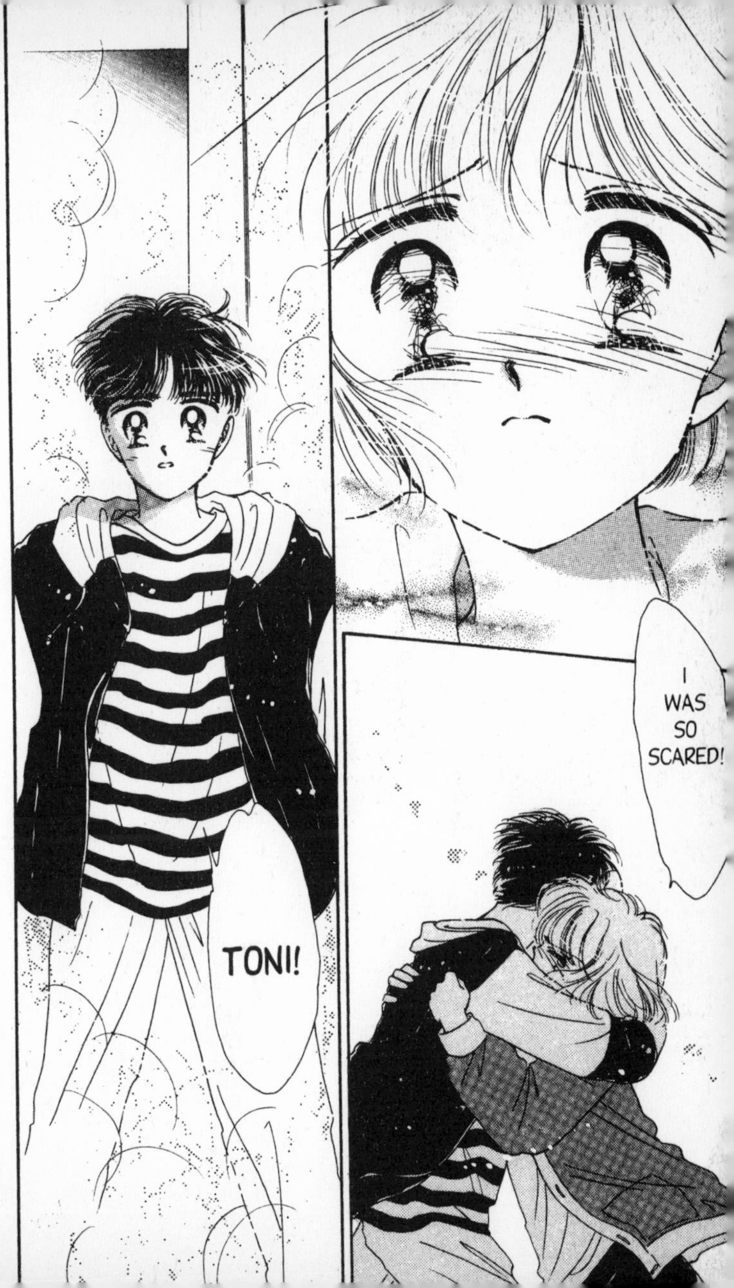
TONI!
I WAS SO SCARED!

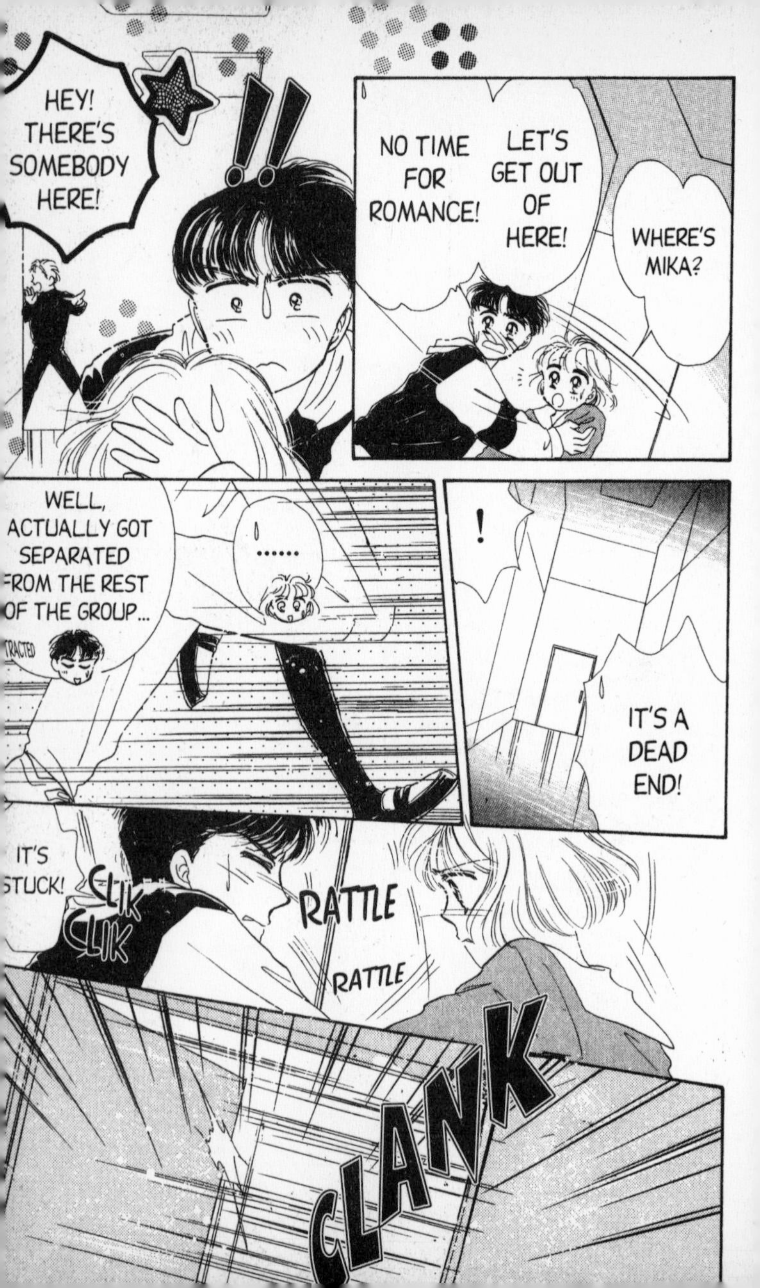
HEY! THERE'S SOMEBODY HERE!
!!
NO TIME FOR ROMANCE!
LET'S GET OUT OF HERE!
WHERE'S MIKA?
WELL, ACTUALLY GOT SEPARATED FROM THE REST OF THE GROUP...
TRACTED
......
!
IT'S A DEAD END!
IT'S STUCK!
CLIK CLIK
RATTLE
RATTLE
CLANK

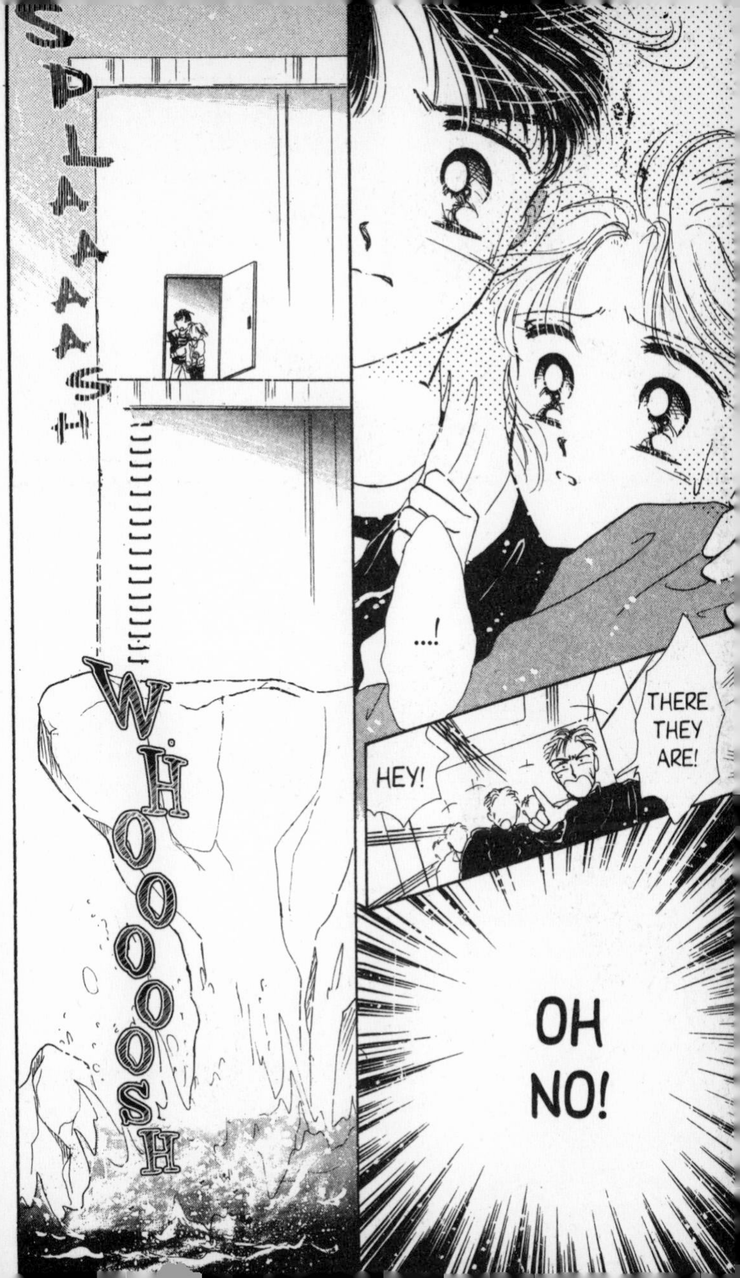
SPLAAASH
WHOOOOOSH
...!
HEY!
THERE THEY ARE!
OH NO!

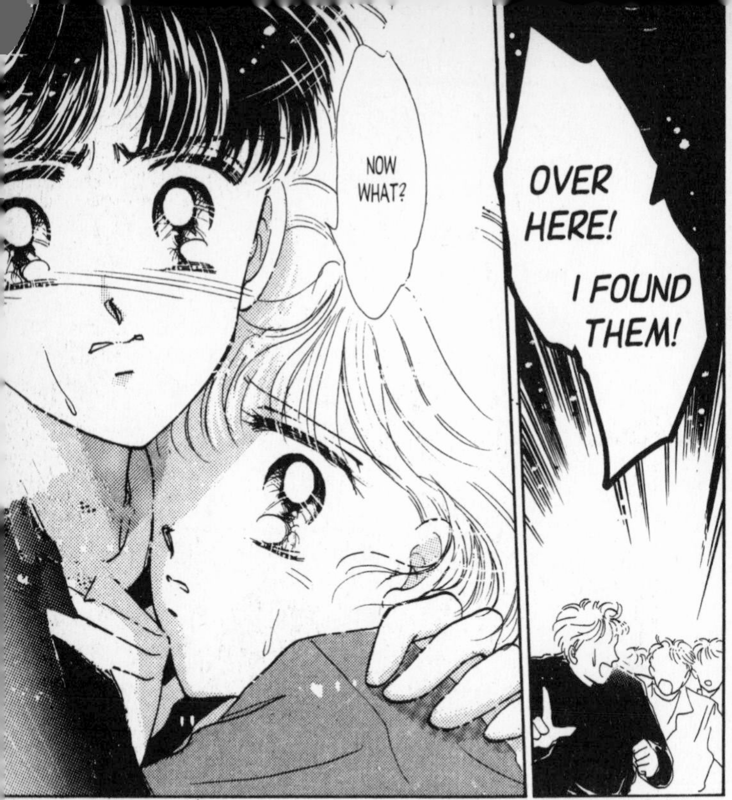
NOW WHAT?
OVER HERE!
I FOUND THEM!

This is a ticket for the "Carnet" subway. You can use it on the bus too.

JORHCA

SCENES D'INTERIEUR

Moving

SESSION SEPTEMBRE 1992

The "Moving" market was awesome!

ok at this receipt! Isn't it cute!

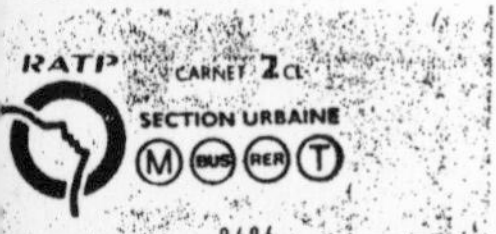
RATP
CARNET 2 CL
SECTION URBAINE
M BUS RER T
0404

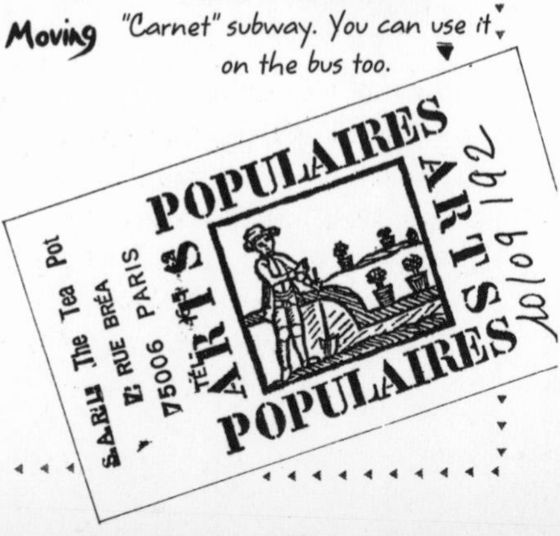
POPULAIRES
ARTS
ARTS
POPULAIRES
POPULAIRES
S.A.R.L. The Tea Pot
2 RUE BRÉA
75006 PARIS
10/09 1992

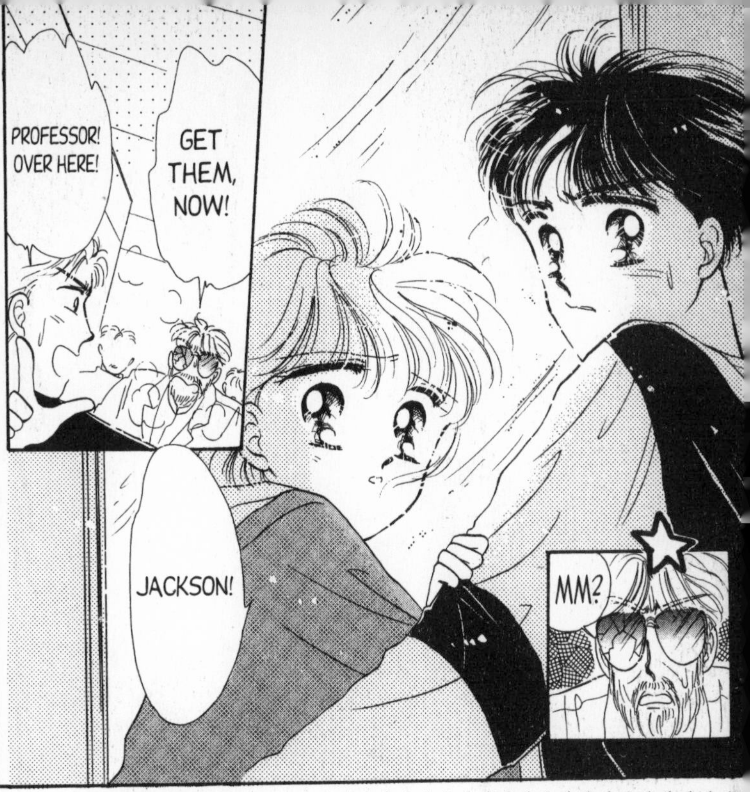
PROFESSOR! OVER HERE!
GET THEM, NOW!
JACKSON!
MM?

BONUS

Paris Part 2

I visited the "Moving" open market. There were so many cute and pretty things! Each booth was so jam-packed, I could stay there all day. I wasn't supposed to take pictures, but I was clicking away all day long! Paris is fun during the day too, but at night it's incredible! The Eiffel Tower is beautiful when it's all lit up. The lights are pretty reflecting off of the Seine River. It's very romantic!

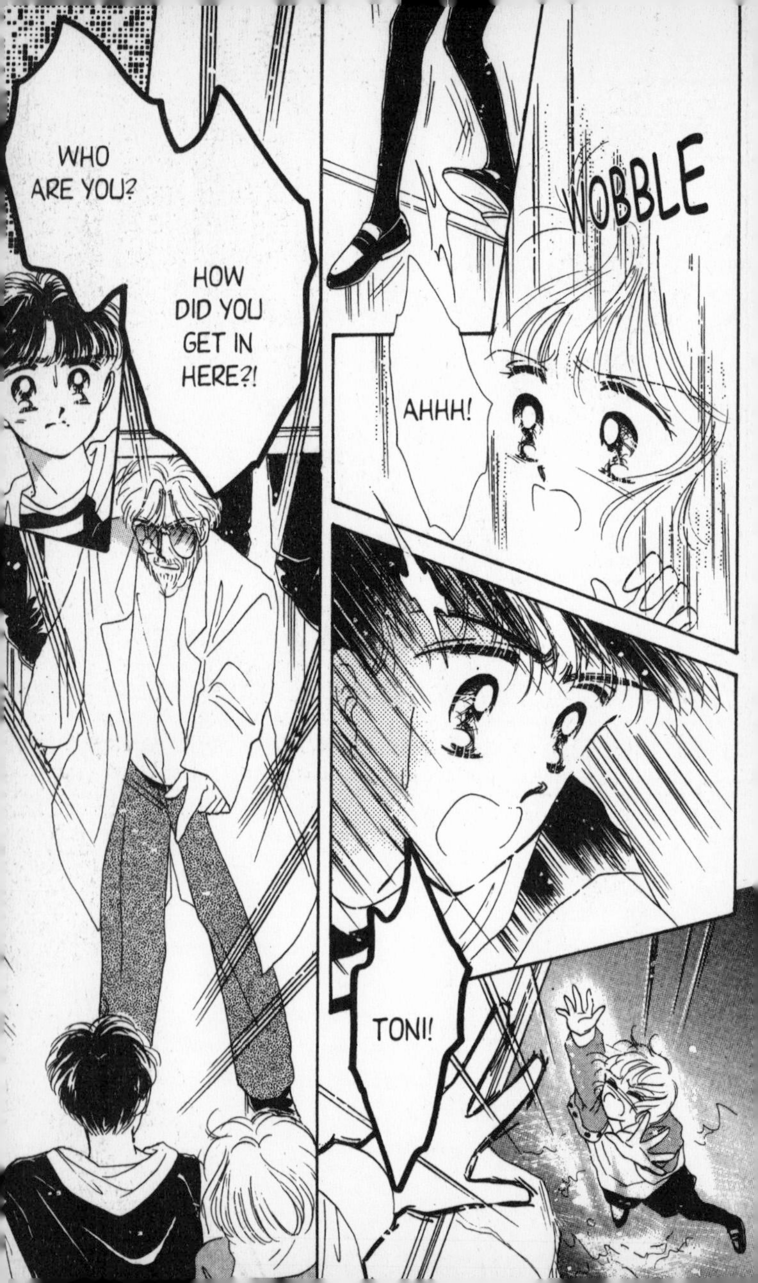
WHO ARE YOU?
HOW DID YOU GET IN HERE?!
WOBBLE
AHHH!
TONI!

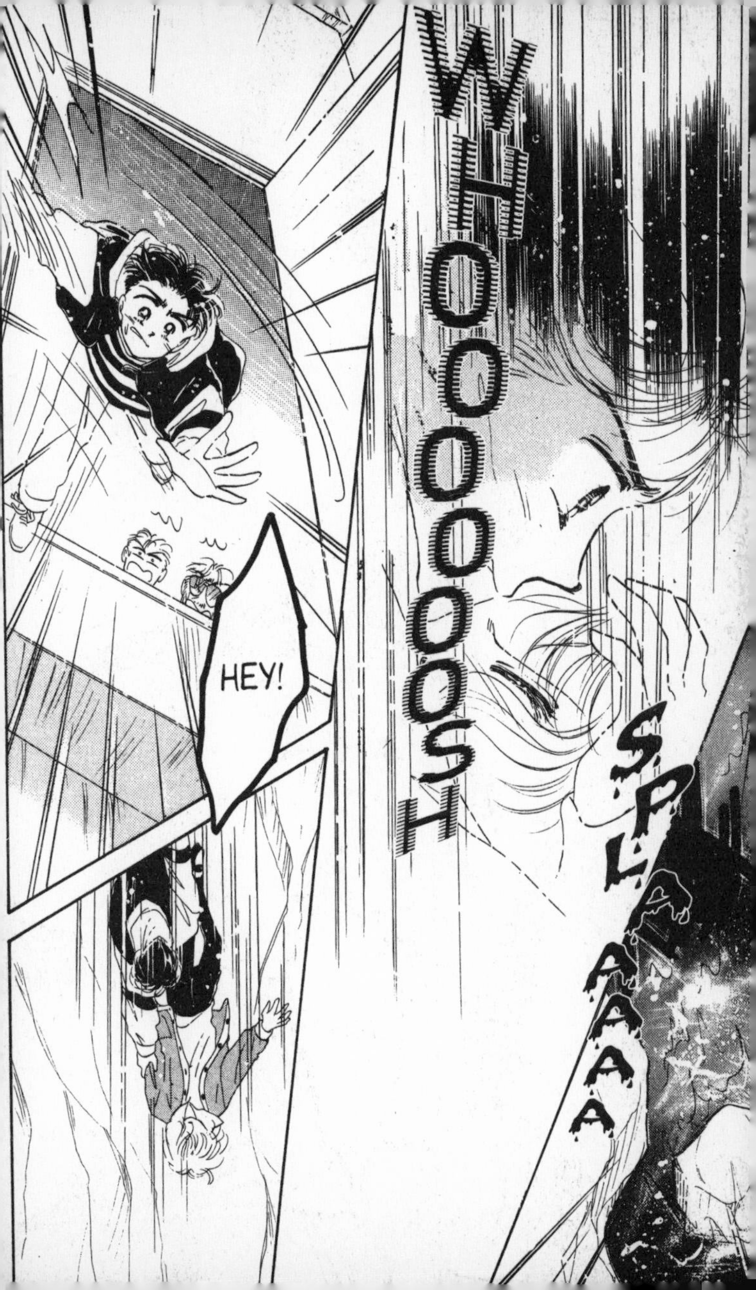

HEY!
WHOOOOOOOOOSH
SPLAAAAA

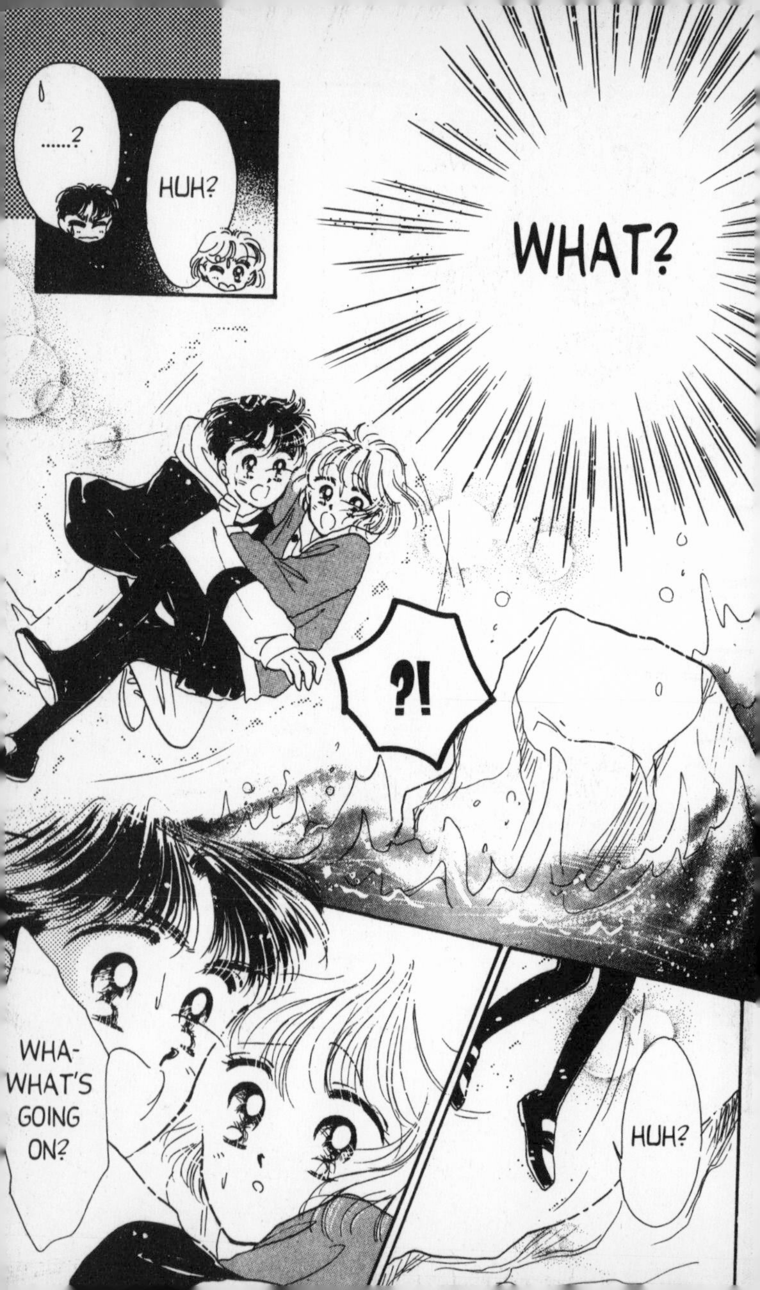
......?
HUH?
WHAT?
?!
WHA- WHAT'S GOING ON?
HUH?

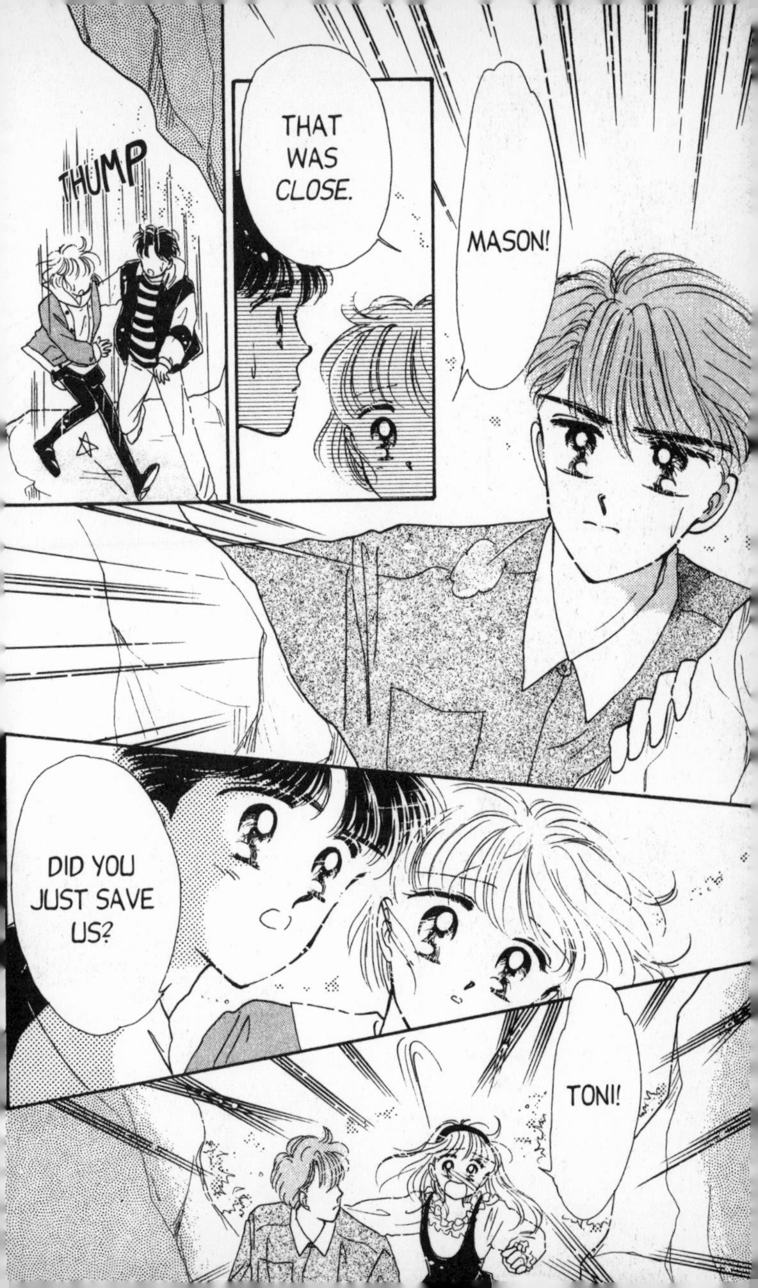
THUMP
THAT WAS CLOSE.
MASON!
DID YOU JUST SAVE US?
TONI!

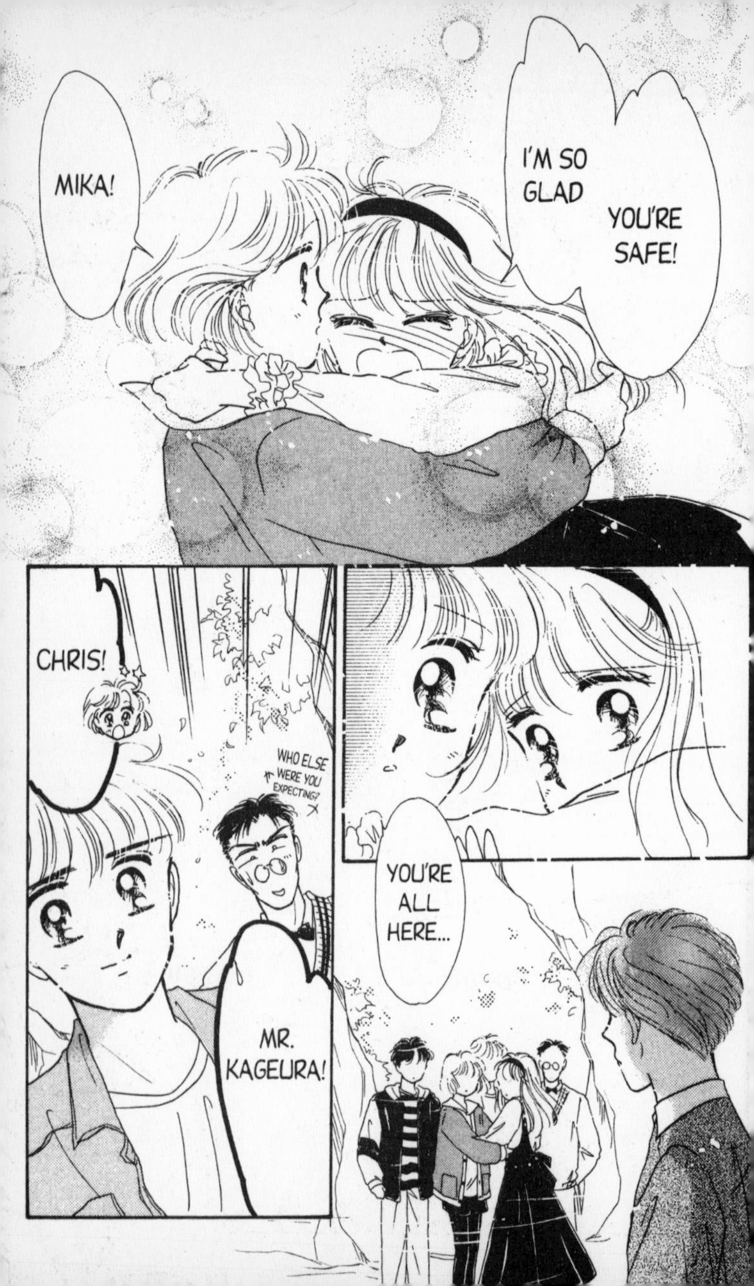

MIKA!
I'M SO GLAD YOU'RE SAFE!
CHRIS!
WHO ELSE WERE YOU EXPECTING?
MR. KAGEURA!
YOU'RE ALL HERE...

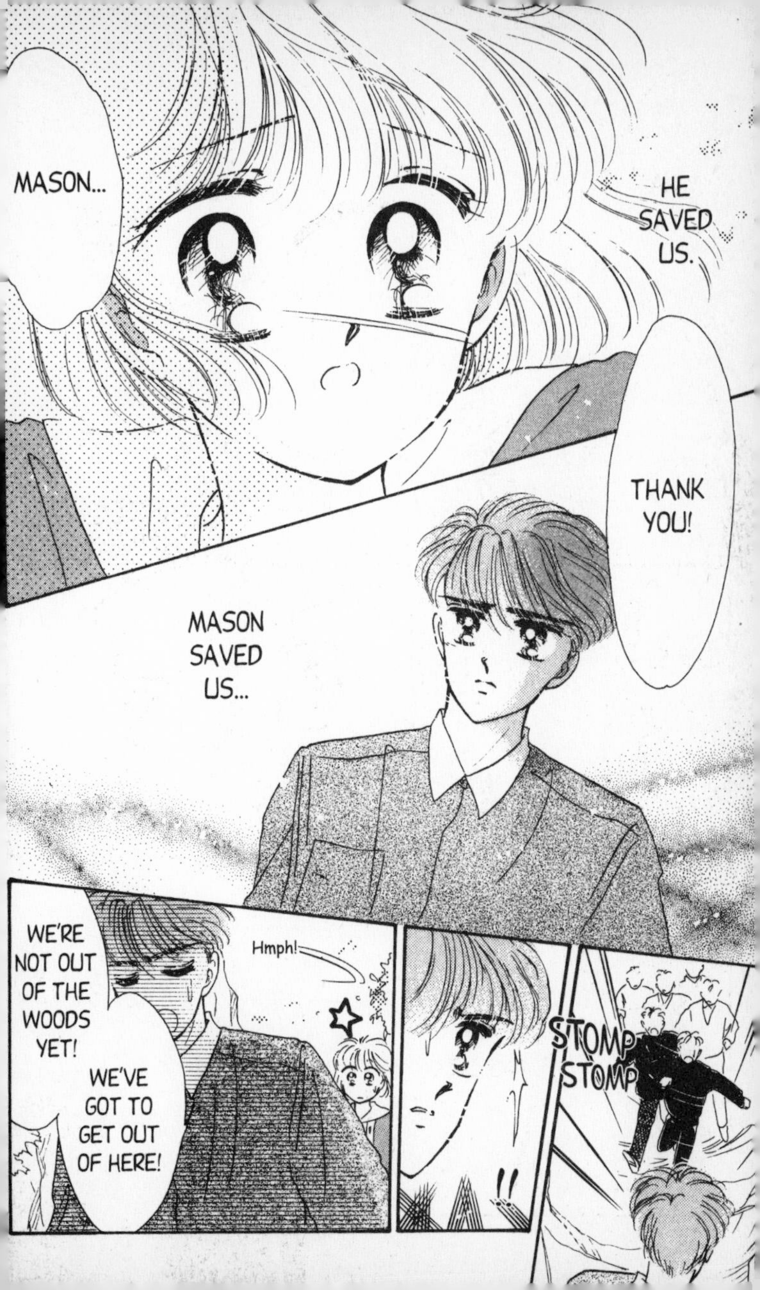
MASON...
HE SAVED US.
THANK YOU!
MASON SAVED US...
WE'RE NOT OUT OF THE WOODS YET!
WE'VE GOT TO GET OUT OF HERE!
Hmph!
!!
STOMP STOMP

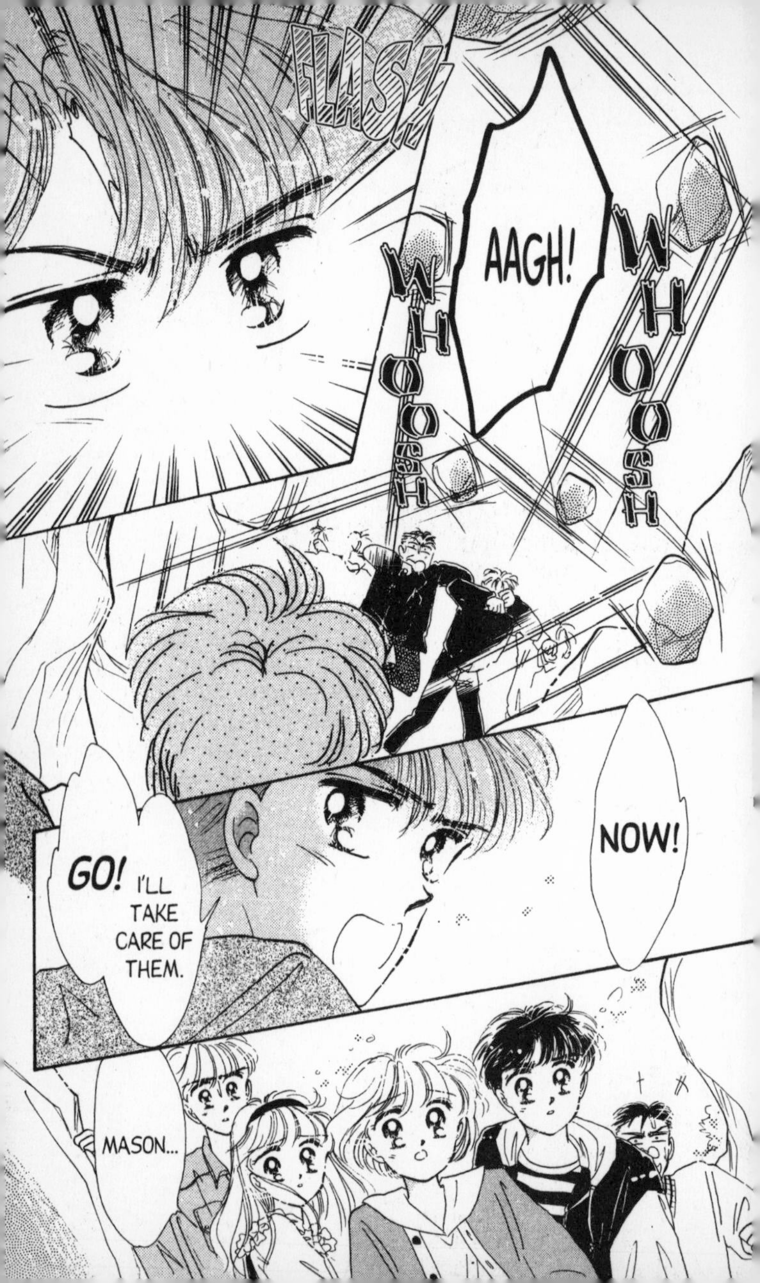
FLASH!
WHOOSH
AAGH!
WHOOSH
GO! I'LL TAKE CARE OF THEM.
NOW!
MASON...

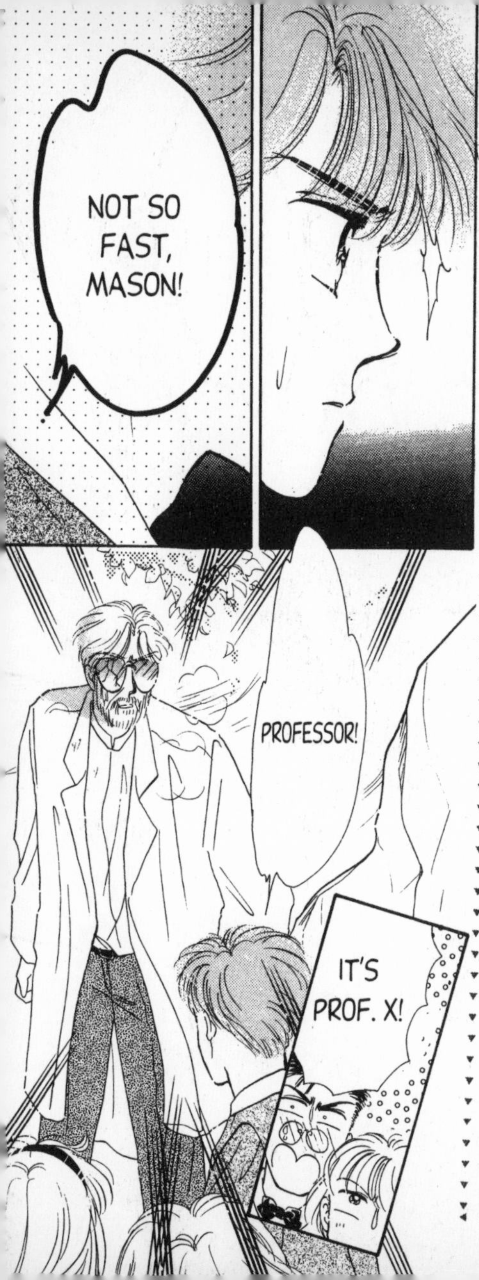
NOT SO FAST, MASON!
PROFESSOR!
IT'S PROF. X!

BONUS

Paris, Part 3.
In Paris, all the shops are really cute! They have hair salons for kids. They're all in red, with toys displayed next to shampoos. The kids sit in these little chairs and they get their hair cut and dried. The candy shop was as pretty as a jeweler's! (The cakes were a little too sweet.) You can often find a lot of nice shops in the smaller streets! And everything tastes so good! I usually don't get too excited, but everything, I mean everything, tastes great! I especially loved eating ice cream!

Because I was so overwhelmed by the sights I wandered into the street and was almost hit by a car... Be careful!

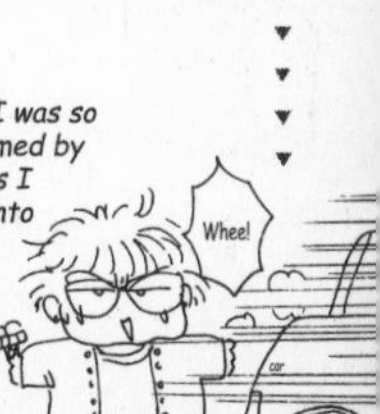
Whee!
car

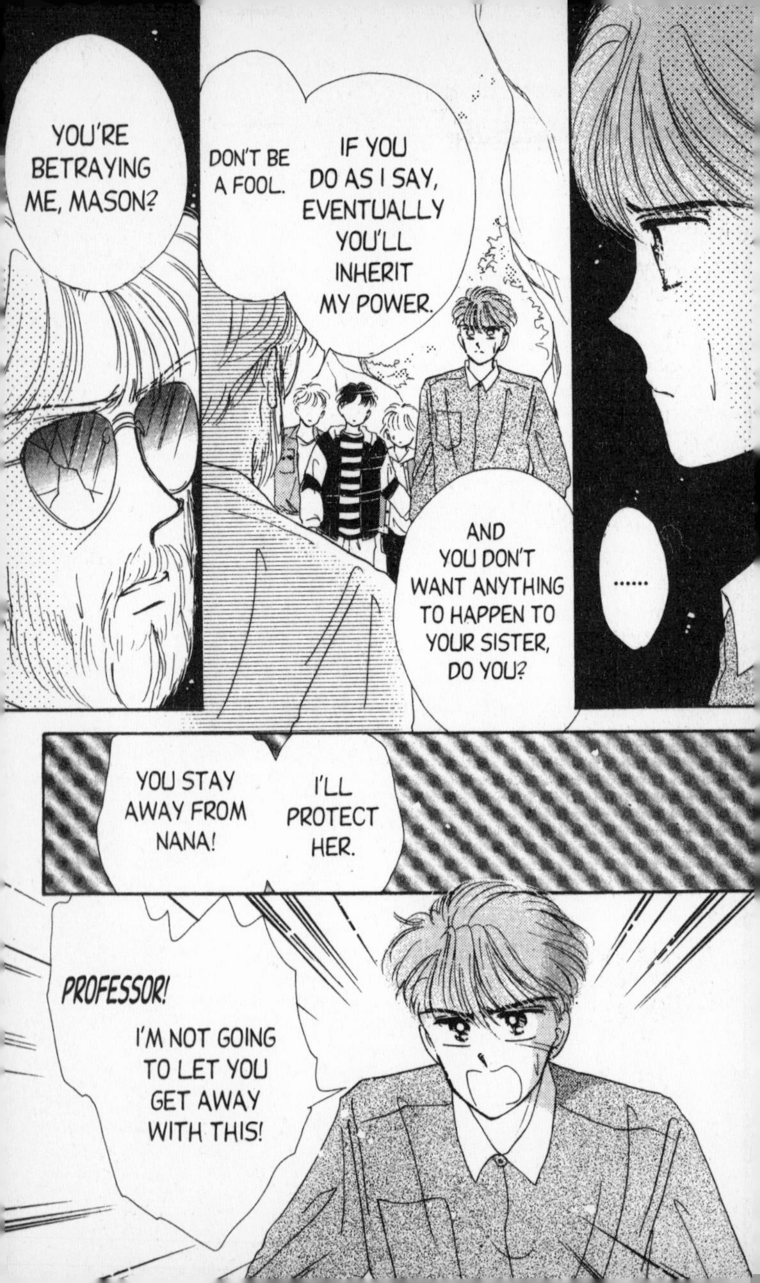
YOU'RE BETRAYING ME, MASON?
DON'T BE A FOOL.
IF YOU DO AS I SAY, EVENTUALLY YOU'LL INHERIT MY POWER.
AND YOU DON'T WANT ANYTHING TO HAPPEN TO YOUR SISTER, DO YOU?
......
YOU STAY AWAY FROM NANA!
I'LL PROTECT HER.
PROFESSOR!
I'M NOT GOING TO LET YOU GET AWAY WITH THIS!

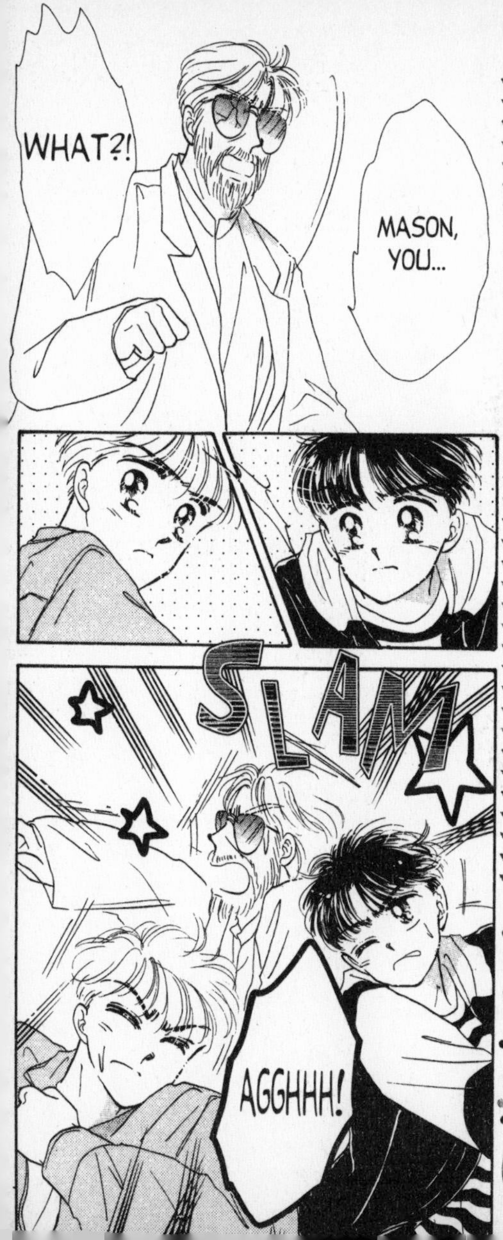
WHAT?!
MASON, YOU...
SLAM
AGGHHH!

BONUS

This trip was really hectic, but I made it home, and I made my deadline, too! (I wanted to relax a little more, but oh well!) We're working hard to prepare the next Miracle Girls story, so thanks for your support! I always wanted to draw castles! And I promise to develop Mika and Chris's relationship, too. See ya next issue!

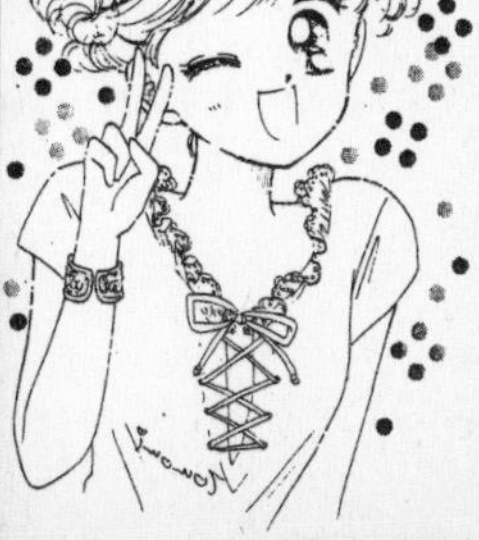

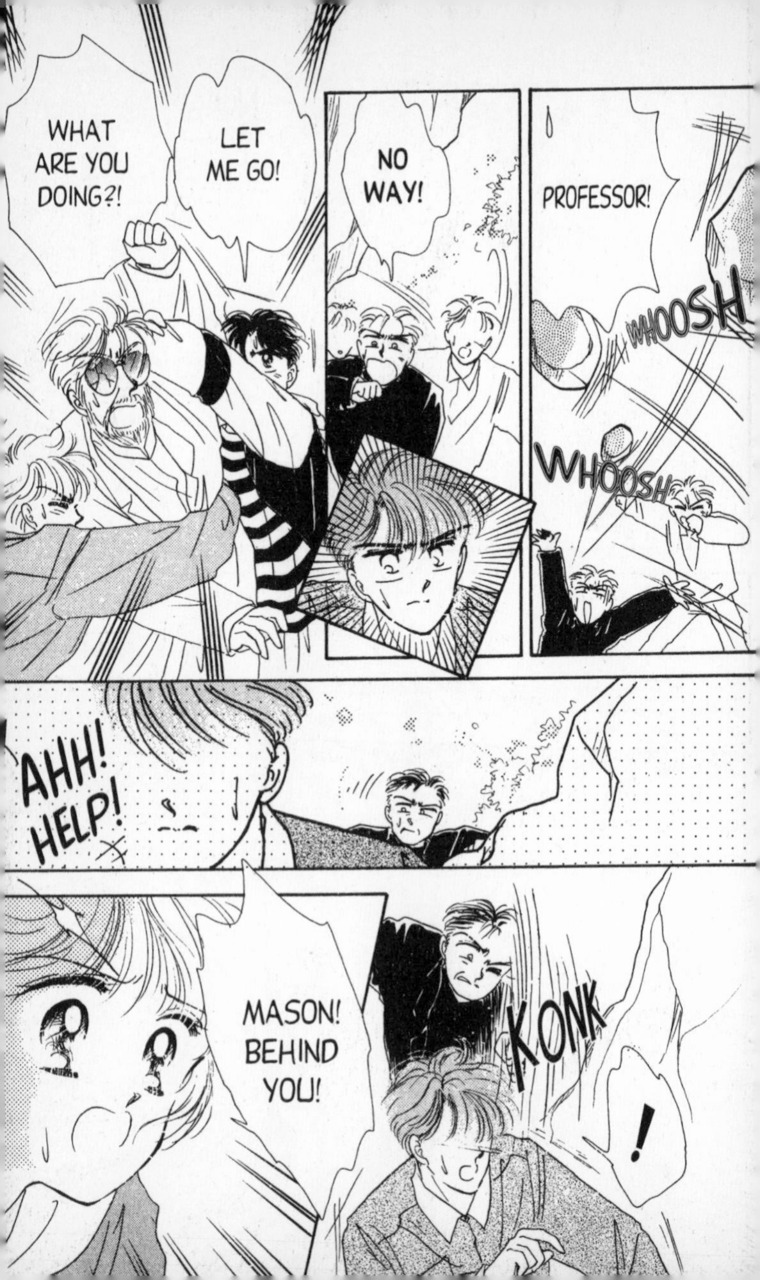
WHAT ARE YOU DOING?!
LET ME GO!
NO WAY!
PROFESSOR!
WHOOSH
WHOOSH
AHH! HELP!
MASON! BEHIND YOU!
KONK
!

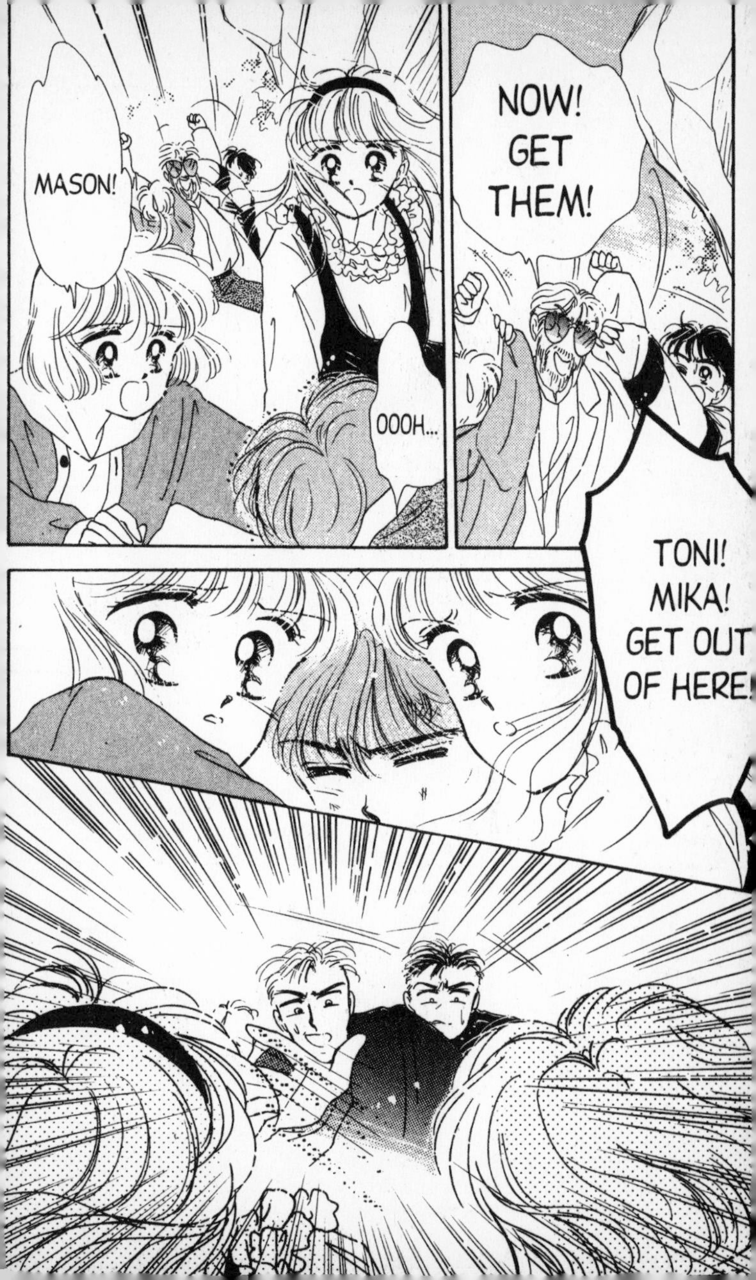
MASON!
OOOH...
NOW! GET THEM!
TONI! MIKA! GET OUT OF HERE!

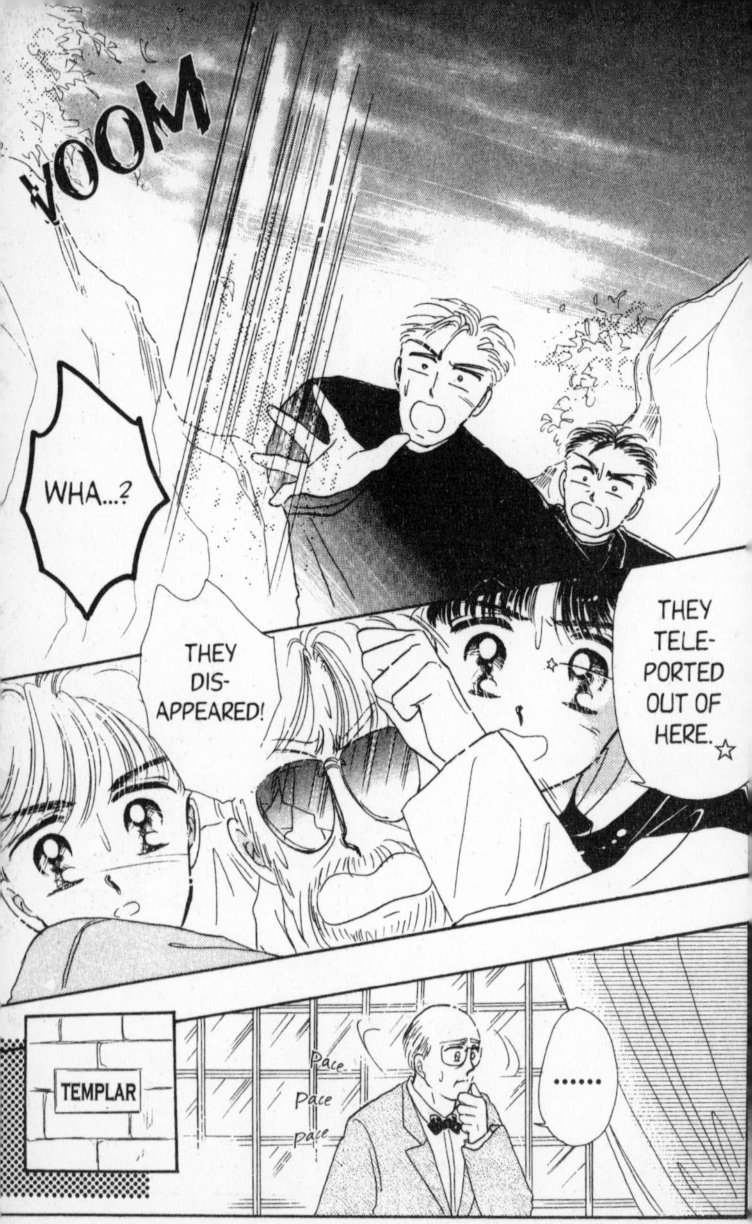
VOOM
WHA...?
THEY DIS-APPEARED!
THEY TELE-PORTED OUT OF HERE.☆
TEMPLAR
Pace
Pace
pace
......

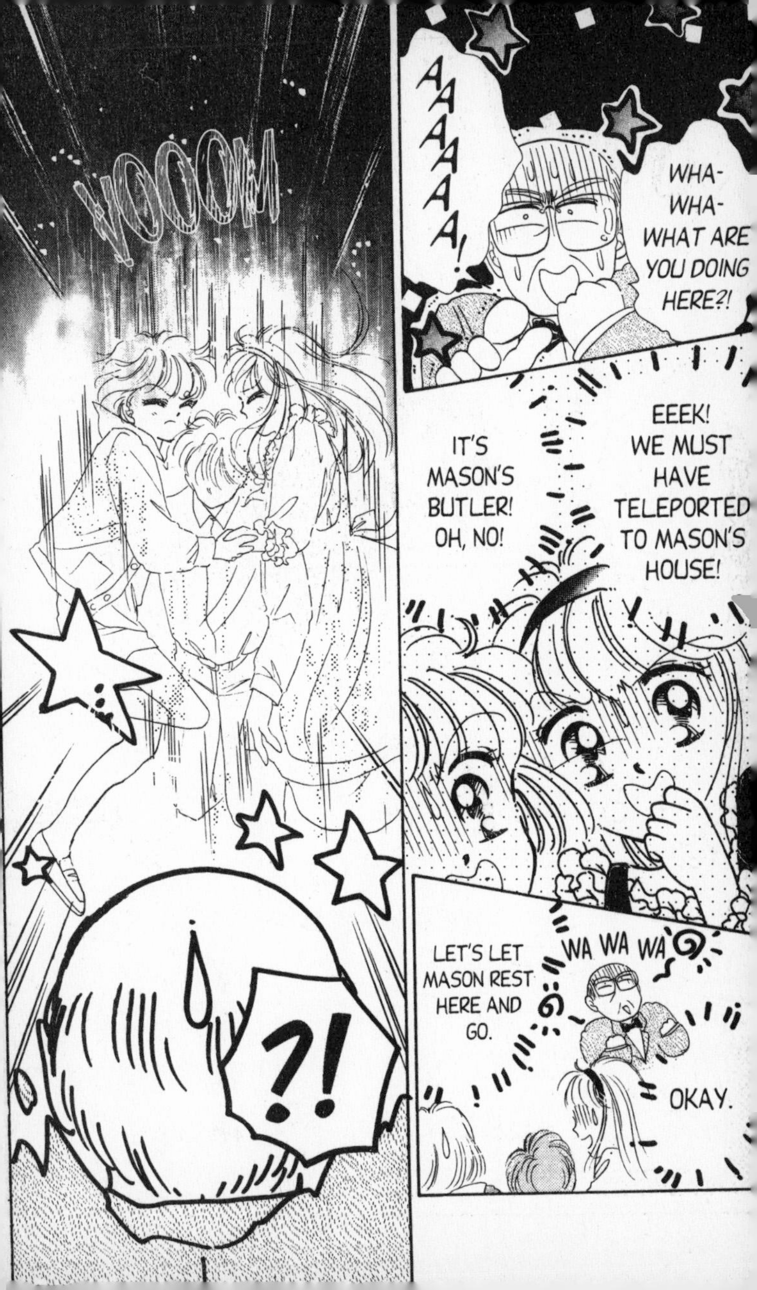
?!
AAAAAA!
WHA-
WHA-
WHAT ARE
YOU DOING
HERE?!
IT'S
MASON'S
BUTLER!
OH, NO!
EEEK!
WE MUST
HAVE
TELEPORTED
TO MASON'S
HOUSE!
LET'S LET
MASON REST
HERE AND
GO.
WA WA WA
OKAY.

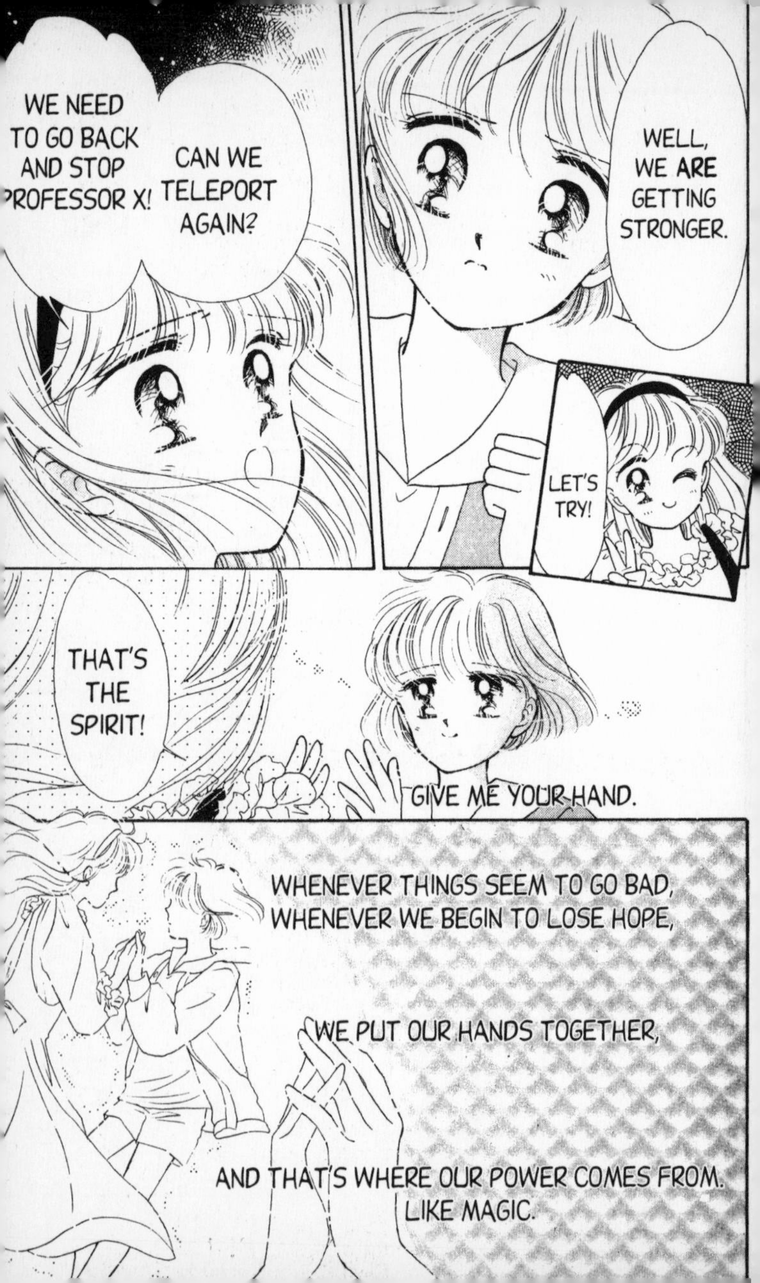
WE NEED TO GO BACK AND STOP PROFESSOR X!
CAN WE TELEPORT AGAIN?
WELL, WE ARE GETTING STRONGER.
LET'S TRY!
THAT'S THE SPIRIT!
GIVE ME YOUR HAND.
WHENEVER THINGS SEEM TO GO BAD, WHENEVER WE BEGIN TO LOSE HOPE,
WE PUT OUR HANDS TOGETHER,
AND THAT'S WHERE OUR POWER COMES FROM. LIKE MAGIC.

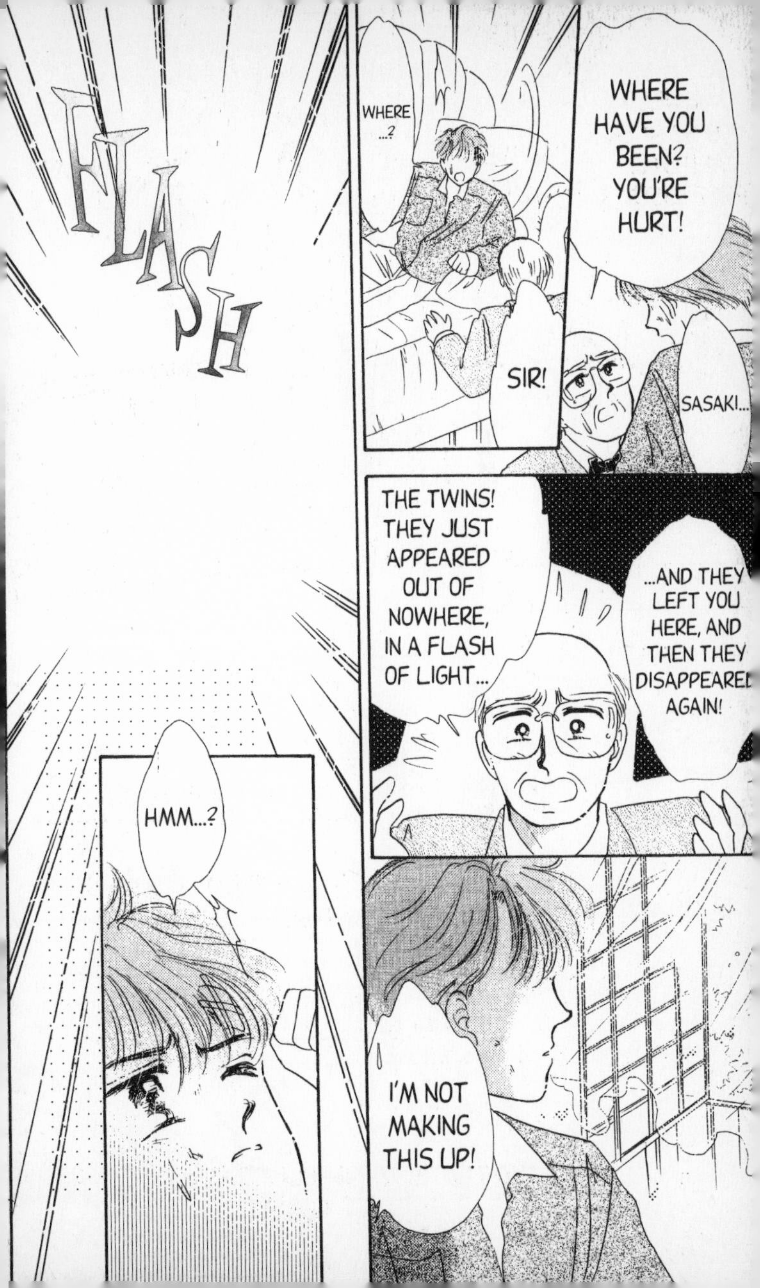
FLASH
HMM...?
WHERE...?
WHERE HAVE YOU BEEN? YOU'RE HURT!
SIR!
SASAKI...
THE TWINS! THEY JUST APPEARED OUT OF NOWHERE, IN A FLASH OF LIGHT...
...AND THEY LEFT YOU HERE, AND THEN THEY DISAPPEARED AGAIN!
I'M NOT MAKING THIS UP!

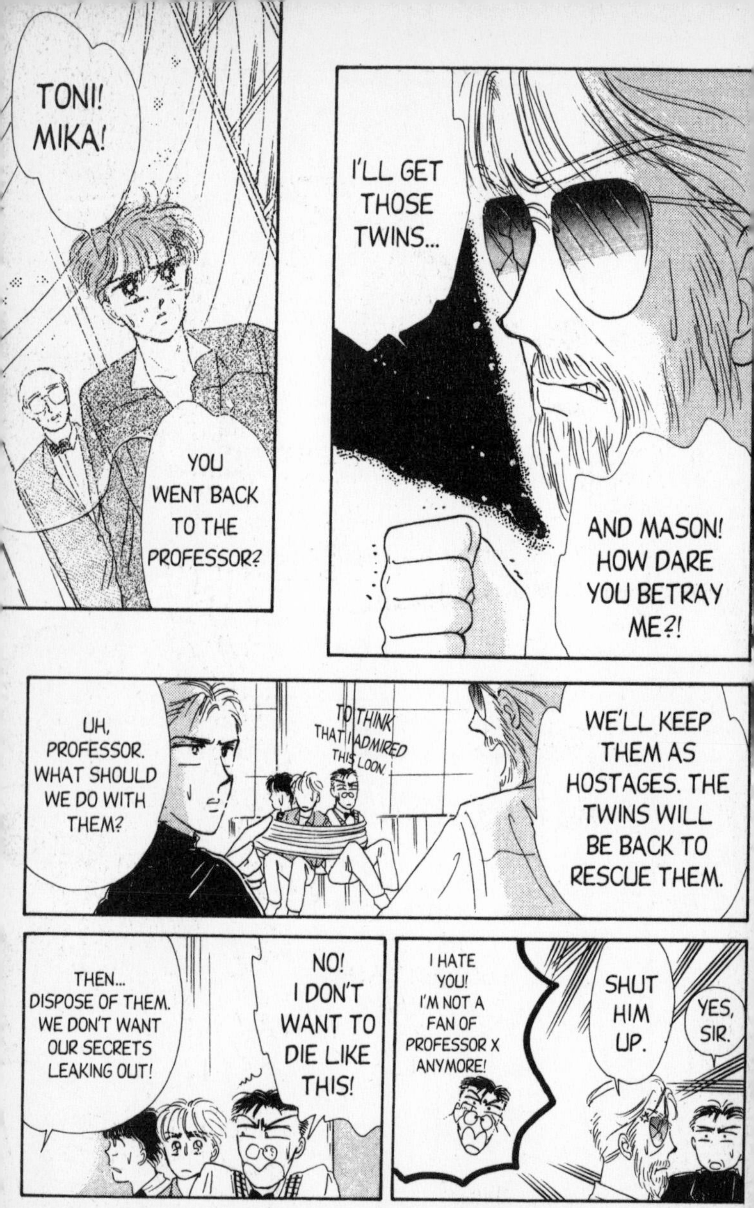
TONI! MIKA!
YOU WENT BACK TO THE PROFESSOR?
I'LL GET THOSE TWINS...
AND MASON! HOW DARE YOU BETRAY ME?!
UH, PROFESSOR. WHAT SHOULD WE DO WITH THEM?
TO THINK THAT I ADMIRED THIS LOON.
WE'LL KEEP THEM AS HOSTAGES. THE TWINS WILL BE BACK TO RESCUE THEM.
THEN... DISPOSE OF THEM. WE DON'T WANT OUR SECRETS LEAKING OUT!
NO! I DON'T WANT TO DIE LIKE THIS!
I HATE YOU! I'M NOT A FAN OF PROFESSOR X ANYMORE!
SHUT HIM UP.
YES, SIR.

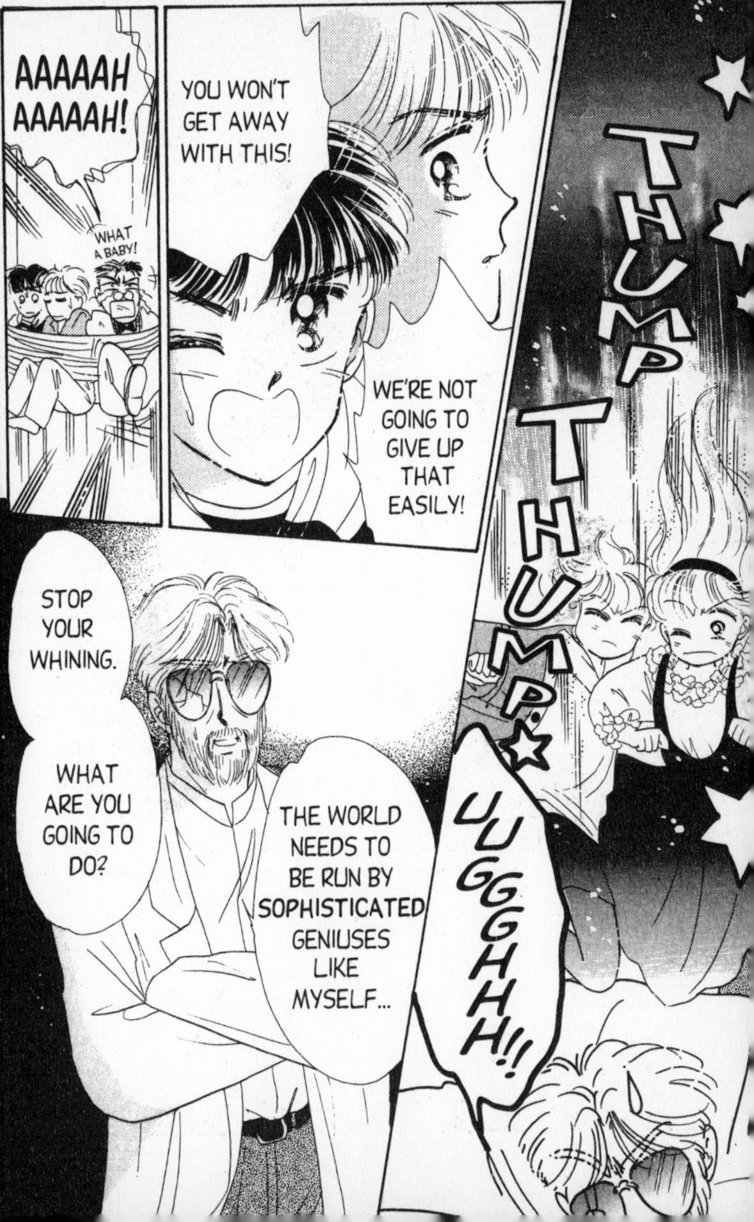
AAAAAH AAAAAH!
WHAT A BABY!
YOU WON'T GET AWAY WITH THIS!
WE'RE NOT GOING TO GIVE UP THAT EASILY!
STOP YOUR WHINING.
WHAT ARE YOU GOING TO DO?
THE WORLD NEEDS TO BE RUN BY SOPHISTICATED GENIUSES LIKE MYSELF...
THUMP
THUMP
THUMP
THUMP.
UUGGGHHH!!

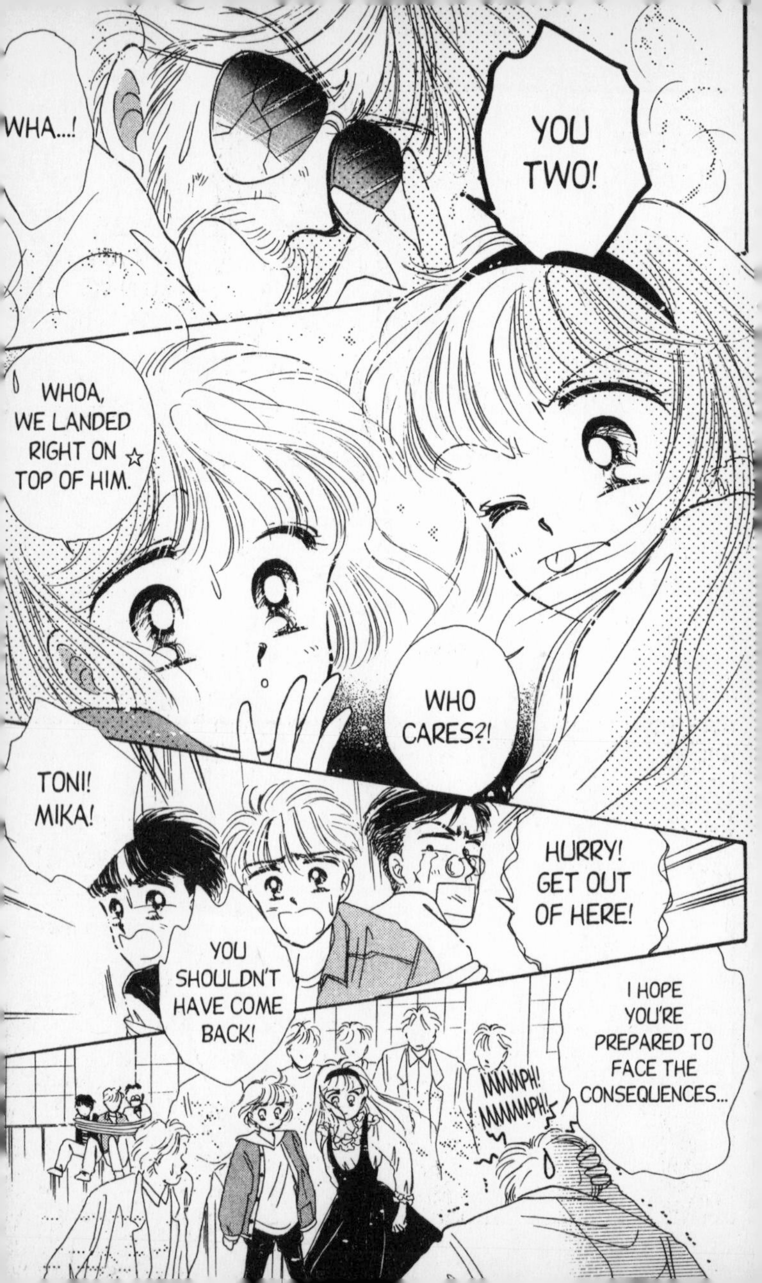
WHA...!
YOU TWO!
WHOA, WE LANDED RIGHT ON TOP OF HIM. ☆
WHO CARES?!
TONI! MIKA!
HURRY! GET OUT OF HERE!
YOU SHOULDN'T HAVE COME BACK!
MMMPH! MMMMPH!
I HOPE YOU'RE PREPARED TO FACE THE CONSEQUENCES...

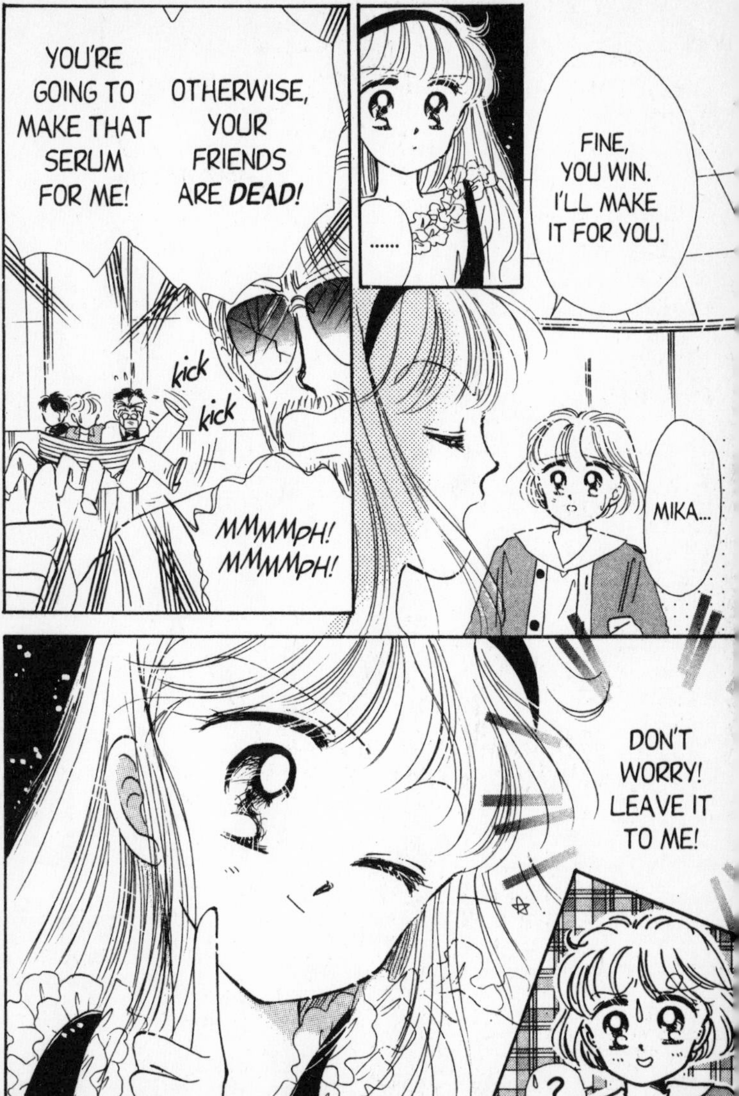

YOU'RE GOING TO MAKE THAT SERUM FOR ME!
OTHERWISE, YOUR FRIENDS ARE DEAD!
kick
kick
MMMMPH! MMMMPH!
......
FINE, YOU WIN. I'LL MAKE IT FOR YOU.
MIKA...
DON'T WORRY! LEAVE IT TO ME!
?

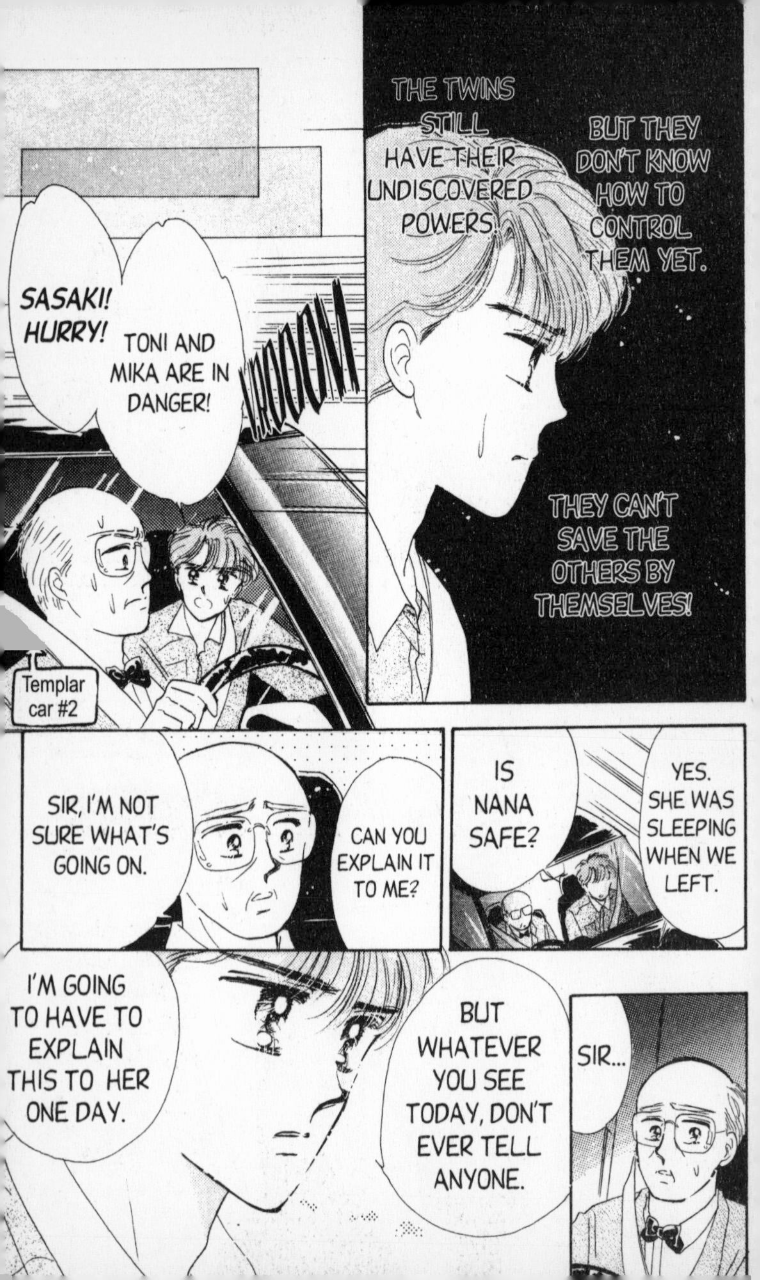
SASAKI! HURRY!
TONI AND MIKA ARE IN DANGER!
VROOOM
Templar car #2
THE TWINS STILL HAVE THEIR UNDISCOVERED POWERS.
BUT THEY DON'T KNOW HOW TO CONTROL THEM YET.
THEY CAN'T SAVE THE OTHERS BY THEMSELVES!
SIR, I'M NOT SURE WHAT'S GOING ON.
CAN YOU EXPLAIN IT TO ME?
IS NANA SAFE?
YES. SHE WAS SLEEPING WHEN WE LEFT.
I'M GOING TO HAVE TO EXPLAIN THIS TO HER ONE DAY.
BUT WHATEVER YOU SEE TODAY, DON'T EVER TELL ANYONE.
SIR...

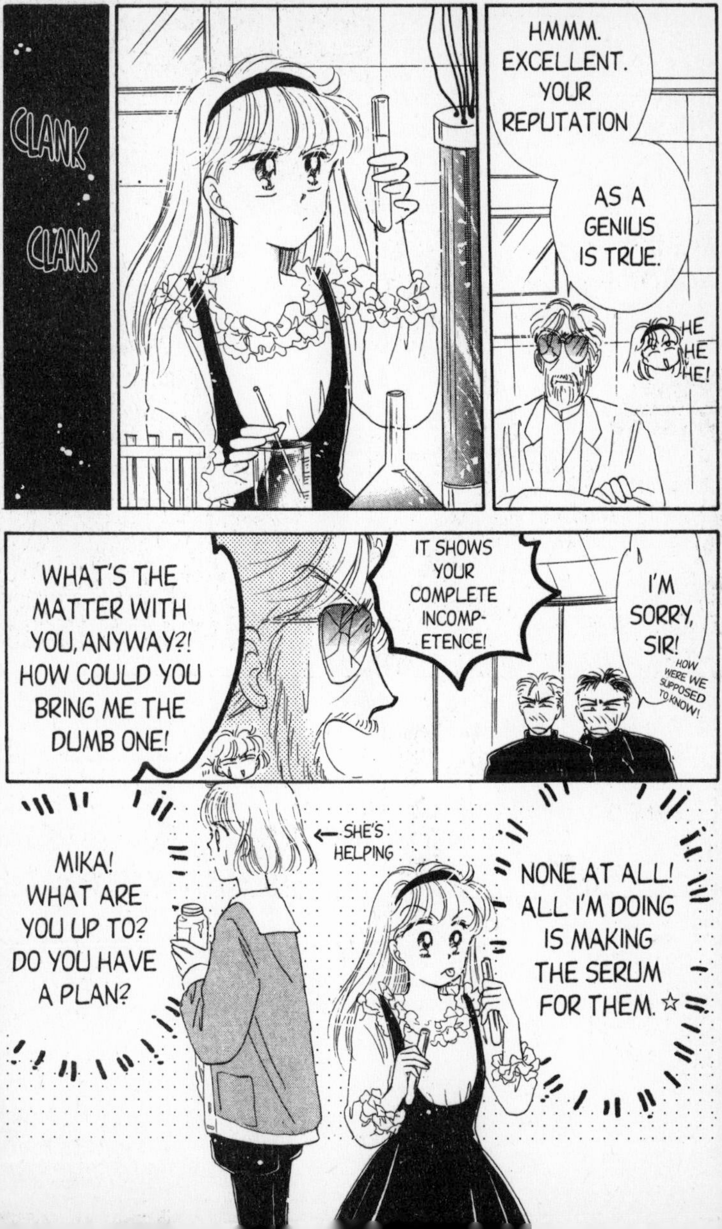
CLANK
CLANK
HMMM. EXCELLENT. YOUR REPUTATION
AS A GENIUS IS TRUE.
HE HE HE!
WHAT'S THE MATTER WITH YOU, ANYWAY?! HOW COULD YOU BRING ME THE DUMB ONE!
IT SHOWS YOUR COMPLETE INCOMP-ETENCE!
I'M SORRY, SIR!
HOW WERE WE SUPPOSED TO KNOW!
MIKA! WHAT ARE YOU UP TO? DO YOU HAVE A PLAN?
←SHE'S HELPING
NONE AT ALL! ALL I'M DOING IS MAKING THE SERUM FOR THEM. ☆

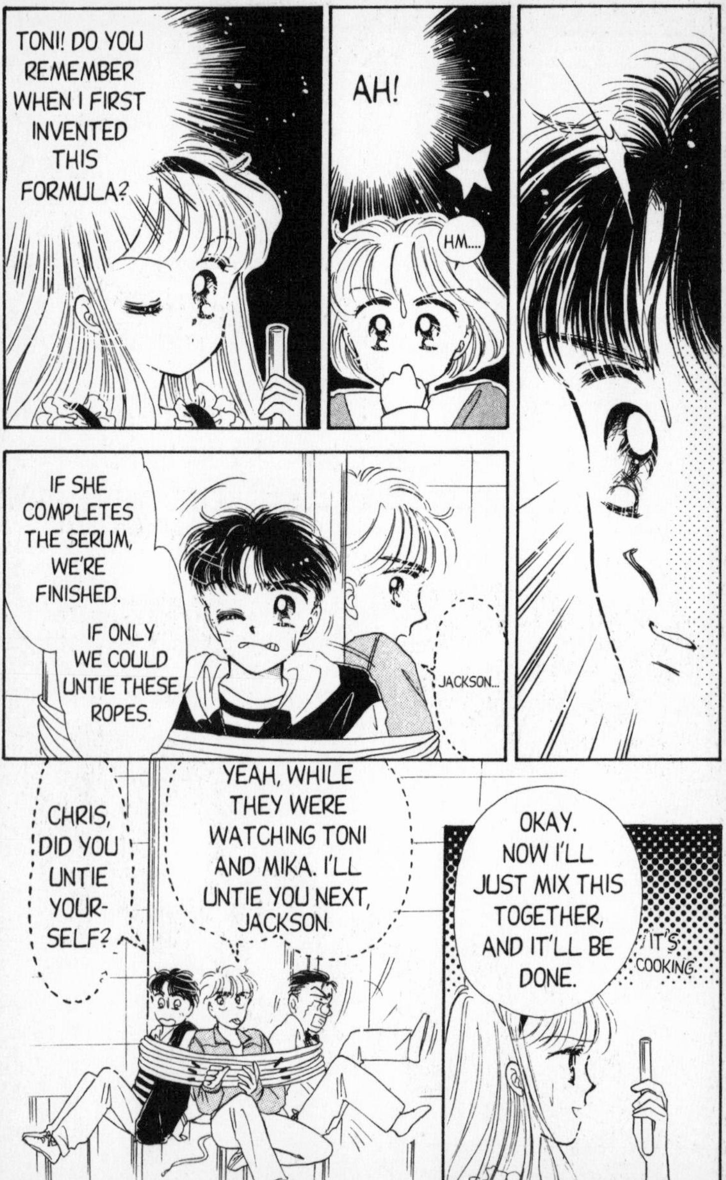
TONI! DO YOU REMEMBER WHEN I FIRST INVENTED THIS FORMULA?
AH!
HM....
IF SHE COMPLETES THE SERUM, WE'RE FINISHED.
IF ONLY WE COULD UNTIE THESE ROPES.
JACKSON...
CHRIS, DID YOU UNTIE YOUR-SELF?
YEAH, WHILE THEY WERE WATCHING TONI AND MIKA. I'LL UNTIE YOU NEXT, JACKSON.
OKAY. NOW I'LL JUST MIX THIS TOGETHER, AND IT'LL BE DONE.
IT'S COOKING.

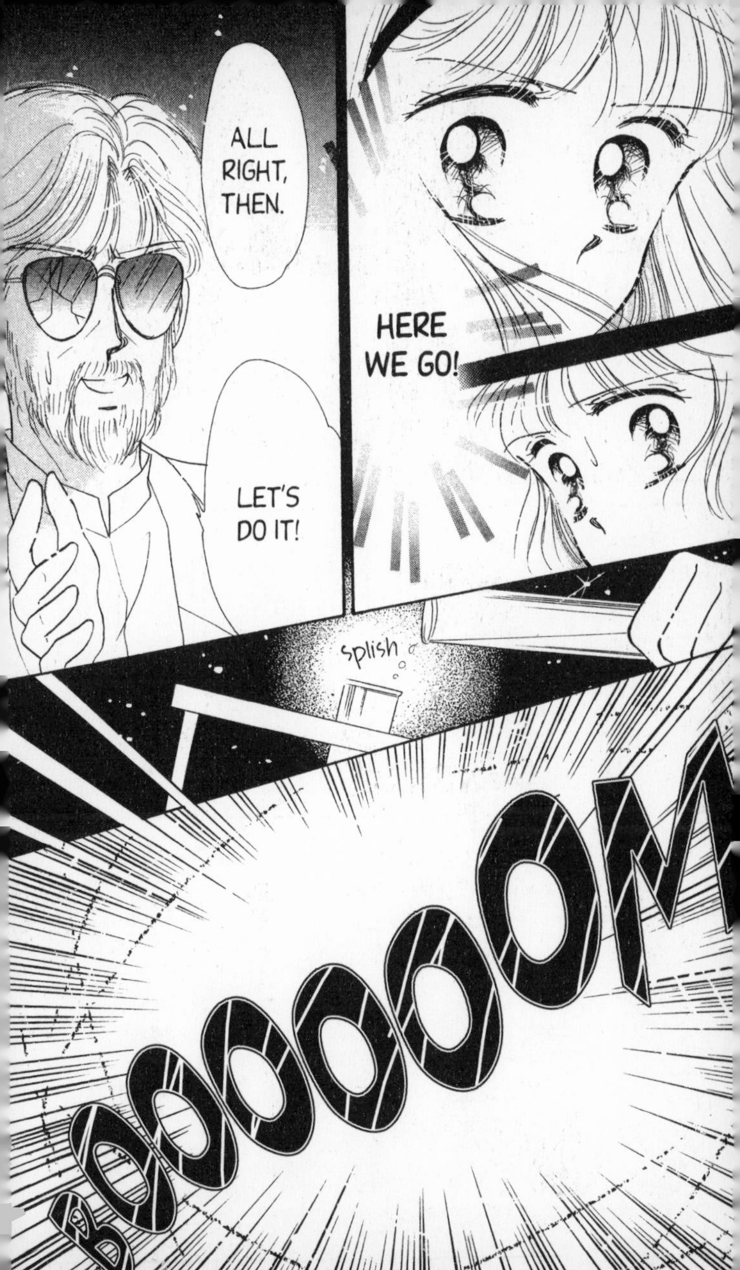
ALL RIGHT, THEN.
LET'S DO IT!
HERE WE GO!
splish
BOOOOOOM

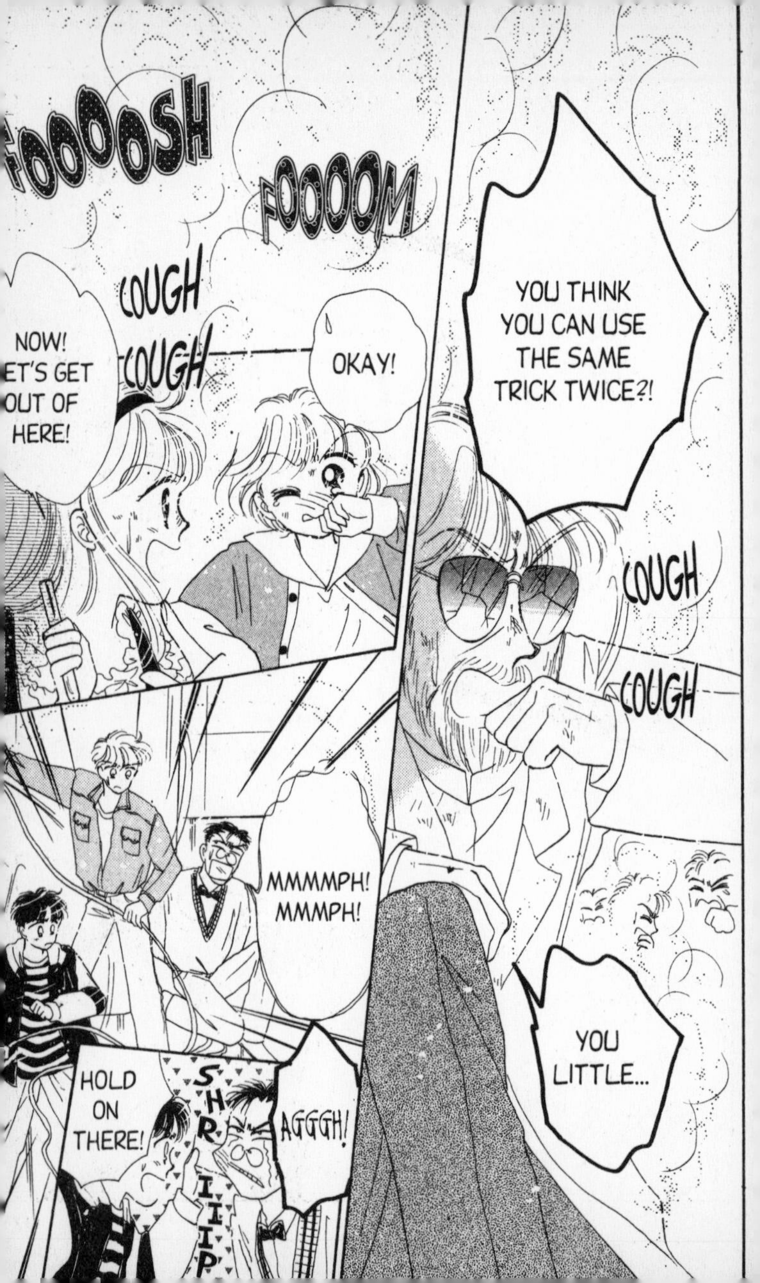
FOOOOSH
FOOOOM
COUGH
COUGH
NOW! ET'S GET OUT OF HERE!
OKAY!
MMMMPH! MMMPH!
HOLD ON THERE!
SHRIIIP
AGGGH!
YOU THINK YOU CAN USE THE SAME TRICK TWICE?!
COUGH
COUGH
YOU LITTLE...

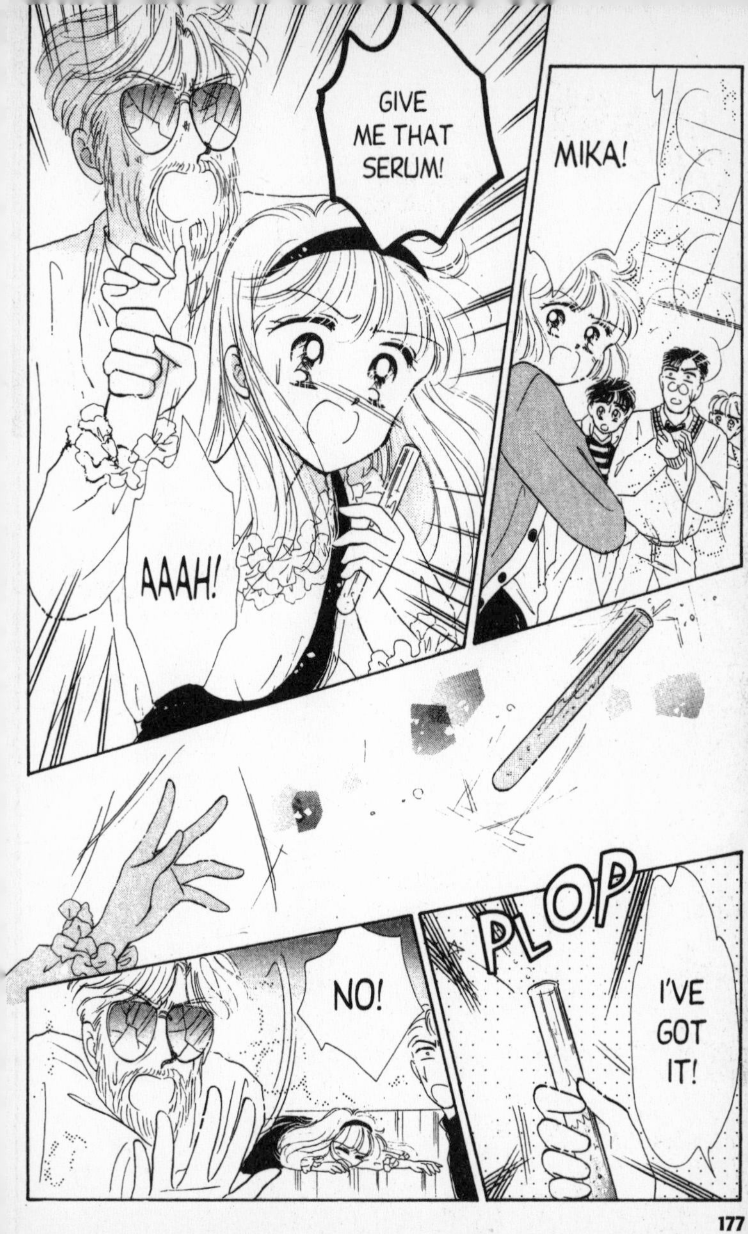
GIVE ME THAT SERUM!
AAAH!
MIKA!
NO!
PLOP
I'VE GOT IT!

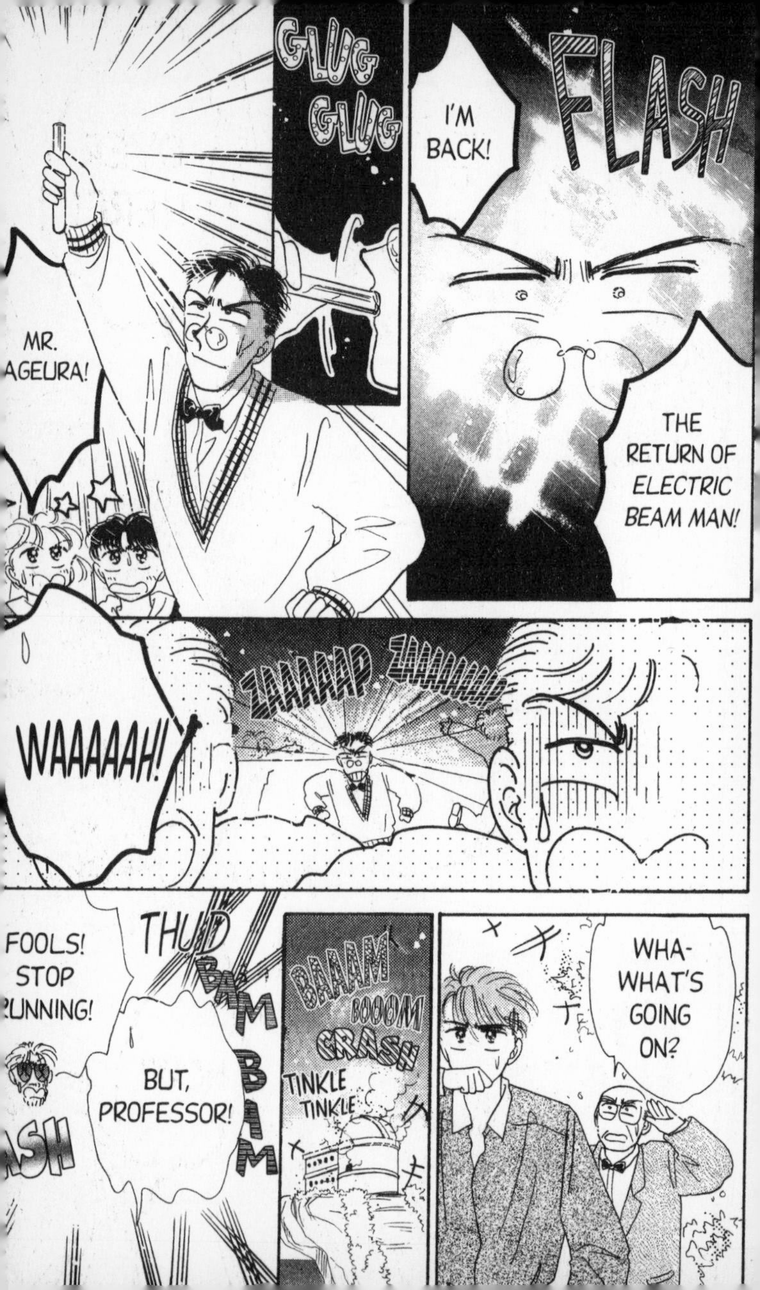

MR.
AGEURA!
GLUG
GLUG
I'M
BACK!
FLASH
THE
RETURN OF
ELECTRIC
BEAM MAN!
WAAAAAH!
ZAAAAAP
FOOLS!
STOP
RUNNING!
THUD
BUT,
PROFESSOR!
BAM
BAM
BAM
BAM
BAAAM
BOOOM
CRASH
TINKLE
TINKLE
WHA-
WHAT'S
GOING
ON?

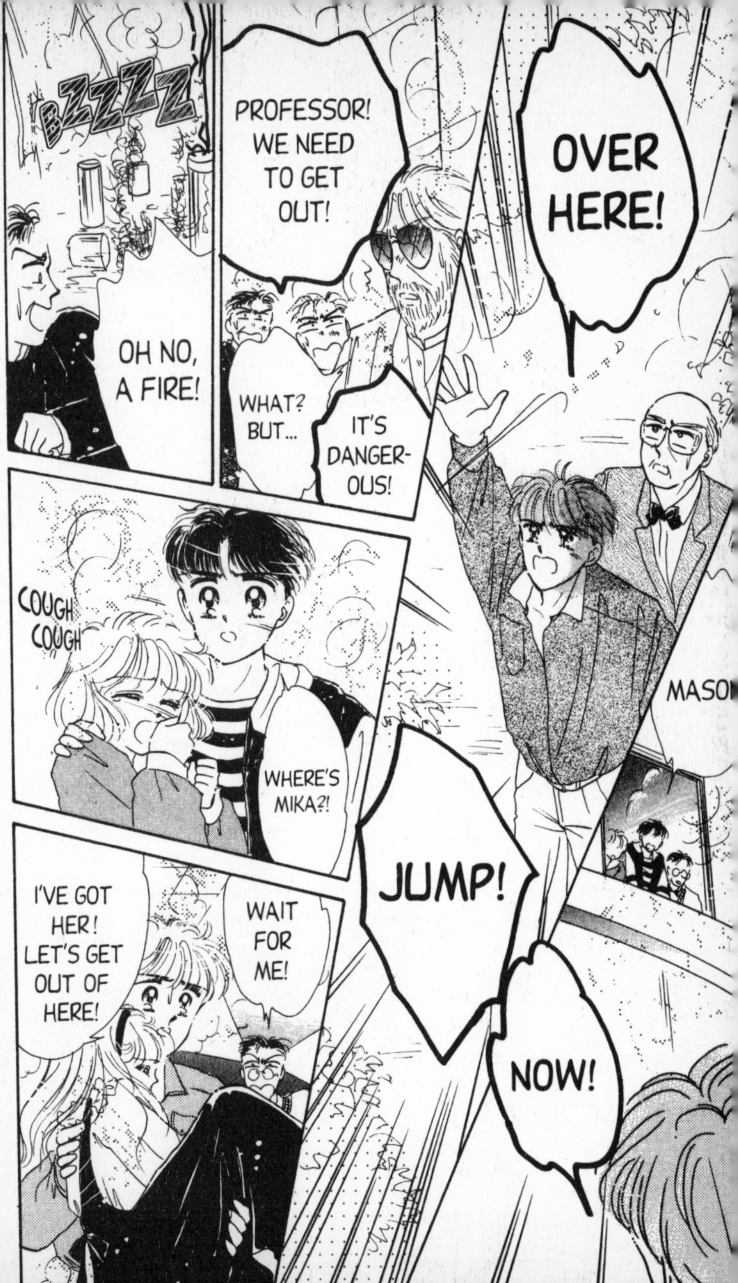
BZZZZ
OH NO, A FIRE!
PROFESSOR! WE NEED TO GET OUT!
WHAT? BUT...
IT'S DANGER-OUS!
COUGH COUGH
WHERE'S MIKA?!
I'VE GOT HER! LET'S GET OUT OF HERE!
WAIT FOR ME!
OVER HERE!
MASO
JUMP!
NOW!

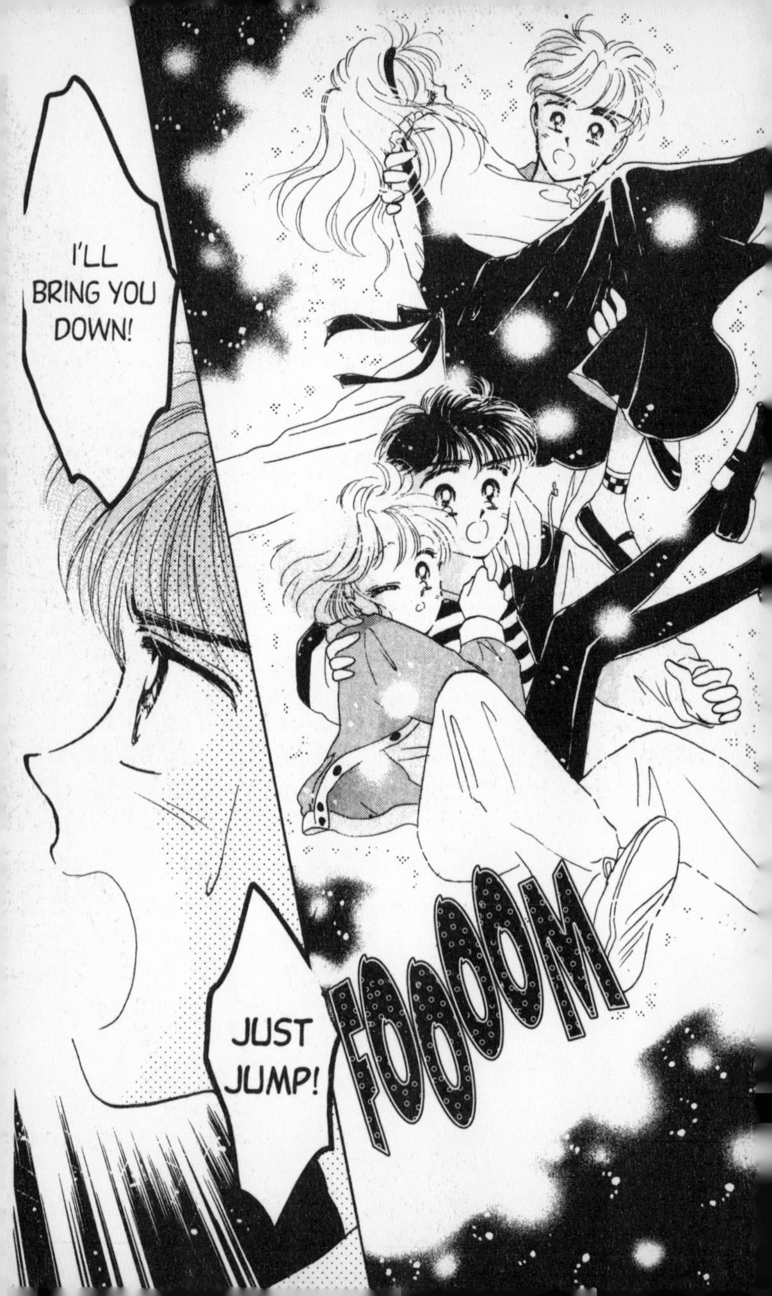
I'LL BRING YOU DOWN!
JUST JUMP!
FOOOOM

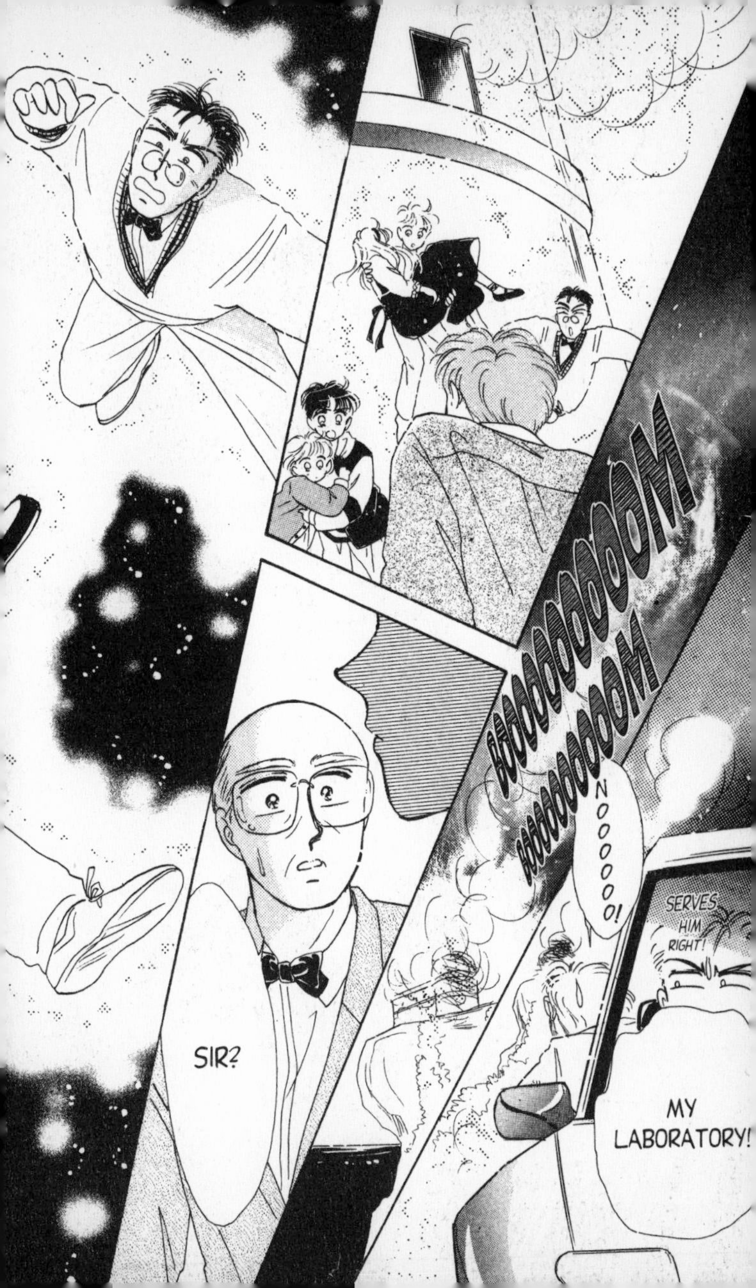
SIR?
BOOOOOOOOOOM
BOOOOOOOOOOM
NOOOOOO!
SERVES HIM RIGHT!
MY LABORATORY!

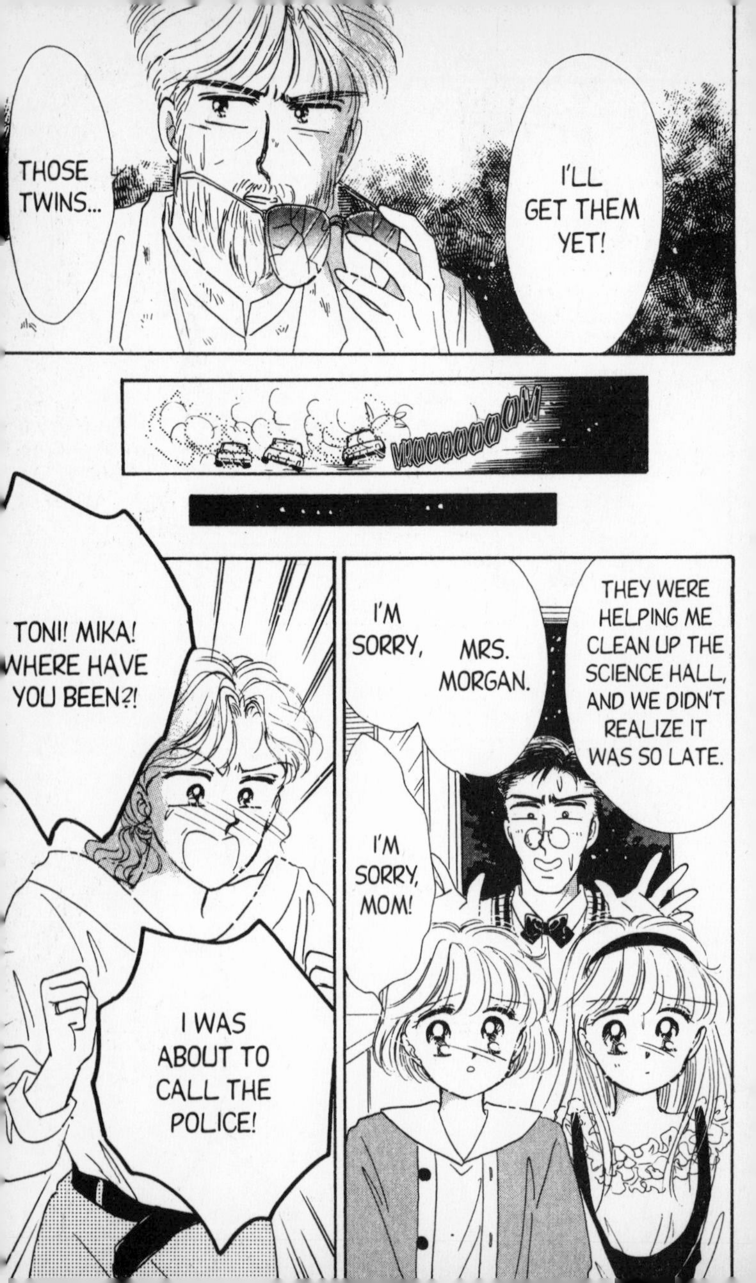
THOSE TWINS...
I'LL GET THEM YET!
VROOOOOOOOOM
. . . . . .
TONI! MIKA! WHERE HAVE YOU BEEN?!
I WAS ABOUT TO CALL THE POLICE!
I'M SORRY,
MRS. MORGAN.
THEY WERE HELPING ME CLEAN UP THE SCIENCE HALL, AND WE DIDN'T REALIZE IT WAS SO LATE.
I'M SORRY, MOM!

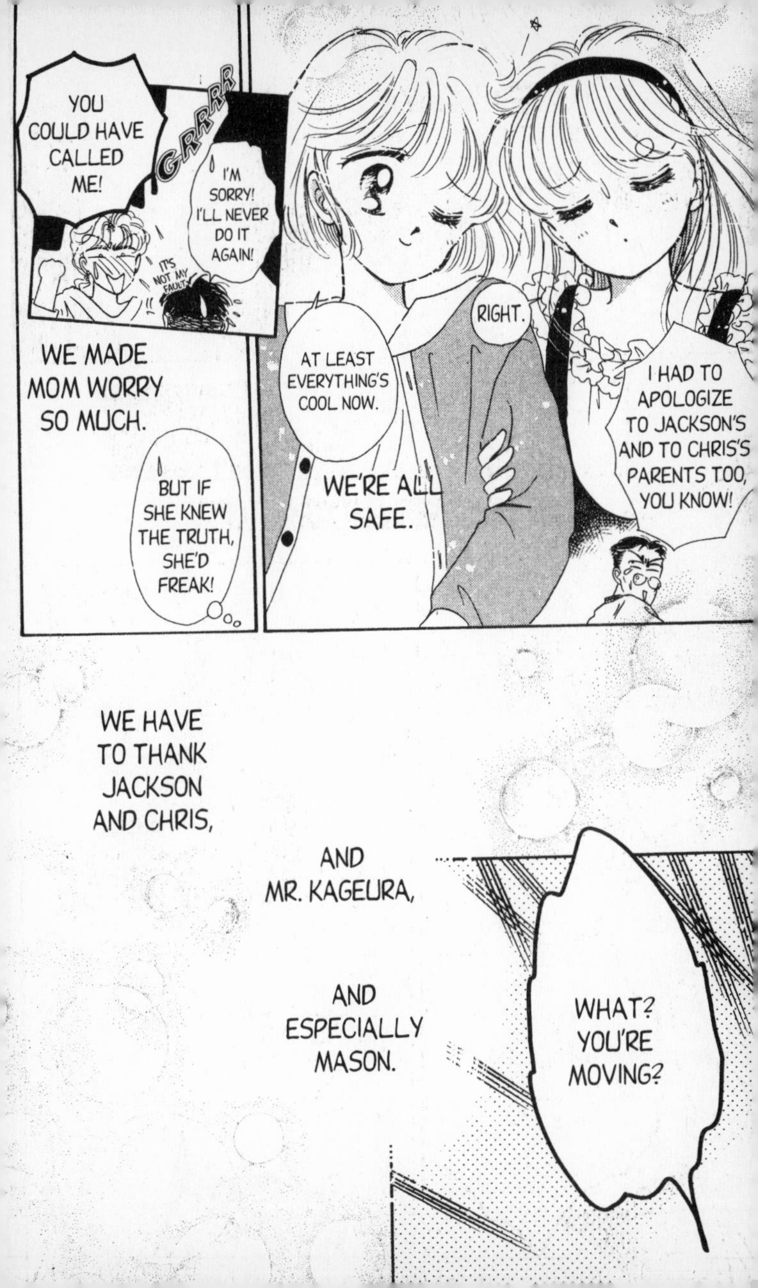
YOU COULD HAVE CALLED ME!
GRRRRR
I'M SORRY! I'LL NEVER DO IT AGAIN!
IT'S NOT MY FAULT
WE MADE MOM WORRY SO MUCH.
BUT IF SHE KNEW THE TRUTH, SHE'D FREAK!
AT LEAST EVERYTHING'S COOL NOW.
RIGHT.
WE'RE ALL SAFE.
I HAD TO APOLOGIZE TO JACKSON'S AND TO CHRIS'S PARENTS TOO, YOU KNOW!
WE HAVE TO THANK JACKSON AND CHRIS,
AND MR. KAGEURA,
AND ESPECIALLY MASON.
WHAT? YOU'RE MOVING?

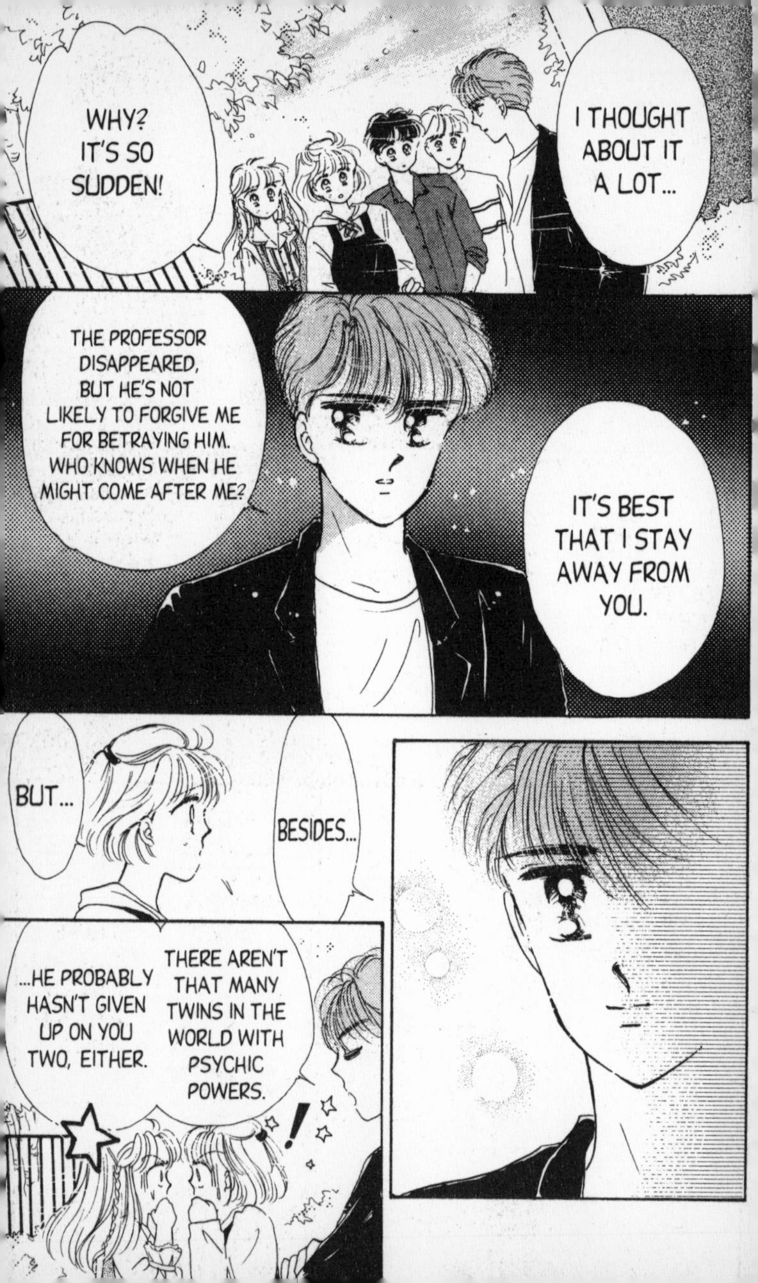
WHY? IT'S SO SUDDEN!
I THOUGHT ABOUT IT A LOT...
THE PROFESSOR DISAPPEARED, BUT HE'S NOT LIKELY TO FORGIVE ME FOR BETRAYING HIM. WHO KNOWS WHEN HE MIGHT COME AFTER ME?
IT'S BEST THAT I STAY AWAY FROM YOU.
BUT...
BESIDES...
...HE PROBABLY HASN'T GIVEN UP ON YOU TWO, EITHER.
THERE AREN'T THAT MANY TWINS IN THE WORLD WITH PSYCHIC POWERS.

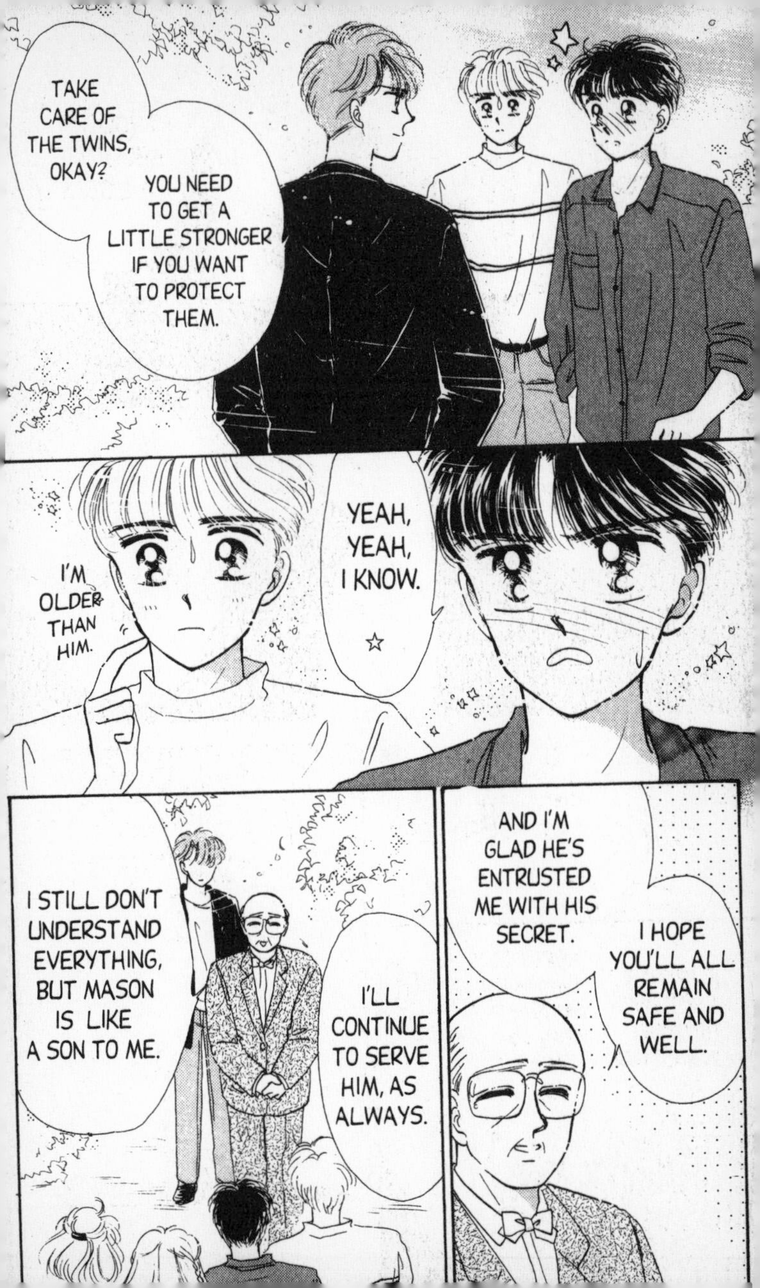
TAKE CARE OF THE TWINS, OKAY?
YOU NEED TO GET A LITTLE STRONGER IF YOU WANT TO PROTECT THEM.
I'M OLDER THAN HIM.
YEAH, YEAH, I KNOW. ☆
I STILL DON'T UNDERSTAND EVERYTHING, BUT MASON IS LIKE A SON TO ME.
I'LL CONTINUE TO SERVE HIM, AS ALWAYS.
AND I'M GLAD HE'S ENTRUSTED ME WITH HIS SECRET.
I HOPE YOU'LL ALL REMAIN SAFE AND WELL.

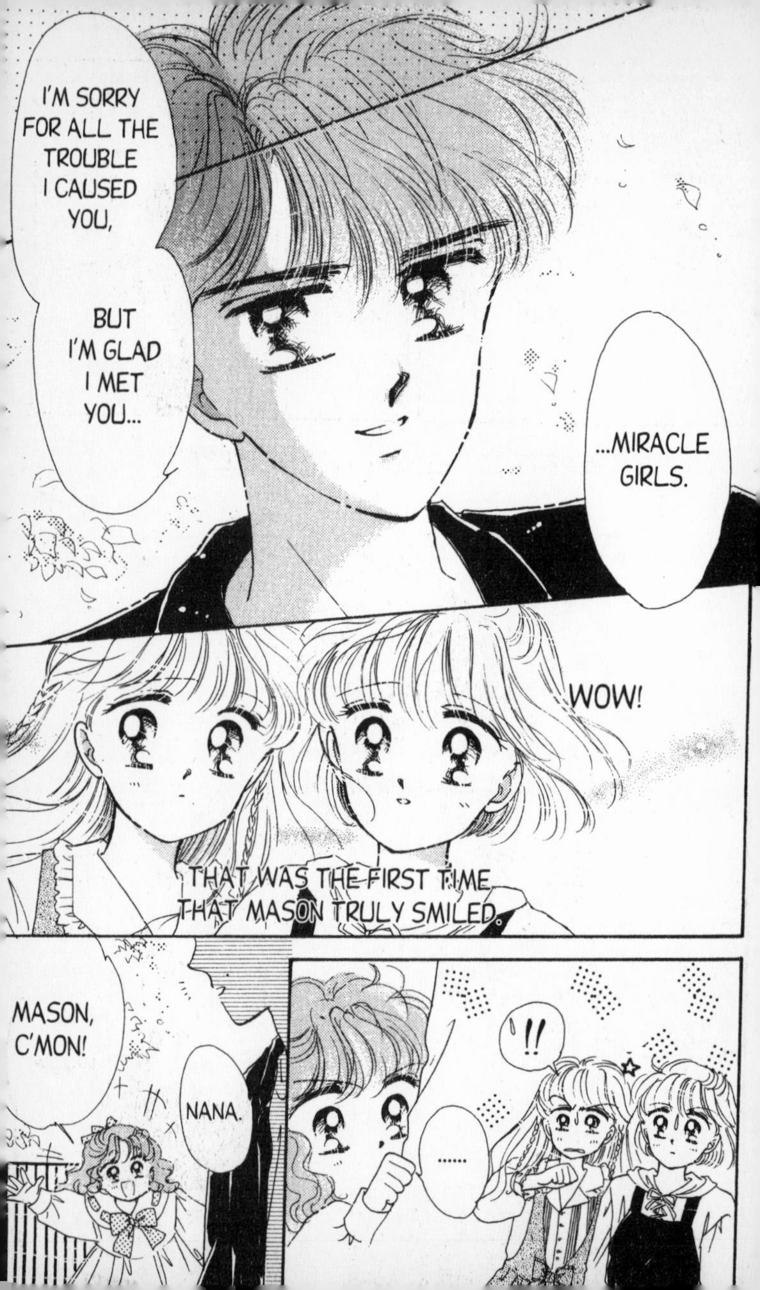
I'M SORRY FOR ALL THE TROUBLE I CAUSED YOU,
BUT I'M GLAD I MET YOU...
...MIRACLE GIRLS.
WOW!
THAT WAS THE FIRST TIME THAT MASON TRULY SMILED.
MASON, C'MON!
NANA.
......
!!

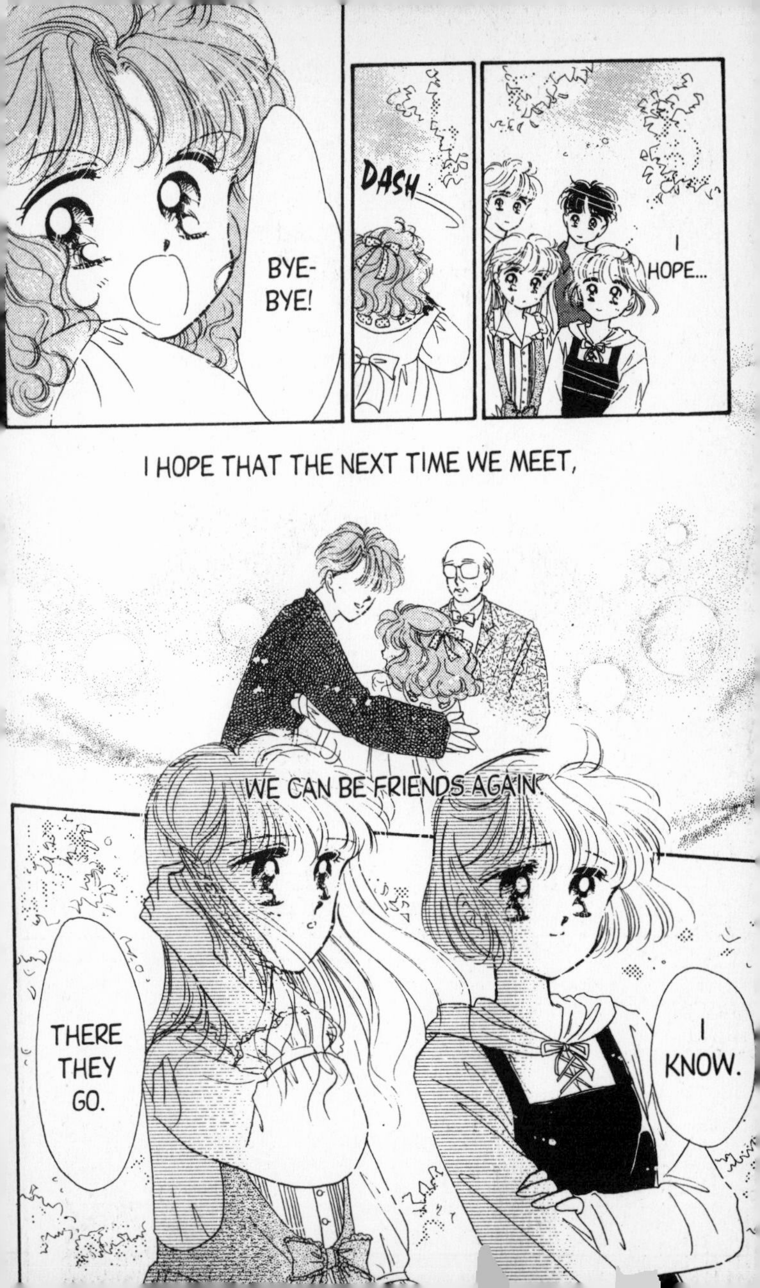
BYE-BYE!
DASH
I HOPE...
I HOPE THAT THE NEXT TIME WE MEET,
WE CAN BE FRIENDS AGAIN.
THERE THEY GO.
I KNOW.

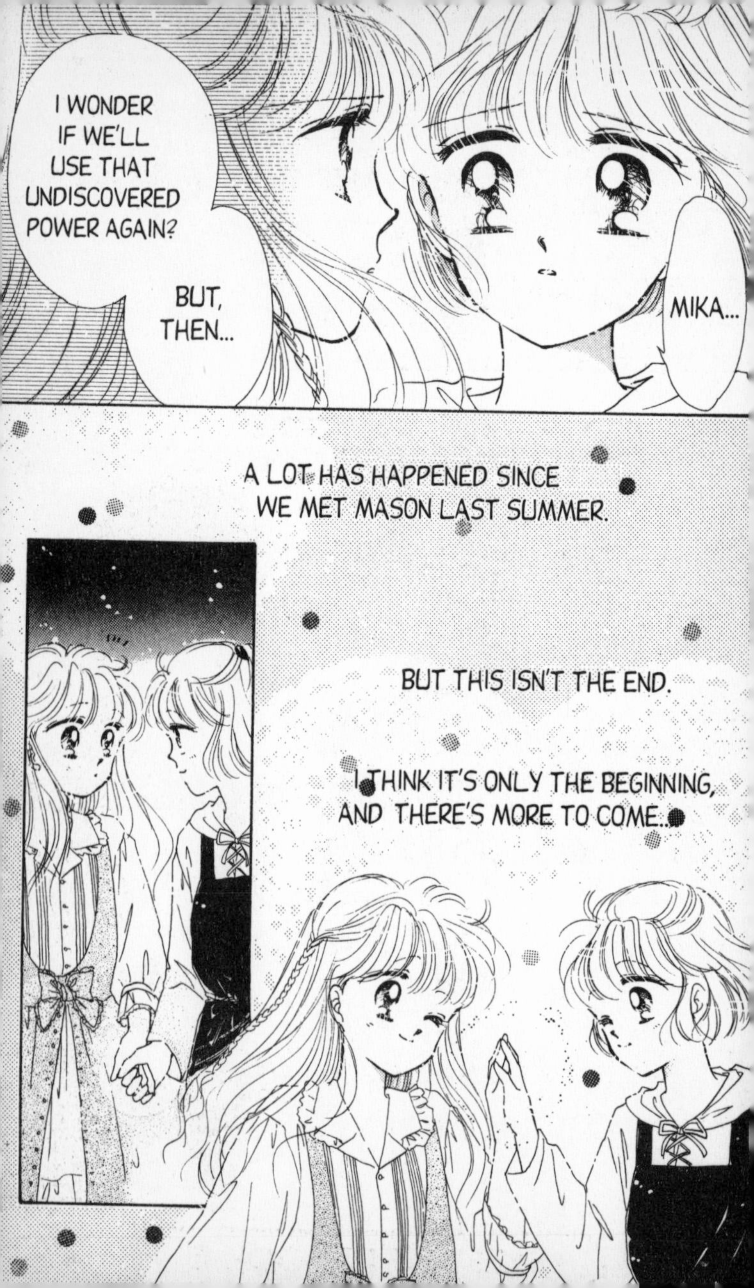
I WONDER IF WE'LL USE THAT UNDISCOVERED POWER AGAIN?
BUT, THEN...
MIKA...
A LOT HAS HAPPENED SINCE WE MET MASON LAST SUMMER.
BUT THIS ISN'T THE END.
I THINK IT'S ONLY THE BEGINNING, AND THERE'S MORE TO COME...

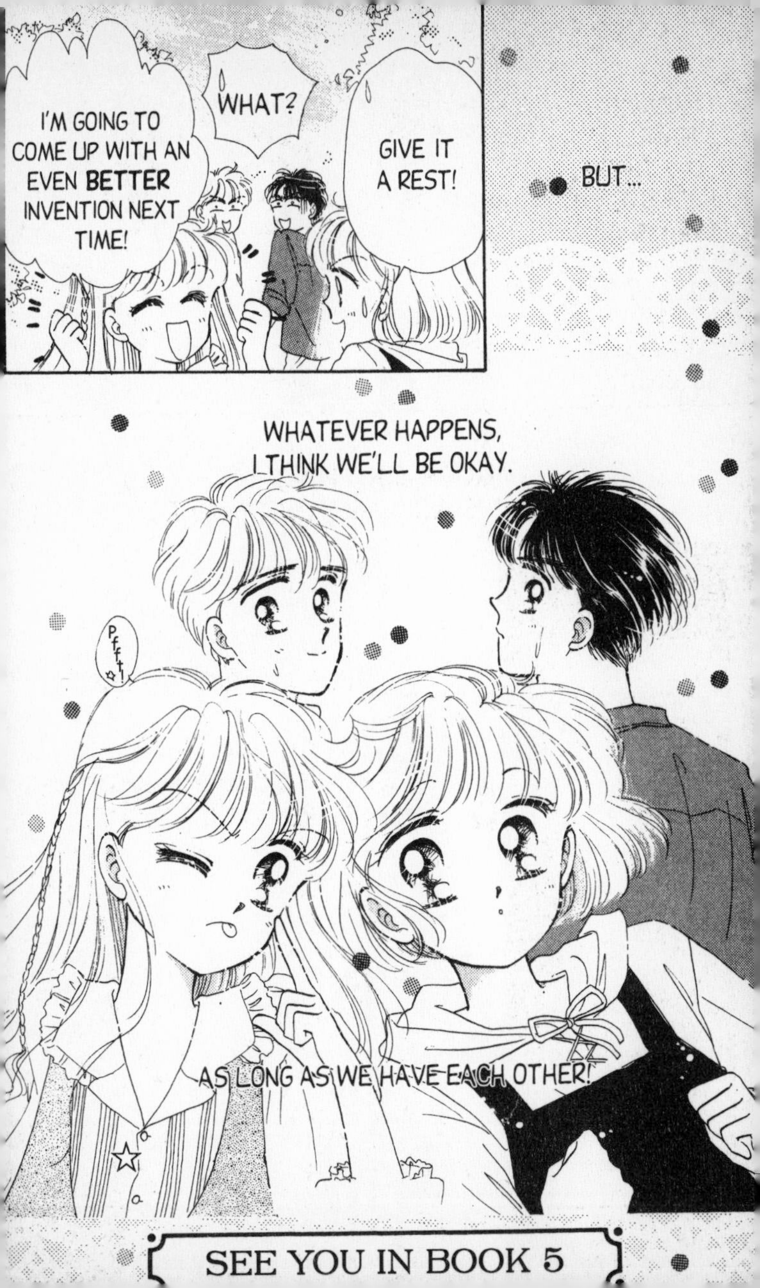
I'M GOING TO COME UP WITH AN EVEN **BETTER** INVENTION NEXT TIME!
WHAT?
GIVE IT A REST!
BUT...
WHATEVER HAPPENS, I THINK WE'LL BE OKAY.
Pffft!
AS LONG AS WE HAVE EACH OTHER!

SEE YOU IN BOOK 5

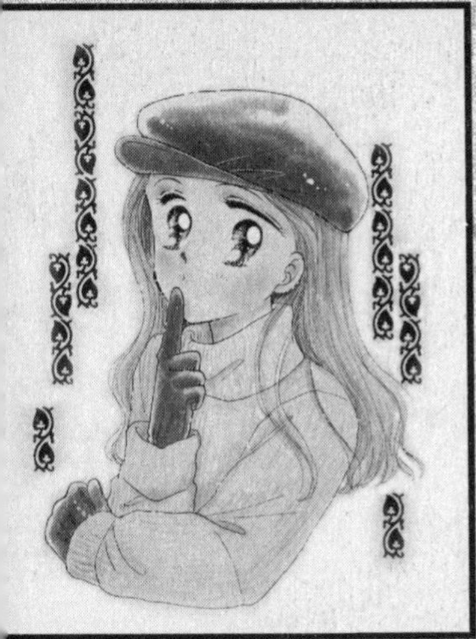

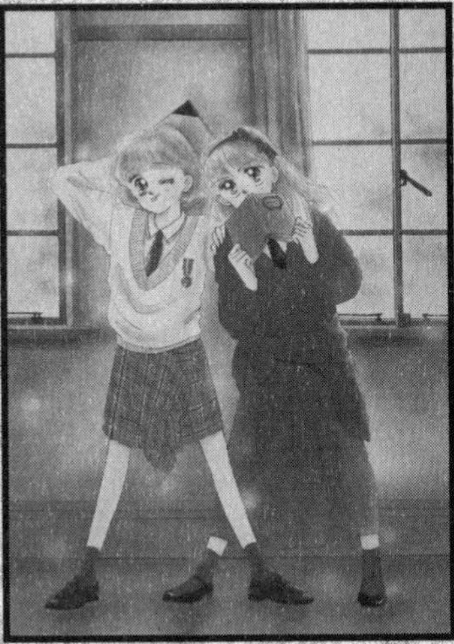

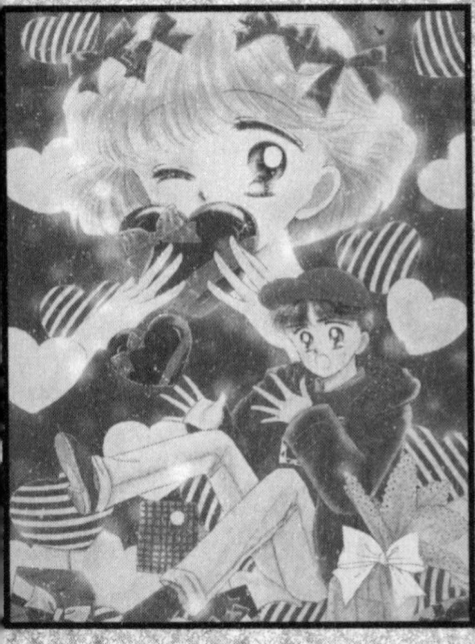

Miracle Girls